Haynes Restoration Guide

MUSTANG

1964½ thru 1970

**by Jay Storer
and John H Haynes**
Member of the Guild of Motoring Writers

From shed to showroom ... *everything you need to know!*

Haynes Publishing Group
Sparford Nr Yeovil
Somerset BA22 7JJ England

Haynes North America, Inc.
861 Lawrence Drive
Newbury Park, CA 91320 USA

ABCDE
FGHIJ
KLMNO
PQRST

CW00642499

© Haynes North America, Inc. 2011
With permission from J.H. Haynes & Co. Ltd.

A book in the Haynes Automotive Repair Manual Series

Printed in the U.S.A.

ISBN-13: 978-1-56392-957-1
ISBN-10: 1-56392-957-0

Library of Congress Control Number: 2011940355

While every attempt is made to ensure that the information in this manual is correct, no liability can be accepted by the authors or publishers for loss, damage or injury caused by any errors in, or omissions from, the information given.

Acknowledgements

We wish to give special thanks to Coker Tire, National Parts Depot and Painless Performance for their assistance with our restoration project.

Contents

1

Introduction   1•1

2

What is a "restoration"?   2•1

What are you planning for your Mustang?   2•2

Resto-Mod Mustangs   2•3

Mechanical skills, shop space, tools
    and experience   2•5

Plan your time   2•7

What to look for when shopping
    for a project car   2•7

3

Organization   3•1

4

Disassembly   4•1

Powertrain   4•5

Body   4•11

Suspension   4•21

Interior and convertible top   4•29

5

Build a rolling stand   5•1

6

Body restoration   6•1

Restoration and paint   6•1

Glass and trim   6•23

7

Mechanical restoration   7•1

Engine assembly	7•4
Transmission	7•31
Driveline assembly	7•39
Suspension and brakes assembly	7•49
Heating, cooling and air conditioning systems	7•77

8

Interior and convertible top   8•1

Interior	8•1
Convertible top	8•21
Headliner	8•33
Instrument panel	8•37

9

Detailing   9•1

10

Now what?   10•1

Car clubs	10•1
More adventure	10•2
Showing off	10•4
Insurance	10•4

11

Mustang resources   11•1

Source list	11•1
VIN/data plate information	11•10

1 Introduction

History

There are many classic cars that are also considered to be milestone vehicles, in that they have exhibited engineering and styling advancements that have influenced the automobile industry and the public. Many of them are legendary names, such as Duesenberg, Packard and Pierce-Arrow. They were advanced and expensive in their day; they were never vehicles for the masses. These large, magnificent automobiles of the Twenties and Thirties are rarely seen today other than in books and museums, or the garages of those collectors who can afford them.

The Ford Motor Company has produced several of these milestone vehicles, including the Model T, the 1932 cast-iron V8, and several significant Fifties cars. This book is concerned with Ford's more recent milestone car, the 1965 Mustang. Introduced early in 1964, the Mustang is still being produced today. It's a brand that has never lost its grip on the public consciousness for sporting great design, fun performance, and lots of value for the dollar.

Though it seemed like there had been nothing like the Mustang before, it did have easily-traced predecessors. Chevrolet had the Corvette, described as America's only true sports car, and this bothered Ford. From 1955-1957, they countered with their own two-seater, the Thunderbird, which was a great-looking car with spirited performance (when the top V8 was ordered). But, it featured a more comfortable ride that sacrificed true sports car handling. It turned out that the Thunderbird was more suited to the country-club market than the racers.

Ford did not have a car to fit the market slot left vacant by the original early T-bird, but there were rumblings in the late Fifties that smaller, thriftier cars from Europe and England were coming to our shores, and none of the Big Three automakers in Detroit wanted to be left without a car to compete against the imports.

Ford's entry was the Falcon, brought out in 1960 with a lightweight, unitized body and frame, clean styling, thrifty six-cylinder engine and even an optional small V8 - the 260 cubic-inch ancestor of the 289.

The Falcon proved to be both practical and enormously successful. Ford was making a killing over its few rivals, the Valiant from Plymouth and the quirky rear-engined, air-cooled Chevrolet Corvair. The latter was an innovative experiment, but the public didn't take to it. So from 1960 to 1965, Ford Motor Company had the domestic, small, affordable, gas-saver market covered, producing almost a half-million in the first year. Models were also produced for Mercury as the Comet, with a few cosmetic changes, introduced as 1960-1/2 models. Ford even downsized their Ranchero to Falcon size and produced the first compact truck. It looked just like the Falcon station wagon without a roof over the rear. This also met with public approval. All of this was during the reign of Lido "Lee" Iacocca as Ford general manager, who was to become a major influence within the company.

The only niche Ford was still interested in scratching was the personal car; something small, nimble, good-looking, fun and affordable.

Although the Thunderbird had sold well only when they made it a four-seater, there was still high interest from the buyers who had purchased the original T-Bird: the youth market.

Early on the decision had been made to utilize the unitized body-frame construction of the Falcon and most of the engine, driveline and suspension components for their new vehicle. This left the stylists to come up with the look and feel of the finished concept. Many versions were brought to life in clay before the one code-named Cougar caught Iacocca's eye. This evolved into a concept called Mustang II, which Ford showed at Watkins Glen in 1963 to the crowd attending the US Grand Prix. They were ready to begin production on the Mustang the following year.

There had been nothing like this on the market before, and its introduction was highly anticipated. The car's debut was earlier than most cars, in order to make the most of the unveiling at the World's Fair in New York. That, plus a total advertising blitz, brought close to four million people into Ford dealerships, where the covers over the new Mustangs were dramatically lifted at the same time in all Ford dealerships. Some dealers sold out quickly, so the San Jose, California plant was turned over solely to Mustang production to keep pace with demand in the Western states, while another plant was opened in Metuchen, New Jersey. Expensive sports and luxury cars have always dominated the spotlight of the media and the public's fancy, but few vehicles in modern times that were aimed at a mass

market audience and with such value for the dollar have made this much impact.

What makes this car so special? Many would say that the immediate visual appeal is the long-hood/short-deck styling (reminiscent of those big Thirties cars) that implied there was a large engine under that long hood. There was nothing else like it on the market. Ford had a lightweight 2,500 pound vehicle, which had benefits for fuel economy, performance and handling, regardless of the choice of engine, delivering a car at roughly a dollar a pound.

Performance was a basic marketing theme for Ford Motor Company throughout the Sixties, and several V8 engines and handling packages were optional on the Mustang. A thin-wall V8 in a lightweight car has always been a winning combination with performance fans. The only other Detroit vehicles promising performance were bigger and heavier, such as

Oldsmobile's 442 and Pontiac's GTO model, while the fiberglass Corvette was in a class by itself. These other performance-image cars were considerably more expensive than the little Mustang whose base price was a shockingly-affordable $2,368!

The styling caught the fancy of the American marketplace and the thrifty six-cylinder cars looked virtually identical to the V8 cars except for a discrete badge on the front fender of the V8 models. Every manufacturer tried to cash in on this new market. Chevrolet brought out the Camaro, and Chrysler Corporation had the Barracuda. The Barracuda had a great fastback roof atop what was basically a Plymouth Valiant and was actually introduced two weeks before the Mustang. Sales figures, however, indicate that it was greatly overshadowed by the Mustang. The Barracuda sold 23,443 units the first year, while the Mustang sold that many the *first day* of release in showrooms! Both *Newsweek* and *Time* magazines featured the Mustang and Ford general manager Lee Iacocca on their covers. The Barracuda was in the marketplace for a decade, while the Mustang has retained its vital position in the marketplace as a fun and desirable car for over 40 years.

Ford had a number of hot cars in their Sixties arsenal, mostly Fairlanes and Galaxies with big engines, but the top two V8s in the production 1965 Mustangs were the 289 with four-barrel carb and 9.0:1 compression, rated at 210 hp, and the 271 hp 289 Hi-Po (short for high-performance) with a host of internal and external changes for higher-revving power and durability. Many books and articles have chronicled the period of what Ford called their Total Performance decade, so we will not go deeply into performance, except for one special model that deserves to be mentioned in any exploration of the 1965-1966 Mustangs: the Shelby GT-350 limited edition.

Carroll Shelby, a Texas chicken-farmer, renowned sports car racer and race-car impresario, was and is a hero to Ford performance buffs, having borrowed the Ford 289 Hi-Po engine that he dropped into a British-built AC sports car, resulting in the legendary Cobra sports cars that won many races, both with Shelby's improved 289s and the 427 cubic-inch, big-block NASCAR engines.

Always looking for more exposure for their products, Ford made a deal with Shelby to produce a racer's version of the 1966 Mustang 2+2 fastback body, shipping the Wimbledon White cars from the San Jose plant to Shelby's facility in Venice, California. The workers at Shelby-American made chassis modifications for better handling, body modifications such as a fiberglass hood to save weight, scoops that ducted fresh air

to the rear drum brakes, and many other changes. Two bold stripes of Guardsman Blue ran from front-to-rear. The badging on the rocker panels read "GT-350". The 289 had a high-rise aluminum intake, tubular exhaust headers and a new camshaft, boosting the horsepower to 306. They did well in racing and added more mystique to the Mustang image.

Shelby also made a deal with Hertz Rent-A-Car for 1000

GT-350's. All fastbacks, the majority were painted black with gold stripes and the lettering changed to GT-350H in gold letters along the rocker panels. Most were equipped with automatic transmissions. Back then a driver over 21 could go in and rent the only-slightly-detuned Shelby for the weekend. More than a few showed up at drag strips on Saturdays, and we're guessing that for some reason quite a few may have been returned by youthful renters with a complaint of "Gee, I don't know what happened, sir, the driveshaft just fell out of the car!"

One of the other brilliant aspects of Ford's marketing plan with the Mustang was the lengthy list of options. It may seem incredible to today's car buyers who have to comb through dozens of dealerships to find the car most suited to their wants and needs, but Mustang buyers in 1965 could have their choice of body styles (coupe, convertible and fastback), engines, transmissions, suspension, interior, instrumentation, wheel treatments, 28 different interior color combinations, and 25 exterior colors. Virtually all Mustangs had bucket seats, although there was an optional bench seat that was rarely ordered, since the average car-buyer of the period considered a small, peppy car with bucket seats and a floor-shift as pretty much the definition of a sports car. The buckets could be the standard ones or the luxury seats with more padding and an equestrian theme - referred to as the Pony interior. You could sit down with the Ford salesman and pick out the Mustang of your dreams. The paperwork went to Ford, which assigned it to a particular regional plant, and a build-sheet was printed that stayed on the car during its trip down the assembly line. A few months later it would arrive at your dealership.

Perhaps in the initial frenzy

of the car's introduction, buyers were happy to obtain the keys to any Mustang they could get their hands on, but the option list allowed such personalization of most Mustangs ordered in 1965 that today's restorers can find unique combinations of options that make their Mustang's story more interesting. There may be no typical or common 1965 Mustang. With a 289, deluxe interior, four-speed, fog lights, white interior with Ivy Gold trim, standard bucket seats, power steering, and Dynasty Green body color, you could have a Mustang that was truly a limited edition, since perhaps only a hundred Mustangs out of the 1965 run had that exact same combination of options. A special Mustang back then is still a very special Mustang today.

From 1967 to 1970, the cars grew longer, wider and heavier, until the 1971 Mustang had little resemblance to the original milestone car of '65. If there's a silver lining, it was perhaps the performance aspect, with Ford offering their classic big-block FE engines in muscle car Mustangs. There were 390's, 428's and even 427's like the big, bad Cobra roadsters. There were also Boss 302 models with free-breathing cylinder heads that were the FoMoCo entries in the SCCA Trans-Am races.

In 1970, the engine choices ran the gamut from the old 200-inch six (pretty weak for the big and heavy Mustangs), a 250-inch six, a regular 302 V8 and a 351 version of the Windsor small-block V8, the Boss 302, a Cobra-Jet V8 and a Super Cobra-Jet, plus the ultimate muscle motor, the Boss 429. It may sound like it was only one cubic-inch bigger than the 428, but this was an engine built purely for NASCAR and drag-racing. Under-rated at 375 hp, most of the Boss 429s wound up in Ford's favored Total Performance dealerships to be drag-raced. The limited-production vehicles are quite rare today and one of the most expensive Mustangs to buy. The FE-optioned Mustangs, particularly the GT-A model, are very popular today, except with mechanics. Changing spark plugs on the wide engine in a narrow engine compartment is not easy at all, and installing tubular headers on one of these cars is a guaranteed knuckle-buster.

Restoring 1965-1970 Mustangs

Our restoration book covers all the details of the restoration of a specific 1965 convertible. This is not to say that the procedures covered do not apply to later Mustangs. Much of what we are going to illustrate for you would apply to restoring any 1965 to 1970 Mustang.

If you are reading this book, you have an obvious curiosity about classic Mustangs. Like the rest of us, you have noticed the appearance of restored Mustangs in movies, television shows and commercials. Whenever the script calls for the hero to be a cool guy (or girl) who follows his own path, they give him a vintage Mustang instead of a new Charger or BMW. We can thank Carroll Shelby and the late actor Steve McQueen

for their contributions to the lasting mystique of the vintage Mustang. The point is that people today still love these cars.

Vintage Mustangs are not seen today as ready for the crusher, even when in a neglected condition. Everyone recognizes that they are of value and worthy of restoration, whether they are seen limping down the road or rusting in an overgrown backyard. Maybe one of the incentives for restoring your old Mustang would be an end to the seemingly never-ending question, "Are you interested in selling your Mustang?" When yours is restored, observers will know that you put a lot of work into it, and plan to keep it for many years of enjoyment.

Seven reasons why a Mustang is an ideal candidate for restoration

1) Millions of Mustangs were manufactured, and a great many are still out there on the road.

2) Restorable examples are reasonably priced. Coupe models are the most affordable, from $1,500 to $5,000, while convertible and fast-

back models can go from $8,000 to $10,000 (depending on condition)

3) Every restoration task or problem that needs to be done on a vintage Mustang has been done by thousands of other enthusiasts before you, so there is an enormous network of shared information in magazines, websites, Mustang clubs and how-to books like this one.

4) The mechanical aspects of the car are super simple compared to current cars, so they're easy to work on, plus they use standard (non-metric) fasteners, so one doesn't need a whole shop full of special tools to tackle a vintage Mustang.

5) The engines do not have a computer or other complicated emissions equipment, all are carbureted rather than fuel-injected, and the ignition system uses a distributor and plug wires, so diagnosis and tuning is greatly simplified. A screwdriver, a wrench and a timing light are about all you need for tuning.

6) Parts are readily available, unlike most other collectible cars.

7) The Mustang is very popular, whether it's a 1965 or a 2011. The passion and nostalgia for the early Mustangs hasn't abated, and properly-restored examples are holding their own in resale value among Sixties collector cars

All of these factors are important, but let's examine that #6 point in more detail. The process of restoring a classic from the Thirties is not for the faint-of-heart or faint-of-wallet. Missing parts on such vehicles often have to be hand-fabricated at considerable expense, and there is little the owner can do without a team of experts to perform the restoration, which can take years to complete.

It isn't just million-dollar Duesenbergs that have these issues; many enthusiasts restoring fun cars of the Sixties are in the same fix. If you're restoring a 1962 Pontiac Bonneville or even a 1972 GTO, finding such commonly-needed parts as new door latches, instrument panel bezels, outside body trim and many other parts requires lots of time-consuming research and paying high parts prices.

In the case of the vintage Mustang, virtually every nut, bolt, screw, hard part, or soft part on the car is available from a dozen sources. Major body parts can still be found in old school

others are made by companies who comply with the Ford Restoration Parts Licensing program. Almost anything you will need for your Mustang is as close as a phone call or internet click.

When you're looking for a Mustang to restore, don't let parts-chasing be a worry, and also do not be concerned about jumping in over your head when you're unsure of your abilities. There are vintage Mustang clubs all around the country. Once you have your restoration candidate in the garage, find and join a local club or chapter of a regional club. They will welcome you and can give you the benefit of their experience. In many large cities, there are Mustang restoration shops and parts sources. The people who run such businesses usually are dedicated and very knowledgeable. Establishing a good relationship with a shop like this is a great idea, as they can usually provide answers to your questions more readily than a rep at some larger operation or online company.

wrecking yards, or you could be one of the lucky prospectors who finds Mustang gold languishing under a tarp in someone's backyard. Many of the Mustang parts supply companies began with NOS (New Old Stock) Ford parts that were old but never used. Today there are more than 12,000 reproduction parts available, from body pieces to suspension components, interior door panels, carpet sets, and seat upholstery in all the correct colors. Some of the parts available today have been manufactured by suppliers that made them back in the day, some from companies who have the original Ford tooling, and

1.1 Before you embark on your restoration adventure, attend as many car shows as possible (particularly ones featuring Mustangs). You can gain much insight from those who have already gone through the process.

1.2 Initial inspiration for the Mustang was the sporty two-seater Thunderbird of 1955-1957. Although desired by many buyers, critics said it was a cross between a luxury car and a sports car, but not big enough for the luxury crowd nor fast enough to be truly sporty. When Ford built the bigger T-Bird from 1958 onward, it was an overwhelming success with the upper-end buyers. Thankfully, that long-hood/short-deck body design lived on in the Mustangs covered by this book.

1.3 Detroit began looking into the popularity of small import cars, and strategizing to compete with them. Ford had the most success with their 1960 Falcon that utilized a roomy interior with a breakthrough integrated body and chassis, or unibody, which allowed them to build a much lighter vehicle for fuel economy, and peppy with even their small, 90-hp six that delivered 27 mpg, a figure most of us would be happy to have in our family car today (along with the 30-cent gasoline of the day).

1.4 Although designed as an economy car, the Falcon and Comet eventually succumbed to demand and offered performance models of both nameplates. This is a restored '65 Falcon with the 260 V8 and four-speed, with the model being the Sprint. These Falcons were like a Mustang with a bigger back seat and trunk.

1.5 Most of the attention in performance and racing circles was on the big NASCAR models, with the biggest engines in The Big Three's arsenals. Ford did very well in this game with Galaxies from 1960 to 1964 (as exemplified by this '64), but they wanted to be known for performance across the board.

1.6 The happy product that resulted was the 1965 Mustang. The lightweight body/chassis of the Falcon and much of that car's suspension was used for strength with light weight, the proven sixes and small V8's, and a knockout design that appealed then and now. A restored '65 Mustang today is still a headturner and fits in with any group of collectible cars at a show. Everyone loves a convertible!

1.7 As far as body-style options, the fastback (or 2+2) was pretty sexy, although the back seat was even more cramped than the convertible. Like the convertible, the fastbacks are hard to find today as restoration candidates.

1.08 A rear seat passenger complaint (from adults) for the fastbacks was baking under the sun from that large, untinted back window over them.

1.9 Mercury was building their version of the Mustang, the Cougar, but not in the numbers of the Mustang. The Cougars had a little more room, a little more comfy interior, a slightly better ride from added weight, and were pushed by salesmen more as personal luxury cars than as racy models. These are also great cars to restore today.

1.10 Some 200,000 of the 1965 Mustangs were sold with the 200-cubic-inch inline six well-proven in the other FoMoCo product lines. This offered 120 hp, so that this base engine exhibited more power than the Falcon sixes.

1.11 Part of the fun of buying a Mustang was the almost overwhelming choices of options a buyer faced. In the drivetrain, you could opt for the 260 V8 (early models), the 195-hp 289 with two-barrel carb, the 200-hp 289 with four-barrel carb, or the enthusiast's choice, the 271-hp 289 Hi-Performance.

1.12 Although this is the standard interior package, it looked very deluxe to buyers in 1965. Just having bucket seats in those days seemed a very sporty thing, plus every Mustang had a floor shift.

1.13 The major option on Mustang interiors was the Deluxe package. Because of the running horses embossed in the upholstery, this interior choice is often called the Pony interior. Restorers often apply this interior to their project, even if their car didn't come with the Deluxe option. Reproduction interior pieces are available from several sources.

1.14 The fastback body was late to the game, but once Carroll Shelby discovered it, his company Shelby-American modified 110 of them to become the highly-collectible Shelby GT-350, with a host of engine, suspension and exterior modifications. The GT-350's cleaned up in SCCA racing, winning the B-Production Championship three years in a row.

1.15 Although this red convertible is not a true Shelby GT-350, the engine compartment illustrates the Hi-Po 289 (271 hp in stock Mustang form) brought up to Shelby specs with hi-rise aluminum intake and larger four-barrel carb, hotter camshaft, and tubular exhaust headers that combined to achieve 306 hp at 6000 rpm. Two suspension mods seen here are the Monte Carlo bar (front) and the one-piece export brace (rear), both designed to stiffen the shock towers.

1.16 Where the original Ford serial number was placed on Mustangs on the left front fender panel, Shelby stamped the GT-350 serial number on an aluminum plate and riveted it over the original VIN number. A clone Shelby can carry this repro plate for conversation purposes, but it lacks the Shelby serial number. Most of the collectible Shelby Mustangs and Cobras are accounted for and listed in an official register to prevent fraudulent sales.

1.17 Most of the production Shelby GT-350's were Wimbledon White with Guardsman Blue stripes, like many of the Cobras. The models furnished by Shelby to Hertz for their Rent-A-Car fleet were almost all black with gold stripes, and gold stripes along the rocket panel. The car on the right here has the open front racing apron below the bumper, an item which probably never appeared on a true rental Shelby.

1.18 One of the most popular sporty option packages in the day was the GT package, which included special stripes along the rockers, a GT badge on each front fender, a GT gas cap, several handling improvements, and two fog lights in the grille area. Many Mustang owners today pick through Mustang supply catalogs and pick-and-choose today as if they were back in the showroom in 1965.

1.19 Here's where the GT badge goes on the fender, and the stripes for the rocker panels. Some had the Mustang letters, while others showed the letters GT in the blank space.

1.20 At the rear, the GT items include the GT gas cap and the special exhaust tips that go through the valance panel.

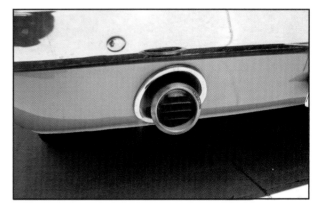

1.21 The stainless-steel surrounds in the valance ostensibly protect the paint in that area from the exhaust heat. Here you can see that the tips have slats inside to force the exhaust to go downward and not bounce back to dirty the car.

1.22 The GT gas cap is slimmer and cooler than the big standard gas cap on '65 and '66 Mustangs.

1.23 Another popular optional item with Mustang buyers was the Rally-Pac, a pair of instruments clamped to the steering column. It only included a tach and a clock, but the clamp-on attachment and the location right in front of you when driving made it seem like something only real sports cars would have. The original units were very scarce for a long time until the Mustang aftermarket came out with decent-quality reproductions.

1.24 Wheel treatment was another simple but popular choice provided to Mustang buyers. This is the simplest standard wheel cover, plus there was an even plainer wheel cover that had long air slots in it.

1.25   Both plain covers could also be ordered with a small, faux three-bar spinner in the center.

1.26   A very nice optional wheel cover was this faux wire-wheel cover. From a distance they looked just like real wire wheels with "knock-offs", as seen on expensive foreign sports cars.

1.27   Probably the nicest wheel appearance option was this styled-steel wheel. It looked like mag wheels of the period, but was chromed-steel, and could be ordered with the car, or ordered as dealer-installed items after the sale.

1.28 The styled-steel wheels looked great on any Mustang, regardless of color or other options. Nice reproductions of these wheels are made today, but are somewhat expensive.

1.29 The 1966 Mustang looks virtually identical to the first-year cars. The most noticeable would be the cleaner grille treatment of horizontal bars, although still utilizing the horse-in-the-corral trim.

1.30 Some '65's had a slim chrome piece in the back of the scooped-out design depression along the body, intended to emulate the look of a brake scoop feeding the rear brakes as on a true race car. The '66s (shown) added three teeth; some people like 'em, some don't.

1.31 Although a number of original Shelby GT-350's are still raced in competition, the ever-increasing value of these cars makes the risk of even a mild crash a serious financial loss. Some 77,000 1965 2+2's were built and another 35,698 in 1966 (not counting true Shelbys). They are still hard to find, but many racers start with a standard fastback and add the GT-350 components, at a racing cost of much less than the real McCoy.

1.32 When a production Mustang is prepped for road-racing, the unibody is treated to improved suspension components and extra stiffening plates added in several areas. Mustangs Plus (Stockton, CA) is one of the leaders in resto-mod Mustangs, offering a number of suspension packages. Here in their shop, a Mustang is on a rotating spit for installation of reinforcement tubes connecting the front and rear subframes.

1-33 The segregation you will see at most larger Mustang events isn't because of any snobbery from either the '65 and '66 crowd or the owners of later Mustangs. It makes things easier for the judges, and if you only like Boss 302 Mustangs, for instance, you can go right to that area. The '67 and later Mustangs kept adding weight, but they also had great performance options like nine-inch rear ends and bigger engines. The '67 and '68 390 GT models are desirable muscle cars with 390 V8's and later even bigger engines. The '67 fastback GT has achieved legend status because of the classic chase sequence with Steve McQueen in the movie *Bullitt*.

2 What is a "restoration"?

The true meaning of the term *restoration* is putting things back to their original form. In the world of high-end vintage automobiles, this is utilized quite literally when cars are judged. If you have a part on your car that is incorrect for your year and model, your chances of it being found worthy of a prize are slim-to-none, as cars start with 100 points, and any deviations from original dock points from your score.

In the wider circle of automobile enthusiasts, it seems as if everyone has a different definition of the term, to suit how they have treated their own vehicle. We recently saw a reality TV show where employees of a wrecking yard restore a collectible car in two weeks and then sell it off at an auction. They pulled the original non-operating engine out of a 1962 Ford Galaxie, then searched through their wrecking yard for a bigger Ford engine that would run. They performed a very basic sand-and-shoot paint job and had new seatcoverings and carpet installed. To them, this was a restoration. Any informed fan of Ford Galaxies would have found the engine they used completely unacceptable, since it was a low-performance smog motor from a decade or more later than the car, and was mostly used in trucks.

While this might not be a restoration in the exact sense of the word, this form of quicker, cheaper restoration can be just as rewarding.

There are many people who fix up their cars with a basic paint job, some new custom wheels and a few cosmetic and mechanical modifications to the engine to get the car looking like new again. Others may take the car back to factory specs, but not necessarily for their exact vehicle, and maybe add an enhancement or two. And we're sure you've seen classic muscle cars that have been souped up and tricked out to be more powerful and cool than they were when they rolled off the line. However, when you see the term restoration in this book, it implies that every possible effort has been made to represent the car as it would have appeared in a dealership showroom when new.

The idea of restoration also implies that the subject vehicle be no *better* than original. For many decades, fine vintage cars, historic race cars and sports cars were routinely over-restored. The underside of body panels were finished with high-gloss rubbed-out paint, many fasteners were chrome-plated where they never were supposed to be, and other license was taken in order to garner points from the judges. Race cars often collected scars, modifications and improved engine and chassis pieces from later models. Fixing or eliminating such unique characteristics would also represent divergence from the car's original status. In more recent times, judging has changed to acknowledge that over-restoration is just as incorrect as under-restoration, and points are subtracted for the practice.

What are you planning for your Mustang?

How you will utilize your vintage Mustang bears heavily on the level of originality you should shoot for. How much do you plan to drive it? A correctly restored car represents a serious commitment in terms of labor, time and expense. When the car is finished, you will most likely treat it gingerly, not take long trips on major highways, and always worry about where you park it. If you intend to exhibit your car in judged shows, you will try to keep it looking showroom new, with all the attendant polishing and detailing that status requires (see Chapter 9).

On the other hand, you may love your vintage Mustang enough to want to drive it all the time, risking the chance of shopping cart dings, gravel damage, paint fade and other consequences of time spent enjoying the open road. For such a car, a meticulous exterior restoration may not be called for. Some owners do all the mechanical work, drive their Mustang for several years, and then do a more thorough restoration when they retire the car from daily use.

There are many enthusiasts who have restored vintage cars, but for whom the driving of their car is half the

enjoyment. Take the Model A Ford (1928-1931) for example. Millions were produced and many survive today. They have been always been popular cars to restore and drive, often on long club tours. Given the low-technology mechanics of the Model A, touring represents some problems for an authentic restoration. For instance, these cars had mechanically operated drum brakes, with no hydraulic master or wheel cylinders to amplify the stopping power. Thus, many Model As are equipped today with hydraulic brakes from V8-era Fords, still not as safe as modern brakes but a technological leap from the mechanical brakes. There are other modifications to Model As that make them more suitable for touring, none of which are stock. In order for these car owners not to be penalized for safety changes, many shows for Model A Fords have classes for Stock and for Touring entries. The modifications do nothing to detract from the outward appearance and nostalgic appeal of the cars.

Resto-Mod Mustangs

Your 1965-1966 Mustang doesn't look anything like a Model A Ford or other antique car, but in some aspects of technology it is still 45 years behind whatever modern car is your daily driver, even if your daily driver is a 2010 Mustang. The level of restoration to which you take your vintage Mustang is totally up to you, based on your considerations of budget, time and intended use.

We have met many Mustang owners who have decided to make some non-original modifications to their Mustang for greater safety and comfort when driving in modern traffic and today's crowded highways. Mustang supply companies have upgrade modification kits for better braking, improved handling with radial tires, modern air-conditioning compressors and other parts that make for an efficient conversion to modern R-134A refrigerant, etc. There are a host of items designed for improved looks or non-stock engine modifications. With enough modifications and changes, along with a transplant of a later 5.0L fuel-injected V8 and T-5 five-speed transmission, you no longer have a restored Mustang but what is called a Resto-Mod. If you really want serious, post-1965 performance and fuel economy when you drive your Mustang, then this may be the path for you. Rest assured that if your modifications had to do with braking or suspension, 99% of viewers would never know your car wasn't exactly stock. There are thousands of Mustangs in this category that look externally stock, yet have numerous modifications. To accommodate such Mustangs, there are events where judged classes are divided into stock or modified, so you won't be penalized if you're on the hunt for trophies.

For purposes of this book, we are restoring our '65 convertible to as close as we can get to original condition, with the original paint color, date-coded wheels, carefully-rebuilt original engine and driveline and a stock interior of the original colors. Every original part that can be rebuilt will be rebuilt, in preference to buying replacement parts. You may decide to simply do your Mustang project as a driver, with any rust or other body problems fixed, a decent paint job applied of a correct color, some engine and chassis work, and new carpeting and interior panels. It will be an enjoyable car and a conversation starter that collects approving looks wherever you go. You can enjoy almost every benefit that a fully restored Mustang would bring you, at considerably less cost and labor and not requiring a complete teardown.

The choices are open to you to carry the restoration to the level that you're comfortable with

in terms of expense and labor time. We would advise you at this point that the bodywork and exterior paint is the most expensive and important phase of the restoration of a vintage Mustang, or in fact of any collectible car. If all you can afford to do right now is the paint, have it done by a shop with a good reputation and references. A Mustang that has no rust or other body damage could be sanded, primed and painted for $3,000 to $10,000. If that sounds like a wide range, it's because the difference is not in the cost of the paint but the amount of tedious labor applied to make the metal straight before the paint is applied. The straighter and flatter the body surfaces are, the smoother and shinier the paint will look when buffed. We've all seen newly painted cars that look good from 20 feet away, but sighting down the side of the body reveals waves and other imperfections. That's the lower end of the paint-job spectrum, achieved with the minimum of metal preparation.

If you are concerned about resale value, we advise you to paint your Mustang only from the factory palette of color choices from the year of your Mustang. Most of these colors are very attractive when professionally applied and buffed. Ideally, everyone who restores a Mustang would paint theirs the original color it was when it was new, but if that doesn't go over, there should be at least *one* factory color that is appealing. You may see a cool color on a new import car in a parking lot,

but don't be tempted to use that paint on your Mustang. Your resale value will be lowered considerably. A buyer who wishes to carry the restoration of your Mustang further than you did will be obliged to sand and repaint the whole car, so he'll pass on your car right off the bat or offer a much lower bid. Conversely, if you at least have a nice paint job and it's a factory color, this is a major plus to a buyer who wants to restore the rest of the car.

The level of restoration that we are representing here is professional quality, and we cover all mechanical and cosmetic aspects of our '65. Of course, the 1967 through 1970 Mustangs exhibit mechanical and styling differences from our '65, but the *process* of restoration will be the same. Following through the various Chapters, you will decide just how far you want to take your project. You may decide to replace all the suspension and braking components, plus rebuild the engine and transmission, with your focus on making the car completely reliable for driving now, but putting off further restoration until you can afford it.

Skills, Experience, Space

Before you even begin the hunt for a vintage Mustang project car, you should ask yourself a few questions. Do you have lots of prior mechanical experience? If you do, removing and replacing most components on a classic Mustang will not be too challenging. If you've worked a lot on modern cars, you'll find that stepping back through four decades in technology and packaging presents a simplicity that makes a car of this vintage a *dream* to work on. On modern cars, everything is squeezed into the engine compartment or under the dash in such a way as if it were purposely designed not to be serviceable. We're not implying that everything is a snap on a Mustang - it's not. Any older vehicle will have frozen fasteners that are a pain to remove. You will cut yourself, you will scrape your knuckles, and that's even while wearing gloves. What is cool about the pre-smog Sixties cars is that there is *room* to get at things and there isn't a giant electrical harness restricting access, and solenoids and vacuum hoses aren't running all over the place. The few exceptions to this aspect are on the '67 and later Mustangs with larger V8's, which can be challenging to work on in the engine compartment. On modern cars, you often have to remove several components just to access the one you're trying to remove, and a comprehensive repair manual such as a Haynes book is a necessity.

Even working on your simpler '65 Mustang, you will still value the Haynes Repair manual (#36048) that covers Mustangs from '64-1/2 to '73 as a companion to this book, with pertinent specifications, wiring diagrams, troubleshooting, maintenance, and repair procedures that are not covered here. If you already have some experience in working on cars, then we can assume that you have at least a basic set of tools, with 3/8 and 1/2-inch drive sockets, ratchets, breaker bar, extensions, combination end wrenches, screwdrivers, etc. In additional, you should have four sturdy jackstands (preferably the lever-adjustable type rather than the type adjusted by pulling a pin) and

a good hydraulic floor jack. There are also some specialized tools you may need, such as a steering wheel puller and a crankshaft dampener puller (these can be rented, as you'll probably only use them once). An electrical multi-meter (volts/amps/ohms) and a continuity tester are both very helpful when tracing electrical problems and are available inexpensively. A quality ft-lbs torque wrench will be necessary for engine and suspension work, where fasteners must be tightened to precise specifications. An engine hoist will be required to pull your engine and transmission, and later on to reinstall them, but these can be obtained at tool rental yards. People who work on cars, either as a hobby or as a profession, dream of having every specialized tool there is. A rollaway cabinet filled with quality tools can cost ten thousand dollars or more, but this isn't a necessity for your Mustang restoration. As you start working on your project, you'll find you may need some different screwdrivers, a small set of folding Allen wrenches, and other miscellaneous items.

Space (inner, not outer) is a hurdle that has to be jumped for any vehicle restoration project. If you live in an area where the climate is dry all year long, you might be able to conduct your work under a carport cover or in your

backyard, but most of us have to work indoors, and having a concrete floor in the garage is a big advantage over working outside over dirt or gravel, especially when trying to use jackstands and a floor jack. Once you begin dismantling your vintage Mustang, you'll find out what every car tinkerer has learned, it helps to have a three-car garage to restore one car! Once you've pulled the interior and stored the parts (see Chapter 3), then removed the engine, transmission and rear end, and finally begin removing the various body parts, such as the doors, hood, fenders and decklid, you have enough stuff to fill the rest of the garage!

If you don't have a three-car garage but have some extra space in your yard, you could get one of those Quonset-style garages with a steel frame that can be assembled and covered in a weekend.

Plan your time

You need to make yourself an honest timetable for your project. Let's say you make a one-year commitment to your Mustang. You should be able to list all the elements of the restoration and assign yourself tasks for each month. Put it all on an erasable white-board. You may have to save-up for some of the parts and outside labor needed for various phases of the restoration and you may not have that extra money every month, but having the jobs spelled out formally on a big chart is a practical way to keep yourself involved. You can see at a glance how much progress you have made and how much remains.

You also need to make written projections of

the expenses for each phase on your chart. For instance, when dealing with the brakes and suspension (see Chapter 6), add up the cost of the new parts you'll need such as shocks, brake components, steering parts and control arms and balljoints and indicate that on your list. This will be a basic guideline for expenditures, since there will be numerous extra trips to your local auto parts store for small parts, brake fluid, fasteners, etc.

Finding your project

Buying the right car for your project is not just finding the right price. If it seems like it's too good to be true, it probably is. Ideally, if you're committed to restoring a classic Mustang, start by joining a Mustang Club ahead of time and learning everything you can. If another, more-experienced club member could accompany you when you're going to look at a potential project, you could save yourself some buying mistakes.

While you're out searching for a restorable vintage Mustang, you've got to keep your emotions in check. The seller can pick up your vibe and may be harder to deal with if he suspects that you're already in love with his Mustang. A poker face is best, neither showing excitement nor disappointment, as if you could take it or leave it.

Check all the usual resources for cars for sale: newspaper classifieds, cars-for-sale publications in the convenience stores, and flyers on community bulletin boards outside supermarkets. Be on the lookout for vintage Mustangs that may be languishing in a driveway or backyard. If the license plates are out of date,

he can evaluate any extra new or used parts the seller is including with the car's purchase price. If your Mustang is going to be your first restoration of any kind, a partially-disassembled vehicle is probably not for you; it's hard for a beginner to know that this pile of disassembled parts adds up to a complete Mustang. If too much is missing, those parts will up your costs.

Check the VIN (Vehicle Identification Number) and compare this to the number on the registration or title. Unlike modern cars, which have their VIN number on the front of the dash panel and visible through the windshield from outside, on early Mustangs, the VIN number is on a plate in the door jamb and also under each front fender. With the hood open, the number appears on the inner fender panel within a cutout in the left front fender. One just like it is stamped into the passenger-side inner fender panel, but this one cannot be seen unless the right fender is removed. If the numbers don't match up to the title, pass on the car. If the car runs and is registered, by all means take it for a ride and see how it drives, listening for any unusual noises.

it could indicate the owner may have lost enthusiasm for his project. On the internet, check Mustang sites and classified ads such as on craigslist. We do not suggest using e-Bay Motors, except for listings that are within a reasonable driving distance from where you live. Photographs in low-resolution taken by amateurs are highly inaccurate at demonstrating the true condition of a vehicle. Lots of car buyers have been stung. Never buy a car from photos! Always make a physical inspection of the car personally. By the time an internet buyer has an out-of-state car delivered on a truck or trailer, and a month later brings it by the body shop he has chosen to paint it, only then will he know if there are expensive-to-remedy defects hiding under old paint. A private-party sale does not come with a warranty of any kind, which is why knowledge is power. Having someone with you that knows what to look for on a Mustang is a big help. He can spot how much restoration work may have been done already, non-stock additions to the car, and

Have the seller rev the engine while you stand near the rear of the car to check the exhaust for smoke. Black usually indicates a stuck choke or other source of rich mixture, white smoke means it's burning oil, and if steam is coming out, most likely there's a blown head gasket. If your state has annual or biennial safety inspections, see if the Mustang has an up-to-date sticker, which would tell you that at least the

basics passed inspection. Look at the tires, they can tell you a lot. Examine the tire-wear patterns shown in every Haynes Repair Manual. Various uneven wear patterns indicate worn balljoints, bushings, wheel bearings or suspension arms. Turn the steering wheel back and forth and see how much it rotates before it actually moves the front wheels.

One problem that you should look for is a rusted-out inner cowl panel. Ahead of the windshield is a panel that extends to the rear edge of the hood. It is louvered for fresh air supply to the HVAC system, and it is not removable from the car. At the front of the firewall is a rubber tube designed to drain any rainwater that might collect in the cowl. This is good in theory, but in practice, dirt, leaves and road grime find their way into the cowl through the louvers. When this debris clogs the drain tube, water collects and over time the bottom of the cowl rusts through, allowing

water to enter the car's interior! If not noticed, it soaks into the padding under the carpet and rusts right through the floor. Unless the owner has a reason to pull up the carpeting, this leakage can go unnoticed for years. To repair the cowl is a serious undertaking that requires a professional bodyman to cut out the top of the cowl to access the rusted area for welding. Always check the trunk floor in a vintage Mustang and peel back the floormat to check for rust. Part of the rear floor is the top of the fuel tank, so if rust develops back there, both the fuel tank and the rusted areas of the floor must be replaced.

It won't be easy to find a perfect specimen. Things like replacing the windshield and its rubber seal should be taken for granted. Forty years of driving is enough to pit and dull any windshield. In fact, every rubber seal and weatherstrip should be replaced.

For some people, restoring a car is considered an investment and they pick their cars on that basis, like a funds broker rather than an enthusiast. This is another factor to consider when you start a Mustang project. You might make some money on your Mustang if you had to sell it, but we can almost guarantee that you aren't likely to make anything on a car that is unfinished, even if it's 80% done. If you purchase a brand-new BMW for $50,000 and drive it for a week, you've already lost a considerable amount of equity and if you had to sell it, you'd take a fair-sized hit financially. The value of a restored Mustang is not related to the odometer reading, it's all about the quality and authenticity of the work. Once finished, you have a car that retains its value.

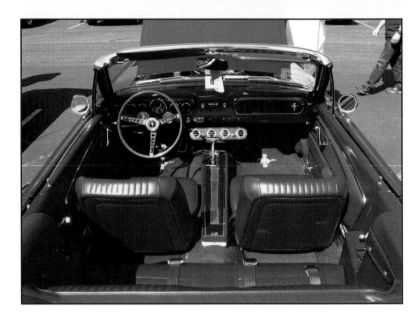

There may be lots of low-mileage BMW's available, but buyers looking for a quality Mustang do not have many to choose from at any one point in time. While not an investment that will turn a big profit, you won't lose much on a properly restored Mustang. Keep this in mind during the restoration process because it will seem at times like you have purchased a money-pit rather than a vehicle, and your family may believe you're ready to set up a bed in the garage next to the Mustang because you seemingly spend all your time out there. When your family takes their first ride in your finished restoration, they will love the car and the attention it draws, and they'll forgive you the time you put in and be proud of your determination to take the project to its conclusion. Everybody on the block will want a ride.

2.1 Where and when are you going to cross paths with your dream Mustang? It could be next week or next year, but only if you are searching diligently. A sharp-eyed vacationer found this one sharing barn space with an old truck and a '49 GMC panel delivery.

2.2 The tires have sunk into the ground and there's a thick coat of dust on the V8-equipped '66 coupe, but the body is straight, the barn protected the paintjob, and within a few days it was up and running!

2.3 Here's another case of looking beyond the little things. This one wasn't for sale, but what do you think? The paint has worn off the trunk lid and there are non-original Shelby-style stripes painted on. However, this *is* a convertible, one of the most collectible of classic Mustangs. Look down the side of the car and see what shape the rest of the body is in. It's **straight** and that is the most important factor.

2.4 If the convertibles are off your budget plan, think about a coupe with a six-cylinder engine. They are much less expensive, but when restored they look just as nice. This coupe with the spotty primer was reasonably priced, and the primer was the guide coat (see Chapter 6) for the bodywork that had just been finished. It remained only for a buyer to pick their favorite color and get a nice paintjob.

2.5 There are some things to look for that apply only to Mustangs. The lower door hinge has a stiff spring that keeps the door check arm in contact with the hinge assembly. The driver's spring usually sees more use and the spring often breaks. The dent indicated here is from the unsprung check bar repeatedly hitting the door edge and fender.

2.6 The six-cylinder Mustang engines in good tune can deliver 24 mpg, and they are unbelievably rugged. If you rebuild one carefully, it will outlast everything else on the car.

2.7 More than one person has shown interest in this Mustang (three phone-number slips are gone), so at this price it must have extensive restoration already performed. Having a Mustang Club friend along will be invaluable for advice. It may be a good buy if the really expensive restoration aspects are already completed.

2.8 Unless you want a road-racer look for your Mustang, this kind of body surgery to fit big tires is expensive and not easily reversed. This is a Resto-Mod style of Mustang, and the Mustang crowd has room for all types of enthusiasts.

2.9 At the other end of the mods spectrum is this nice interior in a convertible. It has aftermarket kick panels that have been molded to accept bigger stereo speakers. Since they can be exchanged for original replacement kick panels very easily, this is not even close to being a deal-breaker on your search.

2.10 It is common to see classic Mustangs with modern aftermarket wheels and tires, and unless the fenderwells have been modified to clear the tires, a restorer will not be deterred. In fact, some people have two sets of wheels and tires, stock ones for Mustang shows and the performance set for fun.

2.11 If you prefer chrome to the basic wheel covers, you can install a set of the Styled-Steel wheels that were available as an option. Reproductions of these wheels are available and very popular.

2.12 Rust is the enemy of all car collectors. Repairing what neglect and the elements have done to car sheetmetal and other parts is expensive. Check out your potential Mustang for rust. Pull up the driver's carpet and padding (with the seller's permission) and inspect for rust. Surface rust can be handled easily, but holes through the car are more serious (check Chapter 6 for how much work it is to replace a floor).

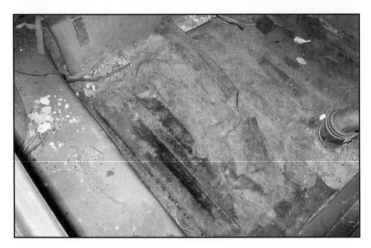

2.13 Perform the same inspection under the floormat of the trunk. Make sure the floor and top of the fuel tank aren't rusted out.

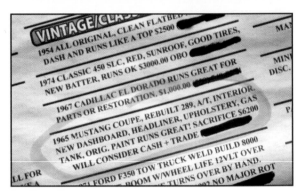

2.14 Most of us don't have the vacation or weekend time to do a large-scale search, but the internet and old-fashioned classified ads in newspapers is where a lot of people find their project cars. Never make an offer without seeing and, if possible, driving the vehicle!

2.15 If you don't mind a longer-term project, you might purchase a non-running car at a reasonable price. This man was taking the project he didn't have time for and giving it to his lucky son! A tow dolly like this makes the light Mustang much easier to tow instead of a large car-trailer.

2.16 Here's a nicely-restored 289. Can you spot the one non-original item here? Yes, it's the dual-chamber, later-model master cylinder. Since this is considered a safety item, no one outside of a judged show would complain, and it is reversible.

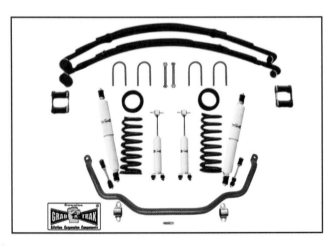

2.17 If you want modern handling under your 40-year-old car, there are a number of suspension kits available, such as this Mustangs Plus Grab-A-Track package of new tuned springs, shocks and front stabilizer bar.

2.18 For external looks, Shelby items are the most popular, such as this racing front apron with large cooling opening below the bumper (Mustangs Plus).

2.19 The famous Shelby Mustangs had fiberglass hoods with a timeless scoop design. Reproduction Shelby-style hoods are available from aftermarket suppliers (Mustangs Plus shown here). Unlike modifications to the actual original sheetmetal, the hood can be replaced in a half-hour if you want to go back to the stock hood.

2.20 Catalogs or wish books abound for the large market of classic Mustang owners. The bulk of the items are direct replacement parts for restoration, plus some custom parts. Most companies have package deals, such as a complete interior kit that is cheaper than buying individual carpet or seat kits one at a time.

2.21 Some of us car enthusiasts like to see and handle restoration parts before buying them. Luckily for us, there are Mustang shops near most any bigger city. This is the parts counter at American Mustang in Sacramento, California where Mustang expertise comes with every part.

2.22 Don't let the size of the counter fool you. After walking through a huge parts storage area, you come to a big repair and restoration shop devoted to nothing but classic Mustangs. It's like a time-warp!

2.23 Not every Mustang part is reproduced, so shops like American Mustang usually have their own small gold mine of original body and chassis parts out back.

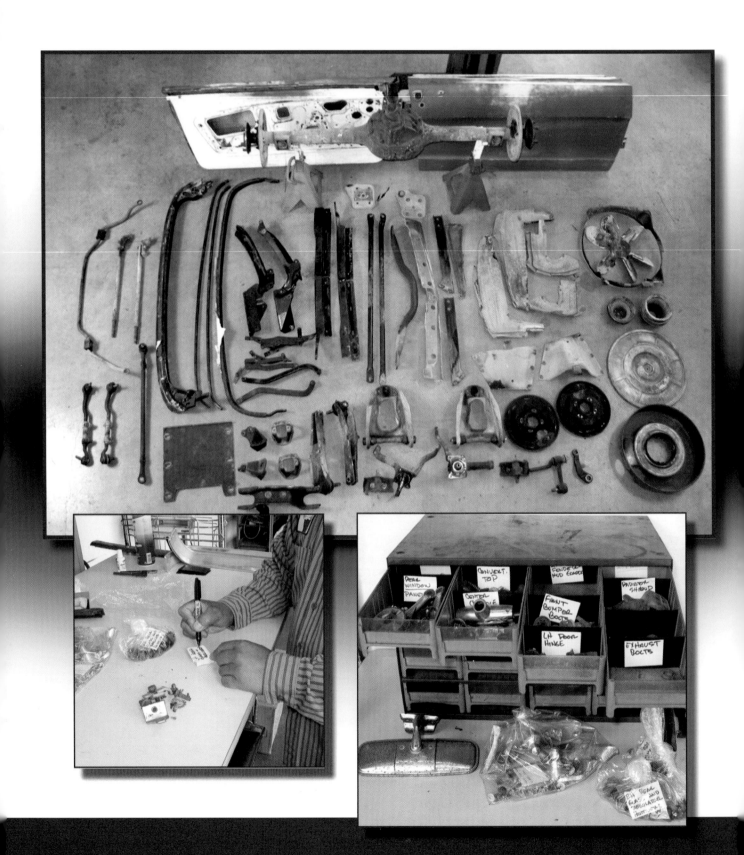

3 Organization

Organization, or rather the lack of it, is one of the most common reasons for a projected restoration of a collectible vehicle to fail and eventually be sold in a pile of unidentified parts. When a vehicle is disassembled to the level required for a thorough restoration, you have to deal with the removal, identification and proper storage of hundreds of parts and pieces, not to mention the thousands of fasteners involved. Anything can happen to us in life, and while your project is on-going, it's smart to identify and protect all your parts. If something happens that requires you to liquidate your project for cash, an unorganized pile of parts is worth a great deal less than you think. Even if a knowledgeable Mustang buyer evaluates your stuff, he may pass on it because he knows better than anyone how difficult it can be to sort out a 5,000-piece jigsaw puzzle.

As mentioned in the previous Chapter, *one disassembled vehicle requires a three-car garage (or an equivalent-size space) to store the vehicle and all the pieces.* You will need to store your parts in a safe spot where nothing can fall on them from overhead shelving, and away from any source of moisture, chemicals or excessive heat. While delicate body and interior parts are stored, you must also protect the items from each other, such as by separating two doors with padding over them, under them and between them. Such body parts must not be stored near the garage door or other entrance and generally should be away from the main traffic paths through your garage. You will be unhappy the first time you are walking into the garage with your arms full and accidentally kick something on the floor, spin it across the concrete and into your grille or other delicate piece. The second time this happens, you'll be cursing like crazy.

It may take some extra time and thought during disassembly to photograph and properly ID each part and put it in a secure storage area, but this investment effort will pay dividends later during the reassembly of your Mustang.

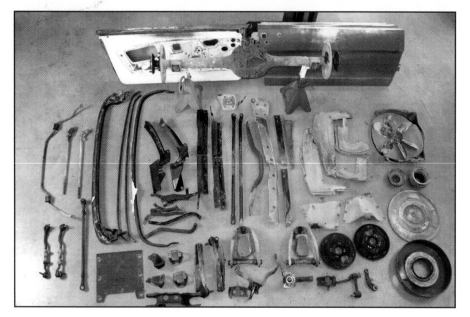

3.1 Organization and identification of the parts you are removing is vital to beginning a thorough restoration. Here a grouping of parts from the early disassembly of our Mustang is laid out, tagged and photographed.

3.2 You'll need plenty of boxes of various sizes to store and protect components. Interior and trim pieces need more protection than rugged pieces like suspension parts.

3.3 Make sure you label the outside of boxes, including such notations as front or right. If you have the room (floor or shelving), keep the boxes open for easy inspection and do not stack other boxes on top.

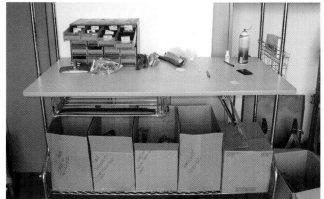

3.4 It's going to be very helpful if you have a clean workbench that can be dedicated to the inspection, restoration and reassembly of smaller components.

3.5 Plastic sandwich bags or cling-wrap are great for storing small items, but only if you identify the contents with tape, markers or sticky notes. For heavier small items such as suspension bolts, use the tougher freezer bags.

3.6 A large box filled with plastic bags is time-consuming to go through every time you're looking for a specific item. Small bags and tagged small parts are best kept in plastic storage bins with tags on the front of the drawers.

3.7 Make good use of your digital camera by documenting how parts were originally installed, especially before you disconnect wires, switches, or the clips securing wire harnesses behind the instrument panel.

3.8 Use your flash when taking photos, and make sure you check after each photo by looking at the display to ensure that you captured what you wanted and that the photo is clear and sharp.

4 Disassembly

As you start disassembling your Mustang, you can start at the front, the rear, or the interior first. What's more important than *where* you start is that each piece is identified and marked (see Chapter 3). It will be easier if you disassemble the drivetrain before the suspension, so the car can still be moved around. The most convenient place in your garage to disassemble the car may not be the most convenient place to have it remain for a year or more as a skeleton. We'll show you later (Chapter 5) how to make a sturdy stand with heavy-duty casters so that even after everything is removed from the unibody, you can still move the car around if you have to.

Even though you are planning to refinish or restore almost every part you remove before the car can be reassembled, treat every part you remove as if it were fragile and expensive to replace. Don't treat the parts roughly even if they will be repainted later. If you're working on the front, then remove the hood first (a two-man job); if you're working on the trunk, remove the trunk lid first. The hood, fenders or trunk lid can easily be scarred when you're dragging out heavy and awkward engine parts or the fuel tank from the trunk.

It is very important that you pick the spot in the garage where all the parts will be stored, then cover that part of the floor with plastic tarps before you begin the storage process. Otherwise, moisture can seep up through the concrete floor during the winter and spring. You could be adding more corrosion to your parts without realizing it.

You will find that there are a number of disassembly tasks that require a second pair of hands. If you can get a friend to help, then stock up on food and beverages and in one day get him to help you on all the items that require a sec-

ond person: removing the hood, the engine, the trunk lid, and the doors. If you have all your identification tools ready such as tags, bags, markers and boxes, have your friend help you move the parts to their safe-storage location. There's no sense dragging a door across the concrete floor by yourself when two people can carry it without a scratch. If you have to move something by yourself, it may help to get it onto a creeper or dolly. It's not worth injuring yourself or ruining parts.

Many people start with the front of the vehicle, removing the hood, headlight surrounds, and grille. If your car has air conditioning and the system still has refrigerant in it, your very first move should be taking your Mustang to a shop to have the refrigerant recovered. It may be easy to just crack the fittings and let it escape, but it's illegal and totally irresponsible, given the harm you'd be doing to the environment.

Not only that, but your car was intended for R-12 refrigerant (replaced today by R134-A), which is very expensive these days, and the shop that recovers your R-12 should give you credit for how much they took out. Don't throw money away; R-12 refrigerant costs $40-plus per pound at the time of this writing. If you keep your old AC system, it will be expensive to charge it later on with R-12, but when you're ready, your A/C shop can install

new O-rings and put your "original" refrigerant back in.

Once the more fragile pieces of the front end like the grille, bumper and front body panels, are removed and stored, you can address the drivetrain. Begin by draining all the fluids, including coolant, engine oil, power steering fluid, brake fluid, transmission fluid, and rear-axle lubricant. Here's where you begin taking lots of digital photos. Before taking anything else out of the engine compartment, take photos of the hoses, wiring, radiator shroud mounting, and all clips or components fastened to either inner fender panel, the firewall or the radiator support. Shoot the location of clips on brake lines, coolant hoses, transmission fluid lines and the fuel line. Use masking tape to tag and label the wires you disconnect from the engine, such as the ignition, the starter and alternator.

As you read through this Chapter, you will note

that our convertible isn't pretty, and the more we disassembled it, the more work we knew was needed to be done to bring it to show-car status. When a convertible is left out in the elements for even just a few years without a waterproof tarp over it, the top material rots from the sun, snow and rain. This allows dirt, leaves, rain and snow to accumulate inside the car, ruining the upholstery, and perhaps the interior electrical items. Once the carpet and its padding are compromised, they hold moisture against the floorpan, eventually creating extensive rust. The seats and carpeting are not too difficult or expensive to replace, but the replacement of a rotted floorpan is a job that is usually handled by a professional shop, and it is both time-consuming and expensive (see Chapter 6).

For the purposes of this restoration book, we were actually *pleased* that we had an example of a '65 Mustang that needed this much repair work. That

This book is filled with information to help make your Mustang run, handle and look great, to give you years of enjoyment. Just take from this book what you need. A time may come when you do have to replace or restore something else on the car, and you can then refer to the appropriate Chapters in this book for guidance.

It must be mentioned that although the Mustang is a great candidate for restoration and is easier to work on than most vehicles, you should have basic skills in using tools properly and some experience in working on vehicles. If you don't have full confidence in your abilities, have someone more experienced help you through the process. By the time you have finished your Mustang restoration, you'll be a veteran!

sounds odd, but if our floorpan wasn't rotted, we wouldn't have been able to illustrate the work required to replace a floorpan and perform many other body repairs. We hope your project doesn't need a new floorpan, but the procedure is thoroughly covered if it does.

If your Mustang is in relatively good shape, with no rust and only minor dings, the extent of disassembly we are illustrating may not apply to your project, especially if yours is to be a frequently-driven-but-nice car, rather than a show-winner.

Powertrain

4a.1 We were lucky to find what we were looking for: a desirable convertible with a V8 and an automatic transmission. However, ours was a long way from being a perfect specimen, as you can see here. Our convertible has had a rough life: non-stock parts, low-grade quickie repaint, four flat tires, incorrect wheels, rusted floorpan and a top that is more air than fabric. This is the humble starting point for our complete restoration.

4a.2 There is a stamped-steel cowl brace (A) on each side of the engine compartment, stiffening the shock towers. On convertible models such as ours, there are also two longer, round-tubing braces (B) that mount at the cowl and run all the way to the front of the inner fender panels. All braces have to be removed before removing the engine.

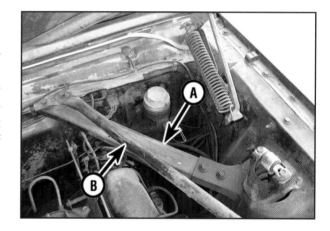

4a.3 Loosen the four bolts (two on each side) that secure the hood to the hood hinge/spring assembly. Do this with a helper.

4a.4 With two people holding the hood, each can remove the last hinge bolt on their side and carefully lift the hood away from the vehicle.

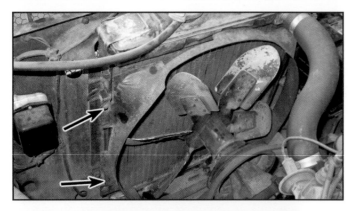

4a.5 Place a drain pan below the radiator and drain the engine coolant. Remove the upper and lower radiator hoses, then remove the fan shroud mounting bolts (two left-side fasteners indicated here) and pull the shroud back over the fan. Shrouds were originally used only on models equipped with air conditioning. Remove the fan mounting bolts and the fan, then remove the shroud.

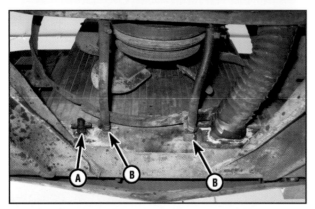

4a.6 The radiator draincock (A) is on the bottom of the tank. Disconnect the transmission cooling lines (B) from the bottom tank of the radiator.

4a.7 Remove the four mounting bolts and carefully withdraw the radiator. Most original radiators are not worth restoring after all these years. Brand new ones are inexpensive and provide good engine insurance.

4a.8 Use penetrating oil on the bolts securing the exhaust pipes to the exhaust manifolds. Let the penetrant soak in, then remove the bolts and lower the exhaust pipes.

4a.9 With a large drain pan under the transmission, loosen the fluid pan bolts and carefully pry the pan away from the transmission case, with one or two loose bolts keeping the pan in position. When no more fluid comes out, bolt the pan back up hand-tight.

4a.10 Remove the small shield at the bottom-front of the bellhousing to expose the converter-to-flywheel mounting nuts (A). There are four, so you will have to rotate the engine with a socket and breaker bar on the crankshaft pulley bolt to access all four of the nuts. One of two converter drain plugs (B) is also shown here.

4a.11 At the rear of the car, remove the nuts securing the driveshaft U-joint to the flange on the front of the differential. Pry the U-joint and driveshaft forward to separate it from the flange. Lower the rear of the driveshaft to the floor and slide the front yoke out of the driveshaft from the transmission. Store the driveshaft properly; a dent or other damage to the driveshaft could upset its concentricity or knock off a balancing weight.

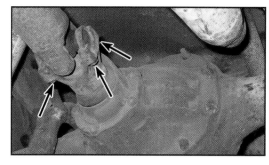

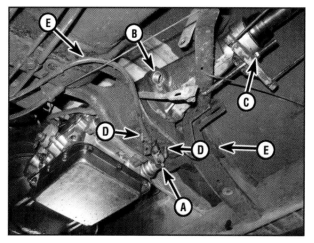

4a.12 Remove the speedometer cable (A) from the tailshaft housing (B), then disconnect the parking brake cable and equalizer (C). With a sturdy transmission jack (these can be rented) supporting the transmission, remove the transmission crossmember by removing the mount nuts (D), then the crossmember-to-chassis bolts (E).

4a.13 Disconnect the electrical connectors at the starter motor, then remove the two starter mounting bolts and remove the starter. ****Warning:** *Make sure the battery has been removed from the vehicle (or at least disconnected) before doing this.*

4a.14 Support the back of the engine to the body with a chain, then gently separate the transmission from the engine and move it rearward enough to access the two converter drain plugs to drain the fluid from the converter. Such a convenient way to drain the converter is one of the perks of working on older cars. Modern cars don't have converter drain plugs.

4a.15 Roll the transmission jack rearward and slowly lower it to the floor. The transmission should be secured to the jack with hooks and chains (or a strap as is being used here).

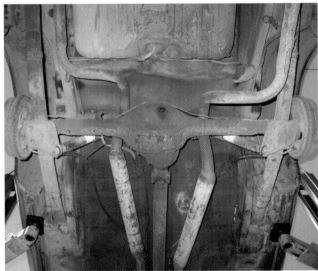

4a.16 Our exhaust system was composed of incorrect muffler-shop pipes and a pair of cheap glass-pack mufflers welded in place. We will be using new, correct exhaust pipes for our car, with the OEM-style mufflers for factory single-exhaust as original on a base V8 like ours. The easiest way to remove our all-welded system was to cut it into sections with a reciprocating saw.

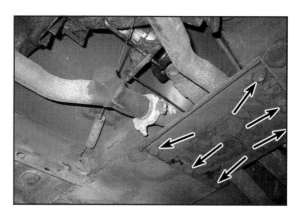

4a.17 This stiffener plate in the floorpan must be removed to get the old pipes out. Install the plate and the six bolts again after the exhaust is removed to retain floorpan stiffness during restoration.

4a.18 Disconnect the throttle/kickdown linkage (A), and the fuel line at the carburetor (B). Disconnect the heater hoses (C) and tag and disconnect the wires at the ignition coil (D).

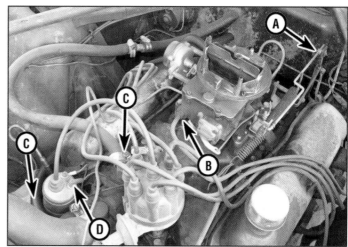

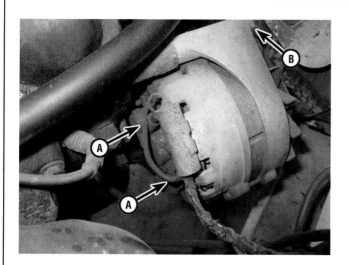

4a.19 Disconnect any ground wires from the engine to the chassis. Disconnect the wires at the alternator (A), remove the alternator adjuster and mounting bolts (B), and remove the alternator.

4a.20 Remove the battery (if not already done) and air filter housing, then attach chains to the front and rear of the engine to begin engine removal. Drain the oil and remove the oil filter, if not already done.

4a.21 With the chains securing the engine to the engine hoist, raise the engine a little to take the weight off the engine mounts. Remove the engine mount-to-chassis nut on each mount. The engine can now be removed. The engine mounts can be fully removed after the engine is removed from the car.

4a.22 Proceed slowly with the engine hoist, checking frequently for still-connected wires or hoses. Raise the engine only as far as you need to clear the fragile front sheetmetal of the body. The engine tends to swing quite a bit, so it's very helpful to have an extra person stabilizing the engine while you pull the hoist and engine away from the car.

4a.23 Once the engine is clear of the car, it can be slowly and carefully lowered until it can be placed on a dolly or an engine stand as shown. Rebuilding the engine or even just dismantling it is greatly facilitated by having it on a stand that allows you to rotate the block.

Body

4b.1 The running horse has been the symbol of the Mustang for more than 40 years. It makes a bold statement on our '65, so it is the first body item removed so it can be stored carefully. Remove the two screws at the top and tilt the horse assembly outward to remove it.

4b.2 Use a plastic trim tool to pry up the left and right trim pieces around the grille opening. Remove the screws (location indicated) before attempting to remove the trim pieces.

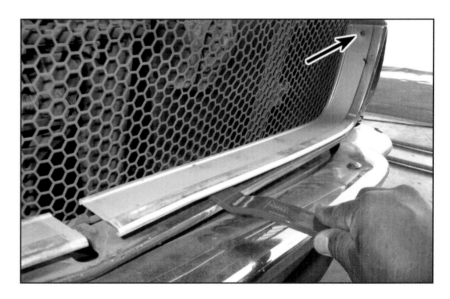

4b.3 Disconnect the one wire at the horn, then remove the horn mounting bolt and the horn from the radiator support panel. There are two horns, one on each side.

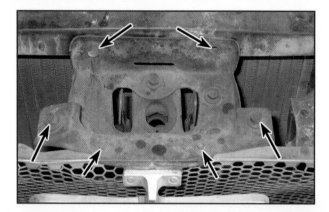

4b.4 Remove the bolts securing the hood latch assembly to the radiator support.

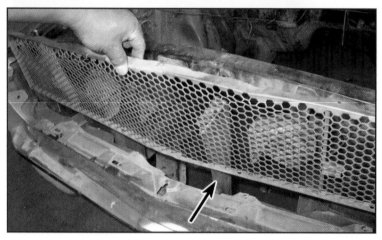

4b.5 Remove the screws securing the bottom of the grille and at the center grille support (indicated). Carefully remove the grille. The '65 grille is a pierced mesh that is fragile and is usually bent or twisted on unrestored cars. Take care when removing it. The 1966 grilles were made of thin plastic bars, which proved sturdier than the flexible '65 mesh.

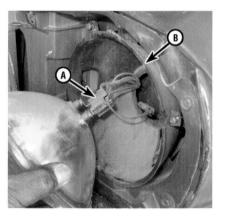

4b.6 Remove the Phillips screws securing the headlight surround. Treat the surrounds carefully, as they are made of cast pot metal and a drop on the floor could break one. Note that our screw holes had worn out and someone used wood screws and washers to retain the surround!

4b.7 To remove the rest of the headlight assembly, loosen the screws securing the stainless headlight retaining ring and rotate the ring until it can be removed.

4b.8 Pull the bulb out enough to disconnect the electrical connector (A), then store the headlight bulbs safely. Remove the screws that secure the headlight bucket (B) to the body.

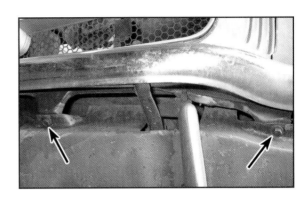

4b.9 Some of the bolts securing the lower front valance panel are accessible from under the front bumper.

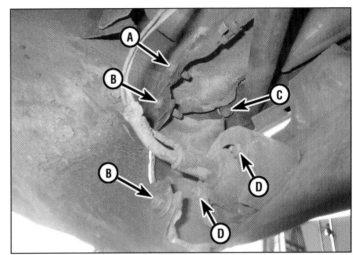

4b.10 From below (driver's side shown), remove the bolt securing the fender to the upper splash panel (A), the fender-to-lower valance panel bolts (B), and one bumper bolt (C). Remove the two nuts (D) holding the front turn signal light assembly in its cavity and disconnect the electrical connector to the turn signal light. Repeat for the other side of the car.

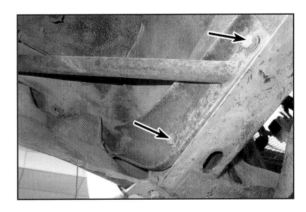

4b.11 Since we are not merely replacing the bumper, the bumper bracket-to-frame bolts (indicated) must be removed so the bumper bracket can be restored and painted. The bumper guards do not actually attach to the bumper, but to the body. Remove the bumper guards.

4b.12 Once the lights and the fasteners are removed, the front valance panel can be removed. These panels rarely stay perfect over the years as they are close to the road and everything on the street bounces up into the panel. The panel is not very rigid, and restoring your original may cost more than buying a new reproduction panel.

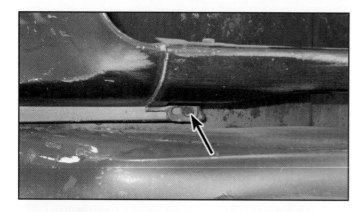

4b.13 Remove the screw on each side that secures the center panel below the grille area. Remove the center panel.

4b.14 When you are sure that you have all the fasteners removed from the upper splash panel, remove the panel. Unless the front of the car has been hit in the past, this panel can usually be restored without too much effort.

4b.15 An air or battery-powered impact tool can be used for quick removal of fasteners, but only during the disassembly phase; never use impact tools during final assembly of body parts or the paint can be chipped. We're taking off the upper row of mounting bolts for the right front fender.

4b.16 Much of the work in removing a Mustang fender is from underneath, not the exterior. Not everyone has a lift at home, but everything can be done without a lift, it just takes longer (and you may have to visit a chiropractor at some time during the restoration process!).

4b.17 Thick undercoating may prolong the life of a unibody car, but finding and removing fender brace fasteners requires you to scrape away (a chisel is used here) to locate the small bolts.

4b.18 The rear of the fender is stiffened by a large sheetmetal brace which is bolted to the fender and the body. Numerous fasteners are used.

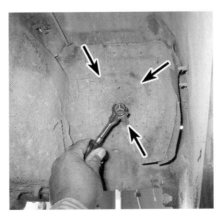

4b.19 Once the rear brace panel is removed, you can access this fender mounting bolt. You can also access this bolt by removing the interior kick panel, removing a rubber plug, and using an extension through the hole in the body.

4b.20 At the front of the fender, remove the three bolts that secure the headlight bucket to the fender from underneath. Bag these bolts and mark the bag as to location.

4b.21 A wire brush like this can speed up the process of cleaning away undercoating to locate fender brace screws. You may have to occasionally soak the wire brush in kerosene (lamp oil) to clear the tar-like undercoating from the bristles.

4b.22 From the outside, remove the screws and the headlight bucket.

4b.23 At the front of the rocker panels, there is one fender retaining bolt. Do not try to remove the fender until all the fasteners we illustrate have been removed or the fender could be damaged.

4b.24 There is a bolt at the cowl that goes through the body into the rear brace of the front fender. It differs from the row of fender-to-body bolts seen in photo 15. If your Mustang has a radio antenna, don't forget to disconnect it before taking the right fender from the vehicle.

4b.25 Open the door to access this last fender bolt. Once this bolt is removed, the fender will still cling to the body due to undercoating, corrosion and dirt. You may have to tug and wiggle the fender to free it from the vehicle. Use masking tape over the edge of the door to protect it from the fender being removed.

4b.26 At last, the stubborn right fender came loose. Off the vehicle, the fenders are quite flexible since the braces are not attached, so store them carefully and don't stack anything on top of them.

4b.27 We performed all of the same disassembly steps on the left, then removed that fender and placed it in storage as well.

4b.28 The doors can be removed at any time, but it is much easier to access the door hinge bolts (indicated) after the fenders are removed. If there were speaker or courtesy-light wires in the doors, disconnect them before removing the doors.

4b.29 It's possible to remove the door by yourself, but much easier with two people. You should pad the top of a floor jack and put it under the door to support it while you are taking out the hinge bolts. If you drop the door on concrete, the damage won't be cheap to fix.

4b.30 Moving to the rear of our Mustang, you'll find you can strip everything at that end in a few hours. As with the front end, removing the trunk lid is the first step, to give access to anything in the trunk. With another person holding the trunk lid, remove the hinge bolts and remove the trunk lid from the car.

4b.31 Since our Mustang is going to need a complete stripping via media-blasting, we're taking out the bolts securing the left and right trunk lid hinge assemblies to the body. Our basic body will be painted, so the areas beneath accessories and small parts need to be painted as well.

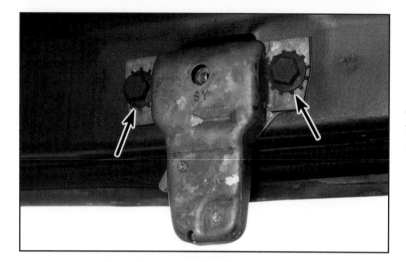

4b.32 The latch assembly is unbolted from the trunk lid, to be stored in a bag with its mounting bolts.

4b.33 Rotate the fuel filler cap, which is retained to the car by a cable. Inside the trunk, remove the nut securing the cable mounting bolt, then remove the cap.

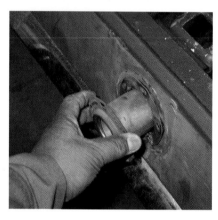

4b.34 Remove the small screws and the ring that stabilizes the gas filler pipe to the body. On our car, there is rust under everything bolted to the body.

4b.35 The top of the gas tank on '65 Mustangs is the actual floor of the trunk. Inside the trunk, remove the mat and the insulation padding over the gas tank. Wear a mask while cleaning out the trunk. Loosen these clamps and remove the filler pipe.

4b.36 Scrape away the old insulation around the tank to uncover the many screws securing it to the trunk floor.

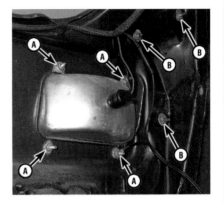

4b.37 Take out the four screws and remove the chrome trim around each taillight.

4b.38 There are two items left to remove here: the red plastic lens and the gasket that seals the lens to the housing. Unfortunately, our housings are going to need work. Since the housing is supposed to be reflective to amplify the bulb's light, this rusty housing must be wire-brushed and painted silver, or replaced with a new housing.

4b.39 Here you can see the four nuts (A) securing the taillight housing, and three of the nuts (B) retaining the cast pot-metal quarter panel endcaps.

4b.40 The bumper comes off readily with its brackets attached. There are two bracket bolts in the rear of the trunk (indicated) on each side. If you don't have a helper, you can use duct-tape to hold the bumper while the bolts are removed, then remove the bumper. Before removing the rear bumper, disconnect and remove the license-plate light.

4b.41 When you have the bumper on the floor, remove the bumper bolts to remove the brackets for cleaning and painting.

4b.42 Remove the screws and pull the back-up lights from the rear valance panel and disconnect the wires. The early '65 Mustangs (so-called 1964-1/2 models) did not have backup lights.

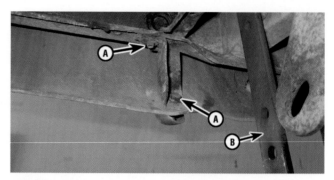

4b.43 The bumper guards can now be unbolted (A) from the rear valance panel from below. Note the Seventies-era non-stock and unsafe long spring shackles (B), installed for a high-rear look or because the original springs had sagged too much, a common Mustang problem.

4b.44 The remainder of valance panel fasteners are accessible from outside. Remove the valance panel. Most of these panels have been punched at least once or twice in a Mustang's life, so a replacement panel may be cheaper than paying a bodyman to straighten your old one.

4b.45 When you are ready to remove the fuel tank, drain the old fuel. You may have to wire-brush the undercoating to remove the drain plug. ** **Warning:** *Gasoline is extremely flammable. Don't smoke or allow open flames or bare light bulbs near the work area, and don't work in a garage where a gas-type appliance (such as a water heater or a clothes dryer) is present. Also, keep in mind that an empty gas tank is just as dangerous as a full one.*

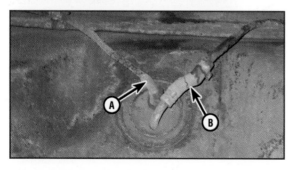

4b.46 Disconnect the electrical connector (A) from the fuel-gauge sender, and disconnect and plug the fuel line (B) before removing the fuel tank. If your tank appears to show no heavy rusted spots or holes, you can have it cleaned at a radiator shop, then sloshed with a fuel tank sealer to prevent future internal rust. New tanks are readily available if yours has seen its last tankful.

Suspension

4c.1 You'll find the suspension and steering components are a little easier to work on after the body panels have been removed, and there is less chance of tools damaging the body. We'll start with the front suspension. The design is simple but effective: upper control arms (A), lower control arms (B), tie-rods (C), center (or drag) link (D), strut rods (E), and a stabilizer bar (F).

4c.2 To remove the brake drums, first use a screwdriver to depress the tang that locks the brake adjuster, while backing off the adjuster with a brake adjusting tool like this, which levers against the hole in the backing plate.

4c.3 The dust cap over the outer wheel bearing can be removed with pliers such as shown, or by tapping a screwdriver between the cap and the drum, moving the drum around to evenly force out the dust cap.

4c.04 Use needle-nose pliers to straighten the cotter pin, then remove it from the spindle using side-cutter pliers leveraged against the hub. Remove the nut lock cage.

4c.05 Remove the wheel bearing adjustment nut and the large flat washer behind it.

4c.06 Wiggle the drum a little and the outer wheel bearing can be removed.

4c.07 The drum should now come off the spindle. From what we've observed so far of our car's condition, it's no surprise to find the brake area a mess. The shoes, springs, and wheel cylinders should always be replaced regardless of how they look. The original drum brakes are no match for the stopping distance of newer cars, so make yours as good as possible.

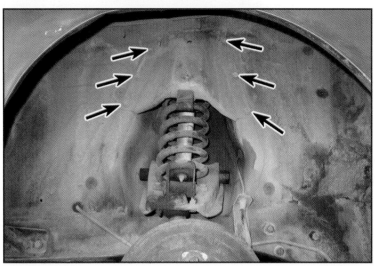

4c.08 The front coil springs must be removed to go very far with front end disassembly. Remove the bolts and nuts that secure the spring cover plate (which helps reinforce the fenderwell and also mounts the rubber suspension bumper). Remove the cover plate.

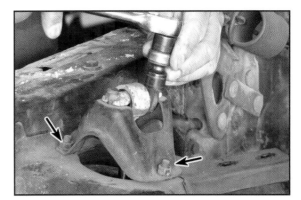

4c.9 Remove the two upper shock absorber mounting bolts in the engine compartment. Since we are performing a restoration, we will also remove the three nuts (two indicated) securing the shock bracket to the fenderwell.

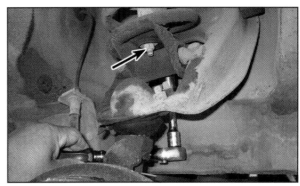

4c.10 From below, insert a short extension and socket to remove the lower shock mounting nuts (one indicated), then the shock can be withdrawn upward from the car.

4c.11 Remove the bolts (A) securing the strut rod to the lower control arm, then hold the head (B) of the stabilizer bar link while removing the nut (C). Use penetrating oil on all fasteners.

4c.12 Remove the nut from the front of the strut rod and detach it from its brace. New bushings will be installed during reassembly.

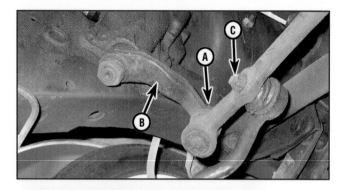

4c.13 Remove the nut and disconnect the center link-to-Pitman arm rod-end (A) from the Pitman arm (B). Also remove the tie-rod-to-center link nut (C), one on each side, then disconnect the tie-rod ends from the steering arms on the spindles.

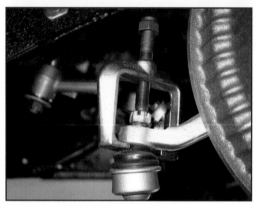

4c.14 When removing steering items with rod-ends, first remove the cotter pin (if equipped), then loosen the castellated nut except for the last four or five threads. Position a tie-rod end removal tool (C-shaped frame) with the point in the hollow dish on the stem of the rod-end, and tighten until the rod-end pops loose. Then remove the nut.

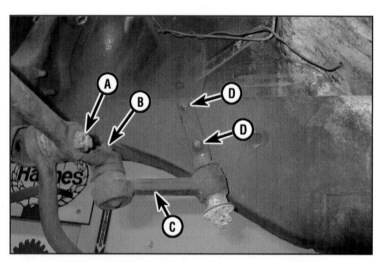

4c.15 On the right side of the front subframe, disconnect the rod-end (A) at the center link, and the rod end (B) at the idler arm (C). Remove the two nuts securing the idler arm bracket to the subframe. The idler arm bushings are generally worn out. A new idler arm will be installed on reassembly to ensure crisp steering.

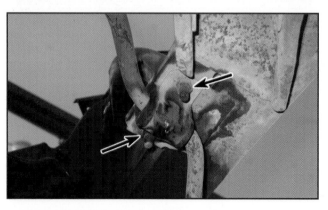

4c.16 Remove the two nuts securing the stabilizer bar frame brackets to the subframe. When both sides are unbolted, the bar can be removed. New rubber bushings will be used on reassembly.

4c.17 The front spring sits in a saddle on top of the upper control arm. You cannot remove the A-arms until the spring pressure is relieved. A spring compressor tool can be rented. The correct tool for our application is one that works inside the spring, not on the outside. The shaft from the upper piece threads into the lower piece, compressing the spring.

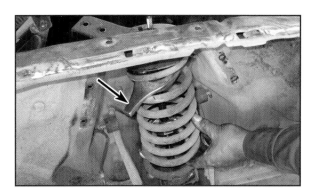

4c.18 When the spring is compressed enough that there is no pressure on the upper control arm, remove the two large nuts (indicated) on the fenderwell that secure the upper control arm.

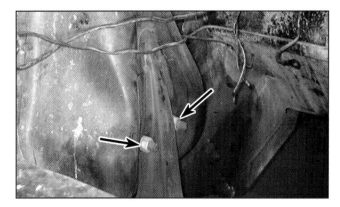

4c.19 Use a crowbar to pry the upper arm away from the fenderwell. Remove the bolt securing the lower control arm to the subframe.

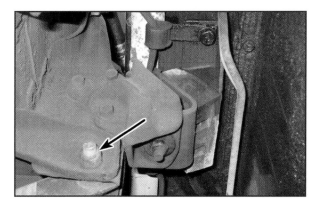

4c.20 At this point, it's possible to remove both control arms and the spindle, and even the brakes (if they haven't been removed yet), in one operation. The components can be separated for restoration some time later.

4c.21 You'll find the rear suspension much easier to disassemble than the front. A basic rear end with two shocks and two springs, that's all there is to it. You can completely disassemble the rear suspension in a matter of minutes if the fasteners cooperate.

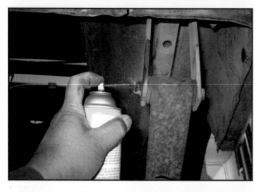

4c.22 But nuts and bolts on a vehicle this old rarely cooperate. Soak all of the rear suspension fasteners with penetrating oil and let them sit for a half hour, then apply more penetrant and begin disassembly.

4c.23 With the back seat removed (see Chapter 4D), you can use a long extension to reach the upper mounting nuts for the rear shock absorbers (on convertibles only). On coupes and fastbacks, there are two small plugs at the front of the trunk floor to remove, providing access to the shock mounting nuts. The remainder of rear suspension removal work will be from below.

4c.24 Use a floor jack to raise the rear end just enough to position a pair of sturdy jackstands under it. Disassembly is easier on the floor than under the car.

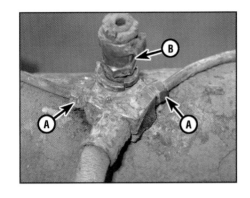

4c.25   Disconnect the brake lines (A) from the brake hose junction block. The fitting on top (B) is a breather (hose is missing here) to vent the rear axle assembly. Remove the breather fitting that secures the junction block to the rear end housing.

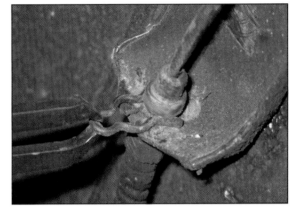

4c.26   On the chassis, remove the clips that secure the parking brake cables in brackets ahead of the rear suspension, then pull the cables back and release them from the parking brake cable bracket, which has been hanging loose near the transmission area since the powertrain was removed.

4c.27   At this point we have only four bolts to remove and the rear suspension comes out, but these spring-eye mounting bolts have been in place for four decades or so and they are comfortable where they are. You might need a breaker bar to get the loosening started. Shown is one of the front spring-eye bolts.

4c.28   The same operation is repeated for the shackle bolt at the rear of the spring. Note that our Mustang had overly-long aftermarket shackles installed to raise the rear of the car, a cheap and unsafe fix for worn-out rear springs (common on early Mustangs). The proper solution is to install new or re-arched springs to restore the correct ride height.

4c.29 If you're using floor jacks, the rear axle and suspension can now be lowered to the floor and removed from under the car for further disassembly. Since we have a hoist, we raised the car, leaving the suspension and axle on the jackstands.

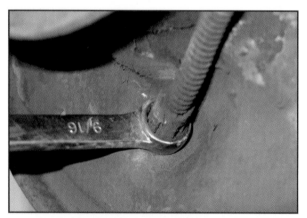

4c.30 Back off the brake shoe adjusters, then remove the brake drums. The parking brake cables can be removed from the brake backing plates by compressing these spring fingers. A small hose clamp tightened around the fingers will squeeze them sufficiently to pull the cable out a short ways, then remove the clamp and remove the whole cable (refer to Chapter 7D for detailed brake photos). A 9/16 box-end wrench, slid over the fingers often works also.

4c.31 We can now remove the lower mounting nut for each rear shock (A). Remove the four U-bolt nuts (B) and the spring can be removed. You will need penetrating oil and a breaker bar.

Interior and top

Even hobbyists who have previously done a restoration or two still may shy away from doing interior work. Thankfully, you have chosen a vehicle that lends itself to the DIY restorer. Except for a very few aspects, the interior restoration of classic '65 to '70 Mustangs is mostly a matter of removing the old upholstery, padding and carpeting, then restoring components you will keep, such as the instrument cluster, the glove box, kickpanels, floor console and rear quarter panel trim panels (where applicable). Not everyone has a convertible Mustang such as our project car, and on those models, it's not a bad idea to have a professional upholsterer install the outer covering after you have removed, restored, lubricated and reassembled all of the folding top components. You will need a few extra tools, such as: a set of small Allen wrenches, a pair of long-handled hog-ring pliers for attaching new upholstery to your seats, a hair dryer, and a pair of side-cutter pliers to cut clips when removing the old seat covers.

You may not be undertaking a full-on restoration just yet, but you will be amazed at what you can do for your project just by installing new upholstery, padding and carpeting, and the costs are not too exorbitant. Other aspects of your Mustang project, such as engine and transmission rebuilding, suspension restoration, and bodywork/paint costs are much higher and the restored mechanical pieces don't look any different that the old parts. Check with the major distributors of Mustang restoration supplies to see what seasonal deals they may have.

Choosing to do your own interior will boost your restoration confidence level, as well as garner admiration from family and friends when they see what you did in only a couple of weekends.

4d.1 From this view, our Mustang's interior looks like it was just brought up from a lagoon. But as you will see in later Chapters, even a worst-case interior like ours can be restored, even if you have never tried.

4d.2 Our top really puts the rag into ragtop! Nevertheless we will demonstrate what you can do with the overhead part of your interior if you are very ambitious and confident in your skills.

4d.3 Everything inside our Mustang had the worst treatment possible, left outside for years, exposed to animals and all forms of weather. This is not something that can be handled by detailing products.

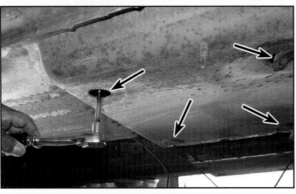

4d.4 The front bucket seats are secured to the underside of the floorpan with four nuts, accessed by removing the four rubber plugs.

4d.5 Pick up the seat and set it down where you can work on it. Up on a workbench is preferred. The outside edge of the bucket seat has a long aluminum cover over the hinge. Remove it and store carefully, as they damage easily.

4d.6 The rear seats are even easier to remove. The seat bottom is kept in place by spring clips. Pull up sharply at each side to release the clips, and remove the seat.

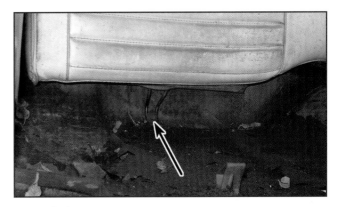

4d.7 The backrest of the rear seat is hung on two clips at the top, and by two bolts at the floor, one on each side.

4d.8 With the bolts removed, just pull upward on the seatback to release it. This can be accomplished by one person. On some models the seatback upholstery is also secured at the bottom with two sheetmetal screws.

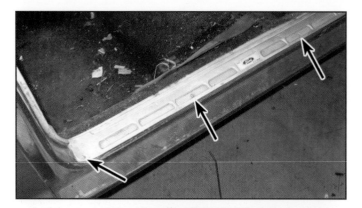

4d.9 The door sill plates secure the carpeting in the door opening, and also secure the front and rear kickpanels. Remove the mounting screws and carefully pry up the sill plates.

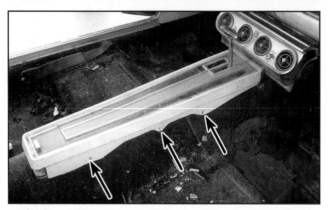

4d.10 With the seats removed, you have access to remove the screws securing the floor console (if equipped) to the floor. Use a small Allen wrench to remove the shift handle. On models with a rear ashtray, remove the ashtray to access two console mounting screws. Models without air conditioning have a small compartment at the front.

4d.11 If your front kickpanels look like ours, replace them! Remove these screws. You cannot replace the padding and carpeting with the kickpanels in place.

4d.12 The quarter-panel trim on convertibles is secured with mounting screws and (above) the snaps that secure the boot cover over the folded-down top. Remove the fasteners to remove the panel. On fastback models, remove the folding rear seat panels to allow removal of the quarter-panel trim. On coupe models, the front edge of the trim panel is secured by the windlace at the rear of the door opening and several screws.

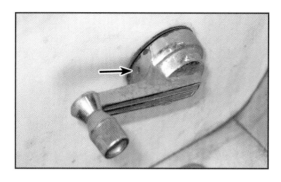

4d.13 A small Allen wrench is required to loosen the setscrew securing the quarter-window handle.

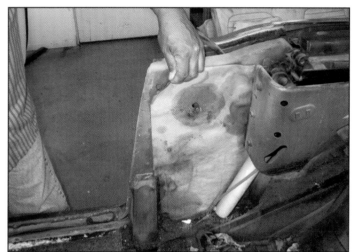

4d.14 After the panel is removed, peel off the weatherstrip paper for access to the quarter-window mechanism. At lower right is the bottom of the convertible top actuating cylinder. There is one on each side of the car.

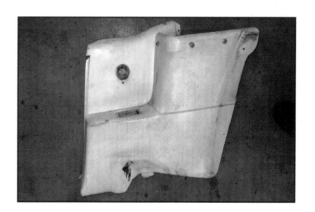

4d.15 Unlike the kickpanels up front, the quarter-panel trim panels are actually covered with upholstery to match the interior. Remove the old material carefully; take it slowly and avoid damaging the panels, which are hard to find. If yours does need repair, see Chapter 8A.

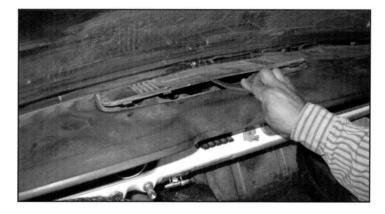

4d.16 To remove the dashboard pad, which will make many other operations much easier in your restoration, first remove the radio grille, using a plastic trim-removal tool.

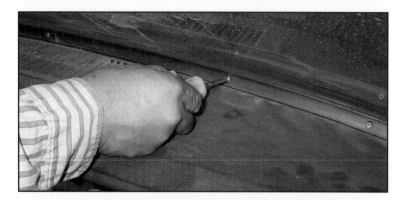

4d.17 A short screwdriver can be used to remove the screws securing the trim panel along the inside-bottom of the windshield. Remove the screws, lift up the speaker and disconnect the speaker wires.

4d.18 Just above the instrument panel, remove the screws, then pry out the dashpad trim with a trim tool to release the clips.

4d.19 Use needle-nose pliers or a trim tool to remove the clips securing the two defroster ducts. Remove the defroster hose/duct from below.

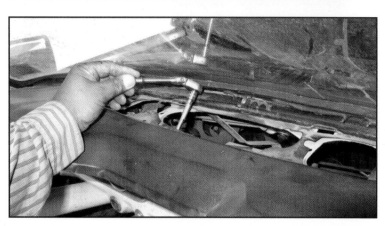

4d.20 There are four nuts securing the dashpad to the body. Two are accessible through the speaker opening and two are accessible at the extreme left and right behind the instrument panel.

4d.21 Remove the dashpad. Installing a new one will prove to be a big improvement from a cracked and warped one.

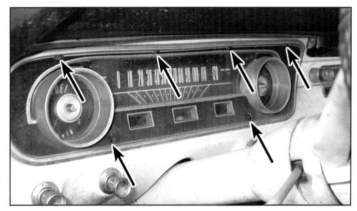

4d.22 Disconnect the speedometer cable from the rear of the instrument cluster, then remove the screws and gently pull the instrument cluster toward you.

4d.23 To remove the ignition lock cylinder, insert the key, turn to the ACC position and insert a straightened paperclip into the hole to depress the tang inside, then pull the key, paperclip and cylinder from the instrument panel.

4d.24 With the ashtray removed, you can use a mirror behind the dash to better see the fasteners securing the heating/ventilating controls to the back of the instrument panel. Remove the temp knobs, then remove the faceplate over the controls.

4d.25 Pull the HVAC control rearward, until you can disconnect the clamps holding the cables. Mark each cable and its original location before disconnecting the cables.

4d.26 With the glovebox out of the way, it is easier to see these wires and components. Use a small digital camera to take photos behind the instrument panel for reference.

4d.27 This is a good time to access the bolts securing the wiper assembly to the interior side of the firewall.

4d.28 At the left side of the instrument panel, you will want to unbolt the fresh-air cable bracket and the bolts securing the parking brake handle assembly. If your brake handle is cracked (as many are) we illustrate the replacement procedure. When the old plastic breaks, it'll be when you're pulling hard on it, and the cut edge can hurt your hand.

4d.29 If you are doing a full restoration, even if the firewall is the only area that needs media-blasting to remove rust, this is the time to tag, disconnect and remove all the wiring behind the instrument panel.

4d.30 Luckily, the Mustang wiring harness is very basic and uncomplicated. The fuse box is as minimal as could be. Rather than disconnect any wires from the fuse box, just unbolt the fuse box from the body and withdraw it with the harness.

4d.31 Tag and disconnect the connectors at electrical components that are to be removed for restoration, such as here at the heater box.

4d.32 The brake light switch is attached to the pedal and the rod to the master cylinder. Use needle-nose pliers to pull the clip, then push the pin out and the switch comes right off.

4d.33 To remove the door panels, remove the two large screws securing the armrest to the door.

4d.34 Use a small Allen wrench to remove screws in the door handle and window crank. Unlike most cars, the Mustang requires no special tool to remove a hidden spring or clip.

4d.35 After carefully prying off the door panel with a trim tool, remove the paper weathershield. After so many years the paper may need to be scraped off.

4d.36 Don't forget some of the smaller details in disassembling the interior. Remove the inside mirror and store it carefully.

4d.37 Another job for a very small Allen wrench is the removal of the sun visors.

4d.38 With the seats out, you can start to remove all the carpeting and the padding under the carpet, as seen here. The original padding soaked up water like a sponge, so anytime you pull up the carpet and padding, you don't know what you'll find.

4d.39 Wear a dust mask when you are dealing with old carpet and padding, and while you are sweeping or vacuuming the floor. There could easily be mold present in the materials.

4d.40 The driver's portion of the floor will probably have the worst rust. Scrape the big flakes off with a putty knife or chisel, then proceed with a wire-brush attachment in an air or electric drill motor to get the rest off. If there are small holes, they can be cleaned and sealed with epoxy. Bigger holes mean replacing that section of the floorpan. We replaced the whole floor.

4d.41 When disassembling the bucket seats, remove the screw and the cover over the seat pivot (console side of the seat shown).

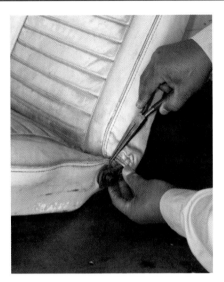

4d.42 Use pliers to remove the clips (one on each side), then pry behind the pivot arm until it comes off the stud on the seat bottom, and remove the seat back.

4d.43 Flip the seat bottom over and examine the seat track mechanism. Take a digital photo to record how the spring and levers are arranged.

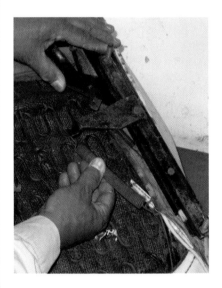

4d.44 Remove the spring and the mounting screws securing the seat tracks. Ours will require media-blasting and painting.

4d.45 At the edge of the seat bottom nearest the center of the car, remove the two screws and the reinforcement plate where the seatback stop-bolt rests. Save in a bag.

4d.46 You'll need a good pair of cutting pliers to cut loose the hog-rings used to attach upholstery to the underside of the seat frame. Where there is a sewn flap in the material, cut the hog-rings securing the listing wire in the flap. Save the listing wires.

4d.47 Hold the seat foam in place while you roll the old material back to remove it.

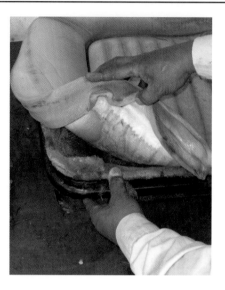

4d.48 Lift up the foam to inspect the bottom. If it's torn or crumbling, install new foam. Even if all the foam pieces look good, at least replace the foam in the driver's seat, where the worst wear will take place.

4d.49 On the rear of the seatback, use a putty knife or trim tool to release the clips securing the back cover. There may also be some small screws.

4d.50 The hog-rings around the seatback cover must all be cut off. Take a digital photo of the spacing and locations for reference when installing new seat upholstery.

4d.51 Here's the underside of the rear seat bottom. Note that burlap material is used between the seat foam and the springs, to keep the metal from abrading the foam or material.

4d.52 After removing the hog rings, off comes the upholstery, burlap and foam.

4d.53 Before we can proceed with our body restoration, we have to remove the old convertible top. Perhaps in a another week or two it might just collapse on its own! The exterior chrome trim strips that secure the back of the top must be removed first.

4d.54 Our trim screws were so corroded, many had to be drilled out to remove the chrome strips.

4d.55 Pry out the rubber weatherstrip that fits between the top and the quarter glass.

4d.56 Around the rear of the top bay, remove the bolts and the strip securing the bottom rear edge of the top material.

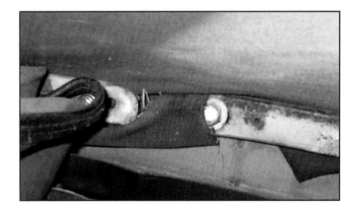

4d.57 Disconnect the cylinders from the top assembly, then remove this pivot bracket just ahead of the top well on each side. Have a friend help you lift the top assembly from the Mustang.

5 Build a rolling stand

As we know, storage is an issue in any restoration project. Once you have disassembled your car to the bone, it becomes an immovable island on jackstands. You have to pick your location carefully because it's going to be some time before you have the car rolling again. This can complicate both working on the body itself as well as accessing parts that may be stored behind the immobilized body. Unless you have lots of garage room, your Mustang is now impeding its own restoration!

One solution can be to create a custom rolling framework on wheels to support the body.

Not only will this rolling stand make it easier to move the car around the garage, it will greatly help when it comes time for media blasting and painting, too. The project requires lengths of 2x3-inch steel tubing, a welder and a chop saw. The whole operation took about three hours. If you have a welder already, you could build a rolling stand like this for your project, or mark your tubing for the cuts you need and bring your tubing to a shop that can cut them for you. Most metal companies that sell steel tubing will make cuts for you at a reasonable price. Alternatively, you could rent a metal cutting saw. It could be done with a hacksaw but you'll

wear out two dozen blades, not to mention your arms.

At all times, think safety! Wear leather gloves when handling tubing, especially with freshly cut edges, and wear a full-face safety mask when cutting or grinding. It should go without saying, but never, ever make even small tack welds without wearing a full-face welding helmet, and preferably one with a leather piece at the bottom that can keep sparks from going down the neck of your shirt.

Follow our construction sequence to fabricate a simple but effective rolling stand. When you begin, block the car to the height you'd prefer for working over and under your Mustang.

5.1 Four tall jackstands supported our convertible in a level position while the cradle was fabricated.

5.2 After measuring from the floor to the front mounting hole for the rear spring, a length of tubing was cut and drilled for a 3/8-inch bolt (minimum) and the tube was bolted in position. Use a lock nut on the bolt, but tighten the bolt only enough to snug it up. You don't want to pinch the sheetmetal or the rear spring installation could be difficult.

5.3 With both rear uprights bolted in place, the project was off and running. Check each tube with a level and a tape measure for squareness.

5.4 The measurement between the bottoms of the tubes should be the same as the measurement at the top, although you'll have to measure the top distance by measuring just below the body.

5.5 A chop saw makes short work of cutting the square-section tubing. If possible, use the saw outdoors, and definitely away from anything flammable; there will be a shower of hot sparks. Keep a fire extinguisher and a hose handy or at least a bucket of water just in case.

5.6 A short length of tubing was cut and drilled to mount where the front lower control arm was attached to the chassis. Again, use a locknut on the bolt but do not overtighten. This piece extends outward to make the front legs the same width apart as the rears.

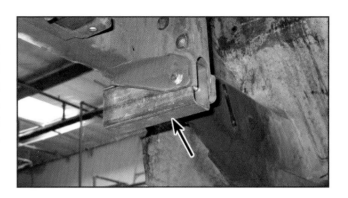

5.7 The vertical tube was clamped against the horizontal piece, the verticality of the upright was checked, and these two tubes were welded. The same procedure was used to mount the left front leg of the rolling support stand.

5.8 With all four legs in place, attention was turned to the longitudinal rails and the tubes to mount between the two front legs and between the two rear legs.

5.9 The four side tubes were checked with a square and then the corners were tack-welded together. After all the corners were tacked, they were checked again for squareness, and the joints final-welded.

5.10 Our convertible unibody gets air, thanks to a large forklift. It's being lifted so casters can be welded underneath the four corners to make our stand a roller. Those of you without a forklift (99.9-percent of you!) will have to resort to a jack, lifting one end at a time.

5.11 Four heavy-duty casters were securely tack-welded to the bottom of our stand, one caster at each corner. They could have been bolted on, but this was the quickest way to begin using the stand. The casters could be cut off in the future if necessary. Keep in mind, though, this stand could become the framework for a nice rolling workbench when your project is finished.

5.12 The Mustang is now rolling and one person can move it wherever it needs to go. When the media-blasting begins, there will be access to the top and bottom of the tub.

5.13 To further strengthen our convertible tub, a length of 1-inch tubing was welded from side-to-side to maintain the proper body width in this area, critical to proper door fit. Since we're going to be replacing our floorpan, it's important to reinforce the body (the floorpan is the main structural member in a convertible)

5.14 The area of the welds is not large, and can be ground smooth after the car is together again. The welded area is covered by the interior panels.

5.15 The paint was carefully ground from the windshield header.

5.16 Two tubes were tack-welded to the windshield header and the cross-tube. This is necessary for the stability of the body when the floor is cut out.

5.17 Two additional tubes were welded into the door opening for further stiffening of this critical area.

5.18 Not only does the rolling stand protect the unibody from stress or twisting, it simplifies loading it on a ramp-truck if it has to go somewhere. Ours had an appointment for media-blasting, and after that another move to the bodyshop.

6 Body restoration

Restoration and paint

Let's take look at several different candidates for restoration. Mustang A exhibits no rust, but has a faded old repaint and a few typical small dents. Mustang B is like ours, rusted panels are everywhere and a cheap repaint covers sins unseen. Mustang C is near-perfect, very straight, original but faded paint, never been hit, never suffered any amateur bodywork, but the engine and transmission are missing.

Which would you think was the better project to purchase? In terms of the expenses, Mustang C will cost you less. The expense of media-blasting, expert metalwork and panel replacements will far outstrip the cost of obtaining a replacement engine and transmission. The cost of a paint job alone, on a car that has already been bodyworked to achieve a straight body, can vary from $3,000 to $15,000 plus. The former is for an inexpensive paint job where little prep work is performed. The difference between the high and low figures is the amount of time and expertise expended. A lower-level bodyman/painter may have low overhead, working in his own home shop, but he may not have all the modern equipment and newer paint finishes. You generally get what you pay for, and the problem with a paint job is that you can't take the paint back to the store!

Utilize the experience of other Mustang restorers in your area to select a shop that will meet a level of expertise that you can afford. When you see your car in primer, it isn't always easy to tell if the all-important prep work has been done correctly, but if there are problems, they will show up immediately after the glossy paint is applied.

In producing this book, thousands of photos were taken, including a considerable number concerning the bodywork. Once our car was media-blasted, we could assess the Mustang's true condition. We chose to replace the floorpan and several other parts for which new sheetmetal was available. We hope you won't have to have your floor replaced, as it is a big job that should be done by professionals. Remember that the Mustang is a unibody vehicle. If there are

flaws in fitting the floor, welding the floor, and sealing it properly before primer and paint, you could have problems with flexing a few years down the road. In this Chapter, we show enough photos to give you the basic idea of how various aspects of our car were restored, but don't think this is all there is to it. Every step you see here was repeated countless times, sometimes with two or

three bodymen working on it at the same time, and often using a lot of tools to ensure that two mating pieces of sheetmetal are just right before welding. The message is, find the best car you can and save money and aggravation when it comes time to prepare and paint the body. Most of the work you see here would be moderately-to-very difficult to complete at home.

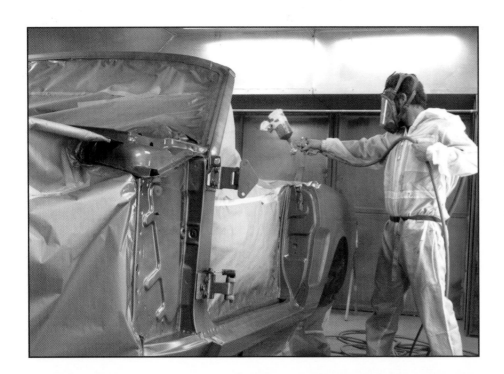

6a.1 Wow - starting to look good! But this car needed a lot of "therapy" before it got to this point...

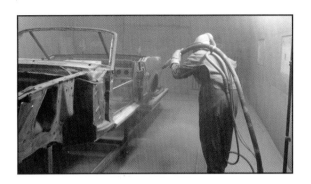

6a.2 For obvious reasons, we took only one or two photos of our car being media-blasted. This is a very inhospitable environment for a camera!

6a.3 Once the layers of old paint, the undercoating, dirt, etc. were erased, the convertible looked like new . . . from ten feet away. All the flaws in the body were laid bare when you looked more closely. However, this is the only right way to begin a total restoration. You have to know what you're dealing with.

6a.4 Here's a typical example of a spot that needs repair. The bottom of the right rear wheelwell was rusted out. On the exterior, the rust area was filled with filler, probably by the same person who did the inferior red repaint, but the rusted part on the inside continued to collect dirt and water.

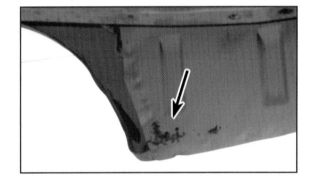

6a.5 With our car trucked to the body shop, the pros could assess the body with experienced eyes and hands. The three main areas that required new metal were the floorpan, the taillight panel at the rear . . .

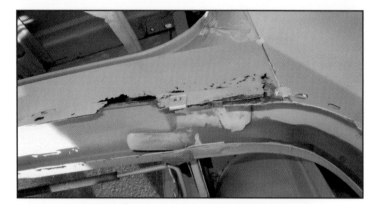

6a.6 . . . and the area just ahead of the trunk lid.

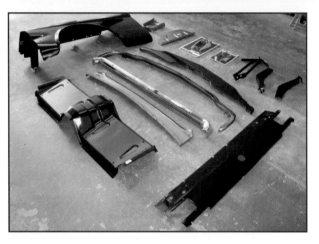

6a.7 There are many sheetmetal Mustang parts made new today, particularly those body parts that are prone to rust or damage. You have probably guessed by now that the bumpers on classic Mustangs are attractive, but really don't offer much body protection.

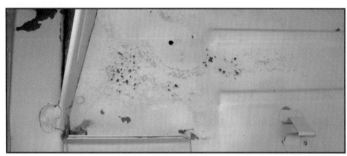

6a.8 It's easy to see here how many little holes there are across our floorpan. They could be welded one by one, but that would rack up lots of professional hours on the project (and the area still wouldn't be very structurally sound).

6a.9 A brand new floorpan, from firewall to trunk, while a lot of work to install, will make for a tighter car in the long run.

6a.10 Careful measurements are taken at various points on the old floor to use for reference when installing the new floor.

6a.11 You can't just cut out the whole stock floorpan at once, so a cutoff wheel in an air tool was used to cut out sections at a time. Of course, you can see how the operator is dressed for this kind of work: heavy welding gloves, full-face safety mask, and tough pants.

6a.12 Removing the floor sections one at a time allows better evaluation of what's underneath, such as the subframe rails they attach to.

6a.13 For purposes of keeping the body from flexing before the new floor is installed, the center-section of the old pan is left in place for now. Alignment marks for the center section of the new floor will help when the old center section is removed.

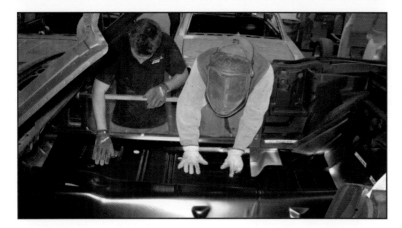

6a.14 The new pan is laid into place and finessed for a good fit before any welding is performed.

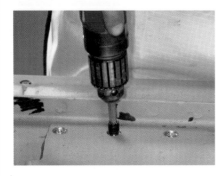

6a.15 The subframe rails and other parts were spot-welded at the factory, and that is what we're doing in the floor installation. To remove spot-welds, you need a hole-cutter like this called a broach. Locate the spot-welds, drill in the center, then use the tool to cut down through the top layer of sheetmetal and leave only a small hole in the other part.

6a.16 The old floorpan attaches to the front subframe rails with two rows of spot-welds.

6a.17 Regular paint will burn off during welding and perhaps initiate rust before long. Weld-Thru primer is made for coating parts that will be welded together and is designed to still protect the metal. We used a lot!

6a.18 At the front of the toeboard area of the firewall, the firewall was cut back to where there was solid metal, leaving a space to fill before the new floor is installed.

6a.19 A cardboard template was made and then traced onto new steel. The new piece was bent in a sheetmetal brake to conform to the firewall and the floor. Before any welding, the inside of the subframe rails was cleaned of rust and the upper flanges ground clean, then sprayed with Weld-Thru primer.

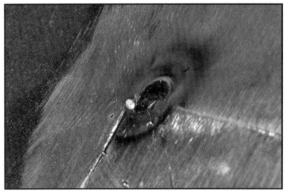

6a.20 Here's a nice tight fit of the new part to the firewall. All four corners were tack-welded and rechecked for movement.

6a.21 The added piece will make for a good strong bond with the new floorpan. With the old center-section removed, all the perimeter parts where the floor will be welded have been sprayed with Weld-Thru primer.

6a.22 Except for all the welding to do, the floor looks like it's ready for the road.

6a.23 The most important thing about joining overlapping or butted panels is that the two pieces must be welded while they are clamped or otherwise kept in direct contact. Gaps could leave a weak or leaky floor, just the thing we've done all this work to prevent!

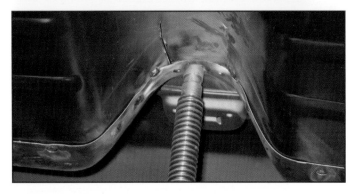

6a.24 A screw jack is very helpful when you have only two hands. From below, this jack is applying some pressure to the top/front of the floorpan. Pressure should be just enough to keep the two metal edges in contact.

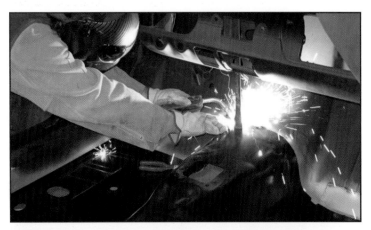

6a.25 Several spot-welds are made inside the car to keep the pan from moving. Spot-welds are usually spaced six inches apart, then to the same spacing as the original spot-welds. Welding too long in one spot will warp the panels with too much heat.

6a.26 When the welder is working under the vehicle, a helper can stand on a section of the panel to tighten the panel gap. He can stand on a brick or block of wood to put the weight where it needs to be. Here he is putting his weight on a long prybar to put pressure only on the spot-weld location.

6a.27 When aligning two pieces for spot-welding such as the subframe-to-floor, use a tapered punch to align matching holes and spot-weld. Only use as much weld as it takes to join the pieces. A bigger blob will not make the joint stronger, but it will leave non-stock looking welds, unless you spend a long time grinding afterwards.

6a.28 Heat usually produces some warpage of thin metals. Here the rear of the new floor is being welded to the remnant of the original floor. After making two or three spot-welds, you may have to use a hammer to flush the fit here or there.

6a.29 A Whitney sheetmetal punch was used to space a set of holes through the new floorpan so the new can be married to the old in the backseat area. A body hammer is used to tighten up the gaps before welding.

6a.30 Once the pieces are welded, the welds can be ground and the seams sealed. It's going to look just like the original.

6a.31 Pressure is applied before each spot-weld to ensure there are no gaps.

6a.32 This piece in the center of the floorpan is a side-to-side brace found only on convertible models. Without a roof to stiffen the car, the floor needs to be stronger. Here all of our floor welding is done, and smaller jobs can now be tackled!

6a.33 Body seam-sealer is what auto manufacturers use where body panels join together. This helps make panels more waterproof and stifles squeaks. Here it's being applied with a caulking gun, but you can get it in a tube for smaller jobs.

6a.34 Trying to make the seams look like they were factory-applied is tricky. One is tempted to run a finger along a freshly sealed seam to smooth it out, but factory seams have more of a rounded bead, rather than flat.

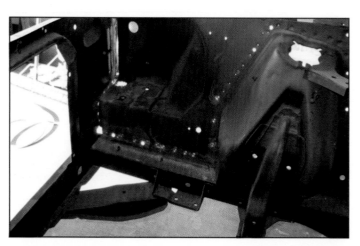

6a.35 The front portion of the passenger-side fender apron on our car had some serious rust where the battery box was (common in many older vehicles). The spot-welds were all drilled out and the front half of a right-side reproduction apron cut and drilled to fit.

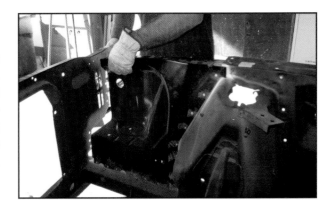

6a.36 You have to drill out the spot-welds at the radiator support before you can remove the apron. In our case the repro apron was cut at about the middle of the shock tower and welded to the original rear portion. The rear portion has the hidden serial number of your Mustang, so you want to keep the original rear portion if at all possible.

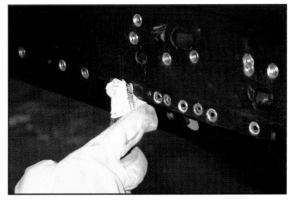

6a.37 The panel between the taillights on our car had taken a beating, and we replaced it with new sheetmetal. Tedious as it may be, the proper way to remove it is to sand the edges until you can see the spot-welds, then drill them out with a broach.

6a.38 You may have to use a hammer and chisel to separate the panel from the braces in the trunk.

6a.39 Once you cut the far ends at the top, you can remove the old panel. Note the rust in all the flanges.

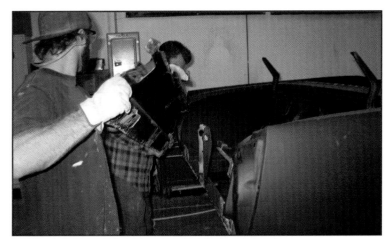

6a.40 Grind the body brackets clean for a good fit, as these secure the bumper.

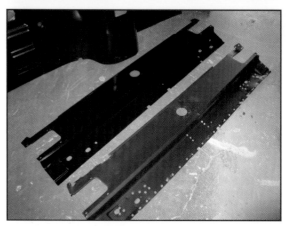

6a.41 The new panel (top) looks just like ours . . . without the holes and dents.

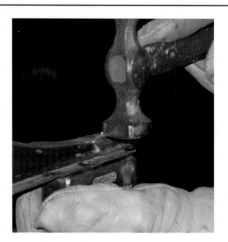

6a.42 Whenever you have cut off a panel by removing the spot-welds, you have some clean-up to do. Use a small sander to remove the paint, then straighten the flange with hammer and dolly.

6a.43 Mark the back of the panel with a bent scratch-awl through holes in the flange.

6a.44 Along the bottom edge of the panel, use a Whitney punch to make a row of holes.

6a.45 Coat the bottom flange on the body and all the cleaned brackets with Weld-Thru primer.

6a.46 One method of temporarily securing sheet-metal parts is with Clecos. Use the special Cleco pliers and insert a Cleco in a hole and release the spring-loaded fastener. To remove, just squeeze it with the tool again and withdraw the Cleco.

6a.47 The Clecos will align the panel for setup, but we also used a number of clamps along the bottom to see how it fits.

6a.48 The trunk lid, end caps and bumper were temporarily installed to check that everything fits well and that the rear panel is adjusted just right. Don't weld it in until this has been checked.

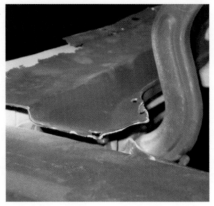

6a.49 This is the kind of damage that is most common, a rusted section that was never attended to, and it grew. On our rear quarters, the filler was knocked out and several small pieces of sheetmetal were welded in place and hammered to the correct contour, then smoothed with a thin coat of filler, sanded and primed.

6a.50 Spot-welds were drilled out all along the front and rear edges of the panel in front of the trunk lid. At the ends, the panel was cut off to where clean original metal would give us something to securely weld the reproduction piece.

6a.51 Once the outer sheet-metal piece was removed and the spot-weld points sanded, the lower part was painted with Weld-Thru primer, and the panel ends straightened.

6a.52 The reproduction outer panel was clamped in place along the front edge only to check for the correct gap between the panel and the trunk lid. Cardboard was placed over the new sheetmetal before clamping.

6a.53 Tack-welds secure the new panel at the trunk lip, while clamps are used to secure the two panels while the spot-welds are made. Note the horseshoe clamp, which is handy because you can clamp on either side of a spot and weld in the center of the clamp.

6a.54 After some sanding over the spot-welds, this new panel will be indistinguishable from the original, and our convertible is one step closer to being ready for paint.

6a.55 Certainly there is no quicker and more thorough way to remove old paint and rust than media-blasting such as we used. The media was able to reach numerous hard-to-access parts of the body, and it essentially sands the rust away, even though sand was not the media used on our Mustang.

6a.56 Hopefully your project Mustang will not need extensive bodywork. If you are trying to remove a lousy over-paint and at the same time find areas that were sloppily repaired with too much filler, an alternative is to use an electric sander such as the one shown here, called a D-A (for dual-action) because it sands in an elliptical motion rather than straight back-and forth, which can take off too much material if you linger on one spot.

6a.57 With the electric sander, you can tackle one part per weekend, sanding to bare metal. If there are no repairs to be made, the part can be primered and put away. Before priming the part, sand it by hand with #320-grit sandpaper, then clean it with wax-and-grease remover, available at automotive paint supply stores.

6a.58 Our Mustang has to be painted in several different colors. Besides the exterior paint color, there are places that receive only the chassis black. Here the engine compartment is getting its color. This is an inside job and the need for a serious, professional breathing mask is extra important in such tight quarters.

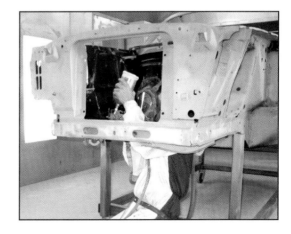

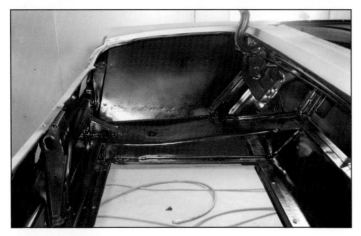

6a.59 The trunk area starts to look a lot better with a coat of chassis black for a uniform appearance. Painting the trunk should be done when the fuel tank is out of the vehicle, as the top of the tank should remain bare metal.

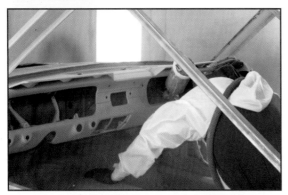

6a.60 Under the dash area is tough to get at with a spraygun. Some painters use a small touchup spraygun for such areas. In our case, our dashboard has to be painted white as original, so the idea is to keep the black off the dash or it could affect the final look of the white interior paint.

6a.61 It's at this stage, almost ready for final paint, that our convertible starts to look like a car again. Once the car is primered, it should be treated carefully, so you don't have to go through the trouble of having to do any more body work!

6a.62 All the removable body parts are painted separately, such as this door being primered in the paint booth.

6a.63 At this point our body-shop chose to hang the doors on the body to check for the fit of components. If you adjust the door hinges to achieve a close and even gap at the rear of the doors to the body, tighten the hinge mounting bolts.

6a.64 One reason for checking is a case like this, where the gap is ok at the front of the door, except where the fender meets the top of the door. Adjustments must be made at both the fender and door.

6a.65 Your Mustang is peppered with places where captive-nut clips are required to install various large and small components. Keep a box of assorted clips in a box. You don't want to have to remove an item because the last bolt-hole doesn't have a clip.

6a.66 Ever wonder how the show cars achieve such beautiful fit and finish? This is one of the techniques of making a perfect transition between two adjoining panels, as this trunk lid is being massaged. The process begins by mounting the part, like this trunk lid, and carefully measuring the gaps around it.

6a.67 It may seem excessive, but the entire top of the trunk lid and the adjoining surfaces around it are covered with a thin coat of body filler, including the gap between the parts!

6a.68 The precise gap desired is made by taking a drywall blade and taping a section of sandpaper to the blade. Pushing the blade back and forth makes a perfect gap. For a smaller gap, use thinner sandpaper, or thicker paper for a bigger gap.

6a.69 A longboard accepts long strips of sandpaper and is very good at taking down a surface you want to come out flat. There are air-powered versions of these, but you have to be careful with these as they sand quickly.

6a.70 There are specialty sanding blocks of various shapes and contours, and ones like this that are actually flexible, for sanding curved areas.

6a.71 By the time the trunk lid was ready for primer, you can see how little of the filler is left, and the surface will look perfectly flat when painted.

6a.72 Wherever you have two mating parts that are meant to flow together, like the headlight surrounds and the front fenders, they almost never seem to fit nicely without a massage. No, we're not gluing them together! That's filler between them. A tiny gap is made between the two parts using a utility blade after the filler has started to harden. Both parts are sanded in place, then the headlight surround is separated.

6a.73 All areas that will be painted with the final color must be wet-sanded by hand using fine (wet-and-dry) sandpaper and a flexible sanding pad. The plastic water bottle is used to supply more water for sanding.

6a.74 When a small flaw is discovered, automotive glazing putty can be dabbed on with your finger. It dries quickly and sands very easily with wet-sanding.

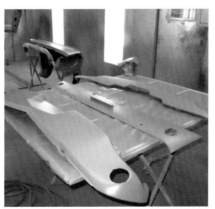

6a.75 The body parts that come off, such as these aprons, are better painted off the car, so no color overspray goes onto areas of the car where chassis black is the final color.

6a.76 Chances are you won't be painting your Mustang at home, but if you were painting a fender or other part, always clean the surface first with a wax-and-grease remover.

6a.77 Just about ready for paint, you can see that not everything on our car is going to be Twilight Turquoise metallic. The finish paint in today's paint systems consists of two coats, a basecoat that has the actual color, and several coats of clear over it, which is what gives the paint its depth and gloss.

6a.78 Today's paint systems are wonderful, with durable products, good technical resources from the paint companies, and paint with depth that makes metallic paints really sparkle. However, today's catalyzed two-part paints are devastating to your skin and lungs, and aren't recommended for home use. You need a large booth with lots of lights and lots of ventilation fans, and most importantly, the proper head-to-toe suit and the best mask you can buy.

6a.79 About half of our Mustang body parts are in another room, awaiting their new paint, while the body looks good even at this stage. It's the reward for all the work that was required to get to this point.

6a.80 After the proper time in the booth, the convertible (still on its rolling stand) was slid outside the body shop to catch a few rays and a few looks! After all the parts are fully cured, they go back in the booth for the application of the clearcoats. Today's HVLP (High Volume, Low Pressure) sprayguns are great for applying paint without a lot of overspray, which makes for a better finish, with less paint wasted.

6a.81 The basecoats and clearcoats are sprayed on the smaller parts, with every confidence that they will look exactly the same as the main body.

6a.82 When the other painting is done, it's time to paint the instrument panel and the interior side of the doors. It's not easy to get under to spray, but still don't try it without a good mask. The correct white for our dash (and all other original colors) are available in spray cans from Mustang suppliers.

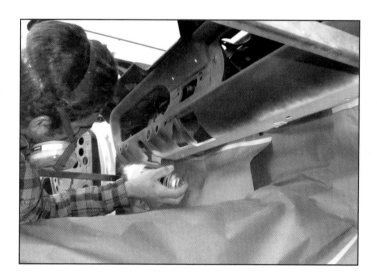

6a.83 The last step in the painting process is the cut'n'buff. Very, very fine sandpaper (wet-and-dry) is used to take out any tiny imperfections in the paint, then it is buffed out with rubbing compound to bring back the shine.

6a.84 It takes a strong and steady hand to buff out the clearcoat. If you let the buffer run too long in one place or nick a sharp body line, you may have to reshoot something. After the first pass, wash the surface of any compound and make a close examination of the surfaces.

6a.85 This is not our hood, but this photo illustrates the last step, using a finer polish, a bigger and softer pad, and a bigger buffer.

6a.86 It was an exciting day for the Haynes 50th Anniversary Mustang to be loaded up for the short trip back to our shop, so we could continue our restoration efforts.

Glass and trim

Finishing the bodywork and paint is a major milestone in any automobile restoration, and you should be proud to have come this far. However, this is no time to rest on your accomplishments, for you should still have a host of items on your to-do list not yet checked off. Most are smaller items, operations that can be tackled in less than a half hour, and a few that require more time and concentration.

We have purposely not shown any great detail of installing parking lights, back-up lights and other items that have only one or two fasteners and only install one way, the better to give more coverage to tasks you might have thought you were going to trailer your Mustang to a shop to have done,

such as installing the windshield. With our photos and captions, we think you can handle this operation and do a great job to boot. Modern windshields are secured by clips and a pile of adhesive sealer, but our Mustang is from the time period where windshields were held in the car by a large, one-piece gasket that has a lip at the interior side and another lip for the exterior side. Installing the windshield is pretty much old-school technology, but you don't need much in the way of special tools. That's one of the reasons older vehicles are more fun to work on!

6b.1 Simple steps like installing the grille and the horse and "corral" makes you feel like you're really making progress!

Windshield

6b.2 There are a number of clips that must be located properly for the stainless-steel trim around the windshield to fit. Where the screw holes are on the body, push a bit of sealant on the hole before screwing the clip in.

6b.3 Here you can see where all the windshield trim clips are located. On a convertible like ours, the top should be down during the windshield installation. You should also remove the rearview mirror and the sun visors.

6b.4 The new windshield comes with a protective tape which must be removed before installation. The bubble-wrap that the windshield comes in makes a good material to place over your work table while working on the windshield.

6b.5 The seal has two grooves; the fat one accepts the windshield, while the other groove fits the sheetmetal lip in the windshield opening.

6b.6 Install the seal around the perimeter of the windshield

6b.7 Check the fit of the seal around the windshield, making sure it's seated completely.

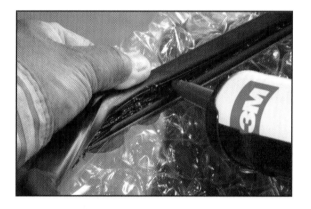

6b.8 Once the seal is on the glass, peel it back slightly to inject a bead of sealant in the groove on the exterior side.

6b.9 This looks like a technique from fifty years ago, but it works just great. A nylon cord is stuffed into the body-side groove in the seal.

6b.10 Protect the paint by applying plenty of painter's tape on the cowl and windshield posts.

6b.11 Squirt a bead of sealant around the windshield lip on the body.

6b.12 Also apply tape around the front of the windshield to help keep the rubber seal in place. Carefully position the new windshield in place and apply hand pressure to seat it against the sealant and the lip of the body.

6b.13 From the inside of the car, begin pulling out the nylon rope at an angle that forces the rubber lip over the body edge. Keep pulling until you have gone all the way around the windshield and the rope comes free. An assistant is helpful. You can push on the outside of the windshield with one hand while you are pulling the rope.

6b.14 If you have the windshield centered in the body opening, there will be a slight gap where the clips secure the glass from shifting. Apply a small bead of sealant in this groove.

6b.15 Remove all of the old sealant from the trim pieces.

6b.16 Remove the old painter's tape from the cowl and masking this area again with fresh tape. The old tape may have traces of sealant on it that we don't want to transfer to the outside of the stainless-steel trim.

6b.17 Snap the bottom trim piece down evenly and centered on the windshield.

6b.18 When the side and upper moldings are ready for installation, turn them over and apply a thin bead of sealant to the backside for a water-tight seal.

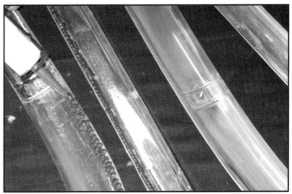

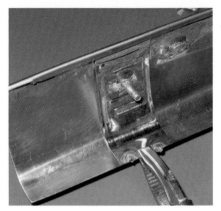

6b.19 Engage the side trim piece with the bottom trim, then push the side trim down so that it snaps when connecting with the clips on the body.

6b.20 Unlike the other stainless pieces, the upper moldings are not secured by clips, but with studs and nuts. Ours had a broken flange that holds one of the mounting studs. We welded ours carefully with stainless rod and a TIG welder on low amperage.

6b.21 The trim and the stud bracket are both thin and easily damaged, so handle them gingerly when welding, you only need a few tack welds. This required a little sanding and polishing on the exterior to remove any evidence of welding heat.

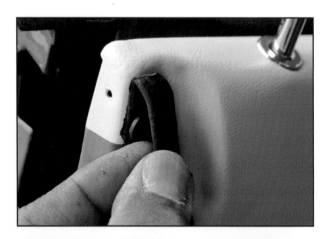

Weatherstripping

6b.22 Unglamorous as it may be, weatherstripping is an important part of interior comfort by keeping out water and cold wind. If you install it properly, it will look like it did as it left the factory decades ago. When your body work and paint was being performed, all traces of the old weatherstripping was sanded or cleaned off with lacquer thinner. The new door weatherstrip starts with a push fastener at the upper rear of the door.

6b.23 Apply the weatherstripping adhesive, making sure to follow the natural nesting ledge for the weatherstripping.

6b.24 Push the weatherstripping into the cement. If necessary, place a few pieces of masking tape to hold it in place while drying, especially under the door. Route it from the starting point, down the door edge, across the bottom and up toward the dash.

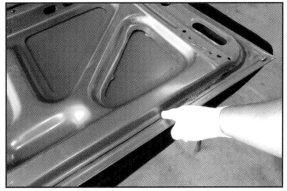

6b.25 The trunk lid can be handled in a similar way, except you should take the trunk lid off the vehicle and set it on a clean, padded surface. Apply a thin bead of cement around the trunk lid.

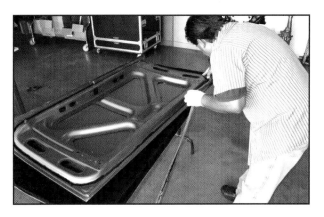

6b.26 Smear the cement with your finger enough that the bead widens to about 1/2-inch wide. Needless to say, you should not touch any painted sheetmetal when you have cement on your hands.

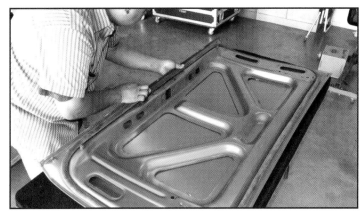

6b.27 When the glue is tacky, start pressing the new weatherstripping around the trunk lid. As you progress around, go back and check that other spots haven't dried out and the strip isn't stuck down.

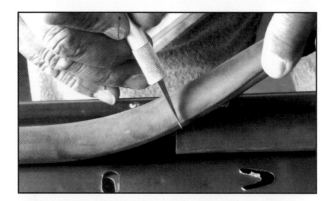

6b.28 It's a little thing, but to do a first-class job you have to cut off the excess strip at the end so both ends meet exactly. Not too short or too long.

6b.29 When the trunk lid weatherstripping has dried, you can reinstall the trunk lid and put in new rubber bumpers at the rear corners.

Grille and horse corral

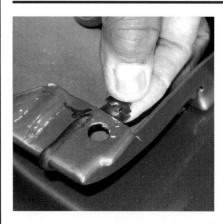

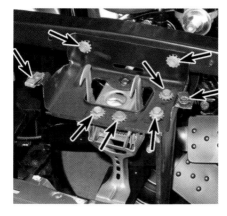

6b.30 These little clips are required in several places around the upper valance. Their purpose is to secure the grille mounting screws.

6b.31 When installing the lower grille bar support, you don't have much room to access the fasteners at the bottom. Use a 1/4-inch-drive ratchet and a long extension. It wouldn't hurt to apply masking tape to the extension and socket so you don't scratch any surrounding painted areas.

6b.32 You can buy an inexpensive package of all the screws and clips for your grille, support and hood latch installation, and they're ready to use (no scrubbing old fasteners).

6b.33 You've been waiting for this for quite some time, but take it slow and steady when installing the grille. The '65 mesh grille is the most fragile of all. We used a new reproduction grille. Lower it into the body and let it sit down completely.

6b.34 Start all of the grille mounting fasteners before tightening any of them.

6b.35 Install the two bolts that secure the top of the grille to the hood latch assembly. By this time the grille should look and feel secure. Do not over-tighten the fasteners.

6b.36 Once again, we bring out the painter's tape and mask the painted areas you will work around while installing the grille opening moldings.

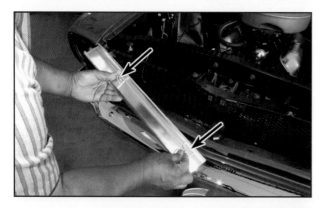

6b.37 The two spring clips on the bottom of the moldings can be moved a little in either direction. Measure the location of the holes in the lower grille bar support in reference to the center, then adjust the clips on the moldings before installing them.

6b.38 Install the left and right moldings. In addition to the two clips on each molding, the top edge of the moldings have a single screw securing them to the headlight surround.

6b.39 The "corral," as enthusiasts call it, is one of the key exterior design features of the '65 Mustang. Bolt together the components: the corral, the running horse, and the two grille bars, then install the whole assembly.

6b.40 The skilled corral wrangler angles the assembly into the opening, then aligns the top and bottom screws that secure the corral.

6b.41 The true beauty of the clean 1965 styling is only fully brought home when the hood is closed, completing the recessed look to the grille and center ornaments.

Exterior emblems

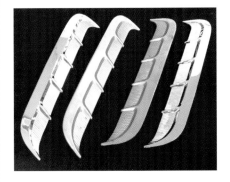

6b.42 The quarter-trim moldings accentuate the racy cooling scoop look. Our originals (at center) are compared here to the new reproduction moldings. Though ours have weathered years of blowing Texas dust and rain, they still look OK, just not restoration quality.

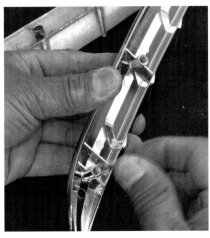

6b.43 Projecting studs on the back of the molding go through holes in the quarter panel. Install the studs in the threaded bosses, then apply a little bit of sealant around the base of the bosses.

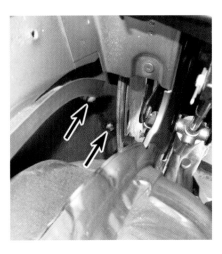

6b.44 Two of the three mounting nuts can be seen in this view of the inside of the quarter panel. Apply a small amount of sealant to the nuts before installing them.

6b.45 Once in place, the decorative moldings add something to the overall look of the car. Imagine how owners felt back in the day getting such a snazzy car for only $2,368.

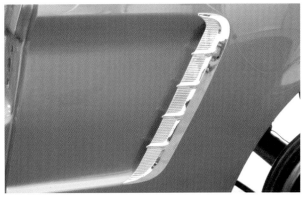

6b.46 If you have all of your original or otherwise used OEM body parts, all of the mounting holes for the various external badges are already there. We did replace the fenders, so we had to run a masking tape baseline on the fender crease line. Measuring from that line down, and from the rear of the fender forward, we used the measurements of the original fender to go by. The patch of tape up front is for the engine badge.

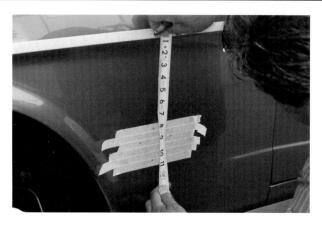

6b.47 The rear of the fender held a running horse emblem and a Mustang logo. We have laid down enough tape so we can mark the locations to drill for both new emblems.

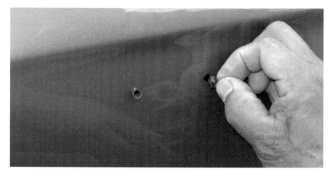

6b.48 You have to be very careful when drilling into the new body parts. Start with a very sharp and small drill bit first, before enlarging the hole until you have the final size, which should match the hole size on the original fender. The little ferrules should just fit into the holes.

6b.49 Unless someone comes by who has a caliper and a sheet of dimensions, no one will ever know this isn't original.

6b.50 With all of the emblems you install, make sure the holes are the right size before you try to install the part. If the hole is too small, the ferrule will pinch and the badge may break when tapped into place with a small plastic mallet. The hood letters are simple. Replacement hoods are already drilled for the F O R D letters.

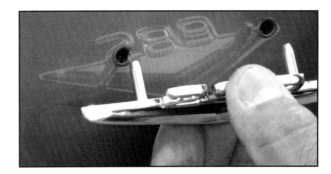

6b.51 The sporty yet thrifty and very smooth 289 V8 was something to brag about in 1965. The many buyers who loved the car but wanted maximum gas mileage chose an even thriftier six. The six-cylinder cars did not have a fender badge like this to show off. Imagine gas at 34 cents a gallon!

Outside mirror

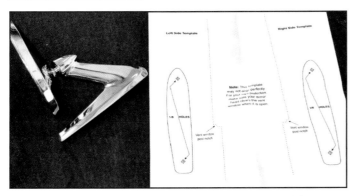

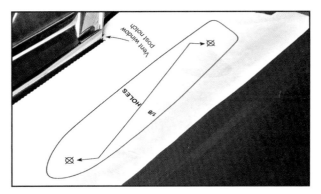

6b.52 It would seem at first that nothing could be simpler than installing an outside mirror with two screws, and if your original mirror was going back on, it would be. Our poor Mustang had holes in the door for several different mirrors, so when the car was at the body shop, all the holes were welded up so we could start fresh. The new mirror comes with simple directions and a template.

6b.53 With the template (one for right-side, one for left-side installations) cut for its destination, it fits against the vent window trim post, providing a guide to drill by.

6b.54 The mirror may need to be moved slightly for perfect location. Keep the mirror centered over the template, but open the vent window to make sure there is no interference with the mirror.

6b.55 Use a spring-loaded prick-punch where indicated on the template.

6b.56 Drilling through the door in the two locations on the template will establish where to place the mirror.

6b.57 Install the two screws, and you're ready to aim it so you can see check out all the cars that are eating your dust!

Mudguards

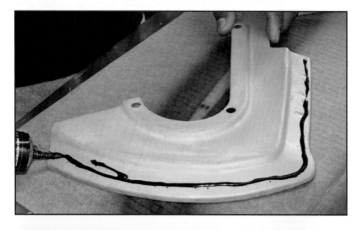

6b.58 The mudguard panel under each front fender keeps road debris from lodging in the cowl and later causing rust. Apply black weather-strip cement to the edges of the steel panel and allow it to dry until it's very tacky.

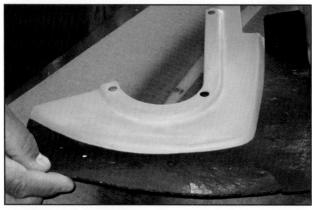

6b.59 Press down the new rubber seal, then peel it back up and let it dry a few minutes. Reinstall the rubber and press it down firmly.

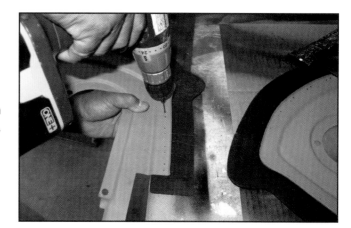

6b.60 Use a small drill bit to drill through the rubber in the original staple holes.

6b.61 Insert the new staples through the metal and rubber mudguard and bend the ends of the staples over on the other side.

6b.62 Coat the assembly with a spray can of rubberized undercoating.

6b.63 Install the mudguard assembly as shown, one in each front fenderwell. The rubber around the plate makes a weatherproof seal against the fender without any squeaks.

Quarter glass (coupe and convertible)

6b.64 Wrap new glass seal around the edges of the quarter-glass. Work on a padded bench when dealing with windows. A chance encounter with a tool or another part could chip or break the glass.

6b.65 A hobby knife cuts a clean edge when removing the excess seal. When you come to a corner on a window, just keep the seal going, then go back and cut the corners to make a watertight junction.

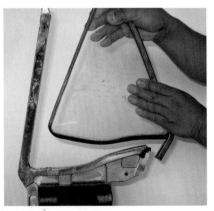

6b.66 Use a rubber lubricant to work the glass and new seal into the chrome strip. Never strike the glass or frame with a metal tool. You can gently persuade the glass with a plastic hammer and a light touch.

6b.67 Lube the glass and push the glass and outer chrome strip into the main window frame.

6b.68 Install these screws to secure the two frame pieces.

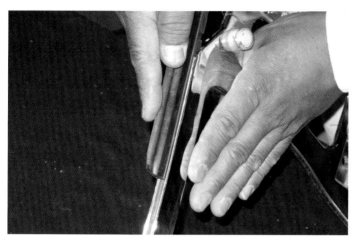

6b.69 Install new weatherstripping along the front edge of the window, sliding it into the groove in the frame.

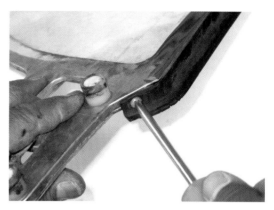

6b.70 Secure the new weatherstripping with a screw at the bottom of the frame.

6b.71 Clean and lubricate the regulator assembly with white grease before installation.

6b.72 Clean and lube the pins the plastic rollers ride on.

6b.73 Angle the window regulator assembly up into the quarter-panel.

6b.74 Install the regulator bolts a few threads in to allow room for adjustment and alignment with the guide plate.

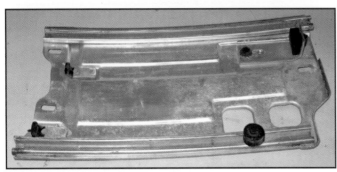

6b.75 The guide plate acts as both a front and rear roller guide.

6b.76 One way to install window rollers is to pull the clip out halfway, slide the roller into the guide, then align the pin to the roller and push it into the roller, then snap the clip all the way on.

6b.77 On the floor below the quarter window assembly, this bracket with slotted bolt holes is used to adjust the upper height that the window needs to be, and also the in/out angle of the window.

Vent windows

6b.78 Wrap the new sealing strips around the glass, then secure them temporarily with spring-type binder clips.

6b.79 Use a hobby knife to trim the seal diagonally in the corners.

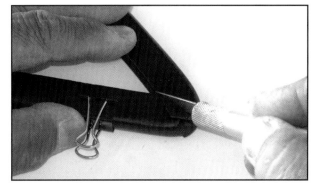

6b.80 Coat the frame and the glass seal with soapy water or rubber lubricant such as exterior rubber and tire detailing product (something that doesn't dry out too fast).

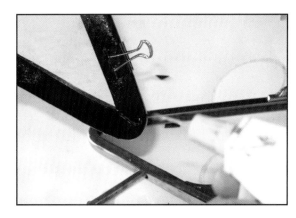

6b.81 With the frame supported on a piece of wood, use a rubber mallet to tap the glass into the frame. Many small taps are better than one big one that breaks glass!

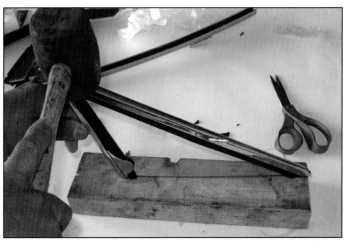

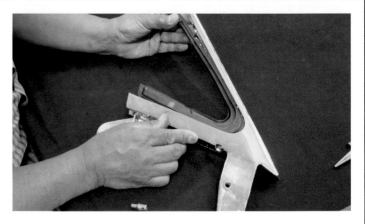

6b.82 Slice through with a hobby knife to remove the excess seal material.

6b.83 Insert a new sealing strip in the exterior vent window frame.

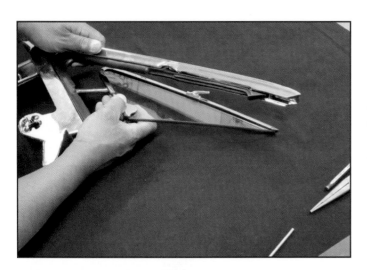

6b.84 Angle the vent window into the exterior frame. Start by aiming the swivel pin on the bottom through the frame, then guide the upper pivot pin into upper portion.

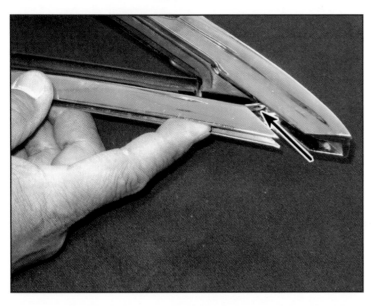

6b.85 By hand, squeeze the two frame pieces together, then insert the retaining screw (indicated).

6b.86 Install rivets in the lower run channel retainer.

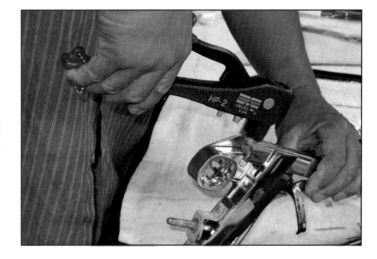

6b.87 Use a narrow rivet gun and secure the rivets.

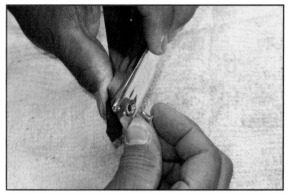

6b.88 The weatherstrip in the upper seal is retained by a smash-type or set-rivet. The rivet is set into the hole where its tapered head fits securely.

6b.89 Place a block of metal on the bench and cover it with two layers of soft cloth or towel. Use a rivet-setting mandrel and tap the end of the rivet until it mushrooms and secures the installation.

Door handles and latch

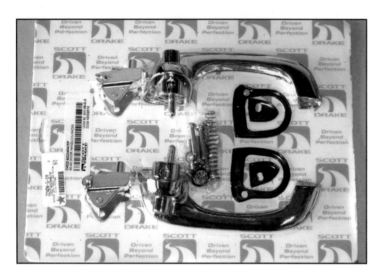

6b.90 If your Mustang is typical, the exterior door handles may have become pitted or turning gray, or the mechanical parts are worn. A new set of handles comes with everything to restore the looks and function.

6b.91 Slip the O-ring over the button and push the button fully into the handle body.

6b.92 The button on the handle is tensioned by this spring and the lock assembly, which pushes on the handle button. This is a trial fit.

6b.93 Lubricate the spring and plunger, compress the spring and install the lock assembly screw to the handle.

6b.94 Install the mounting stud at the forward end of the handle and slip on the rubber gasket.

6b.95 Push the eyelet for the lock rod into the hole on the lock assembly.

6b.96 Put the new rubber gasket on the main body of the handle assembly and push the assembly against the door, then install the rear mounting screw, followed by the forward mounting nut

6b.97 Working inside the door, position the latch assembly so that the side toward the door jamb protrudes like this and the lock rod that goes to the lock button at the top-rear of the door is sticking up through the hole. Install the three latch mounting screws and tighten them. Now install the lock button and ferrule.

6b.98 Inside the door, insert the external lock cylinder and secure it by tapping the large, U-shaped clip into the groove on the cylinder. Attach the lock, lock cylinder, latch and handle rods to the latch.

A To outside door handle

B To key lock cylinder

C To inside door handle

D To lock button

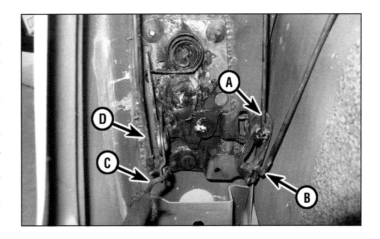

6b.99 Mount the interior door handle mechanism to the door with three screws and snap the actuating rod from the latch to the mechanism.

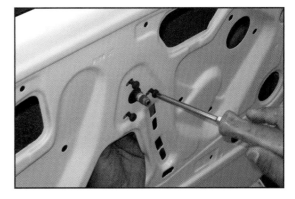

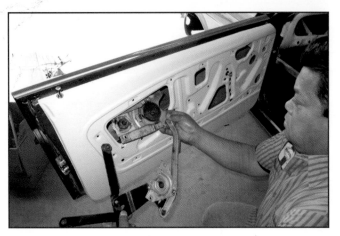

Door glass and door panel

6B.100 If you have big arms and hands, this is going to be a little tough. Working inside a sheetmetal door is one place muscles aren't helpful. When working the window regulator assembly through the door opening, what you need is patience.

6b.101 Get all of the regulator assembly bolts installed before tightening them.

6b.102 Working inside, install the guide rollers (lubricated) to connect the guide channel to the assembly.

6b.103 Note the location of the two glass-stop brackets. Here is where each of these brackets should be bolted to the interior side of the door.

6b.104 Now it's time to address the window glass. Remove the frame retaining screws from the rear edge of the glass frame . . .

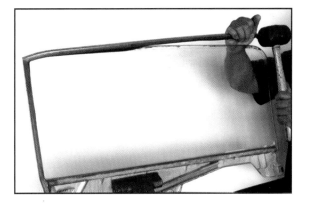

6b.105 . . . then carefully pry up the front of the frame and tap it rearward to remove it from the window.

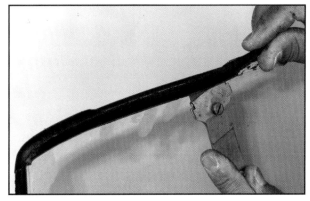

6b.106 Scrape the old seal from the glass, but be careful not to scratch it. Follow up by cleaning the glass with brake cleaner.

6b.107 Wrap the window with the new seal, using binder clips to hold it in place as you work around the perimeter.

6b.108 Lubricate the frame and seal with soapy water and install the frame over the seal, tapping it into place with a rubber mallet.

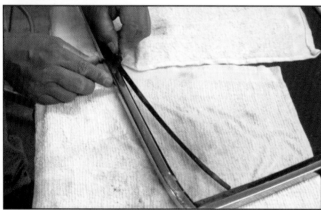

6b.109 Trim the seal flush with the frame.

6b.110 Carefully lower the glass into the door, inserting it into the front run channel . . .

6b.111 . . . while simultaneously engaging the roller of the regulator arm with the channel on the glass frame.

6b.112 Install the rear run channel and guide it into place, cradling the rear edge of the window.

6b.113 Install the run channel bolts and tighten them. You'll have to adjust the run channels in or out to achieve the proper fit against the roof when the door is closed, and this will no doubt take several attempts. Be patient and don't shut the doors with much force until you have the perfect fit.

6b.114 When you're happy with the adjustment, install the water seal and the run channel bolt-hole covers in the end of the door.

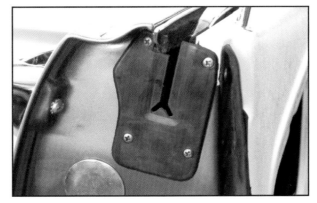

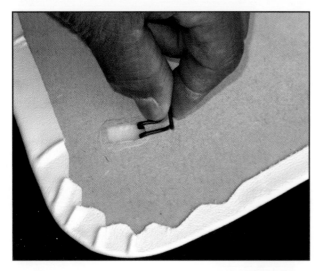

6b.115 The door panel clips fit into these holes in the backing of the door panels. There is considerable room to adjust the location of the prongs to correlate to the clip holes in the door. Don't try to install the panel without aligning the clips ahead of time.

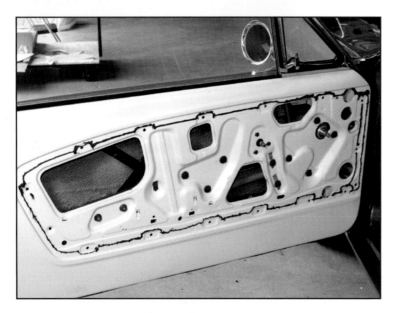

6b.116 Very carefully apply a small bead of weatherstripping adhesive around the door opening as shown here. Less is better than more.

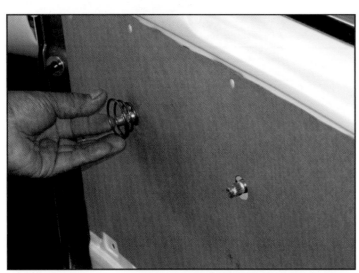

6b.117 Press the new watershield into the sealant to secure the watershield. Install the spring that goes behind the window crank.

6b.118 Making sure that all of the clips align with the holes in the door, press the door panel into place without tools - just the palms of your (clean) hands. Go all around with your hand to ensure that all clips are secured to the door. The window and door handles can now be installed with an Allen wrench. Make sure you install them at the same angle on each door.

6b.119 Feel for the armrest cutouts in the door panel backing, locate the holes for the screws, then cut two small openings with a hobby knife.

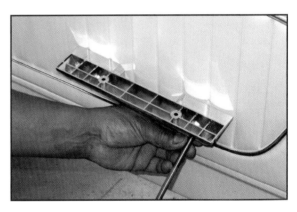

6b.120 Install the armrest base . . .

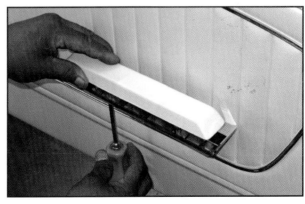

6b.121 . . . followed by the armrest pad.

7 Mechanical restoration

Engine Assembly

The powertrain of any vehicle is extremely important, and no one wants to hear the inevitable embarrassing comments if your classic Mustang has trouble on the road. If your choice is to restore the engine, transmission and rear end versus the flashier choice of spending all your money on the paint job, the car will never let you down. There will be time and finances later on to finally achieve the paint and interior you dream of.

Rebuilding an engine is a formidable task if you don't have much experience at it. Perhaps someone in your Mustang club can act as an overseer if you are determined to learn how this vital component works. Once you have built your own engine, it will change your attitude about driving. You will always be listening to noises you've never noticed before, and stepping on the gas pedal will be a pleasure in a different way than if you had just had your engine rebuilt by a shop.

It is possible to save hundreds of dollars of labor time by building your own engine, and you have the spare time to put it together slowly and carefully. Engines of the Sixties are fun to rebuild, lacking all the complications of modern computer-run engines decked out with sensors and solenoids to operate various engine controls. You'll find that the Windsor small-block V8 engines are relatively uncomplicated and when finished and broken in will offer excellent performance. They are also among the smoothest V8 engines.

If you currently lack the skills and experience needed to rebuild an engine, by all means go ahead and find an engine shop that is recommended by other enthusiasts you know. There are some special tools you will have to borrow or rent. Unless you plan on building other engines later on, purchasing tools that are only used once or twice, such as a crankshaft damper puller, don't pay back the investment. One tool you will need, though, (no. 36048) is the Haynes Mustang Repair Manual - it has all the specifications you will need for your project.

If you have a shop build your engine for you, you are advised to read the warranty on the engine very carefully. Many rebuilders specify that you must have proof of purchasing a new radiator or having your radiator rebuilt. This is for good reason because overheating is one of the major causes of engine failures. A marginal cooling system can damage a fresh engine, because it is going to run hotter than usual during break-in because the rings, bearings and other components are tight, and there is more friction as the components wear into each other. A new water pump and thermostat should also be installed.

If you're worried about keeping your Mustang original, make sure the shop you chose knows. Painting the engine and other parts should be the correct color for your year Mustang, and you may even want to bring them two cans of the correct paint. A beautifully rebuilt engine that was painted late-model Ford Blue or Grey is not going to sit well with you when you go to your first Mustang event. Tell them not to throw away anything from the original engine, like clamps, hoses, brackets and so on. You may need them, even if only for samples.

While you may choose to assemble your own engine, the machine work on the block and cylinder heads will have to be done at a machine shop. You should also have them install new camshaft bearings, which can be tricky to align exactly with the oil holes. Also have them drive in a new camshaft bore plug at the back of the block.

Follow our photos and captions of the important points of preparation and assembly. Remember, Haynes has probably taught more people to rebuild an engine than any other source. We'll examine the cylinder head overhaul first, because it involves many specialized tools and precision tolerances. Since we don't have leaded gasoline anymore, and unleaded fuels are destructive over time to pre-smog-era engines, we are showing some of the steps it takes to install hardened valve seats that make old engines more resistant to damage.

7a.1 Extreme cleanliness is of prime importance when building your engine. When you're not working on it, wrap it up with a large plastic trash bag.

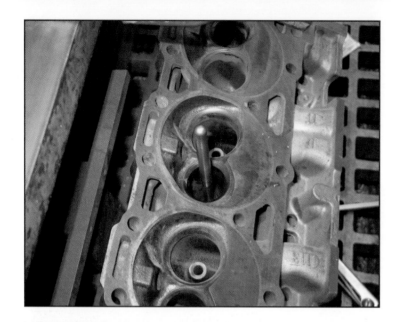

Engine

7a.2 A machine shop will thoroughly disassemble and clean all of your components. The head will spend time in a large machine (like a mill) while its critical aspects are corrected by machining surfaces. The process starts with adjusting the head so that a tool placed in a valve guide will be straight up.

7a.3 A precision level is slipped over the tool in the guide, and when the head is level in both directions, it is locked down tight.

7a.4 This is the hardened seat that will be put into our heads for each exhaust valve (since they run the hottest).

7a.5 This cutter is used to machine a bigger hole to accept the new seat.

7a.6 The cutter is carefully adjusted to very close tolerances in order to cut an exact, centered hole, which is just a tiny bit smaller than the hardened seat that's going in.

7a.7 Here is the new hole (much bigger that the old valve seat size).

7a.8 Here the new seat is being driven into the new hole. Some shops also shrink the inserts a little by freezing them the night before.

7a.9 This tool is slipped into the valve guide and locked in place, where it will act as a steady center for the next operation.

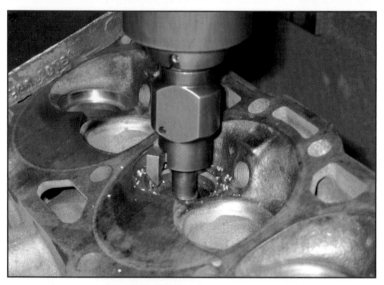

7a.10 This cutting tool can impart several different angles at once to the valve seat.

7a.11 The valves must be renewed as well, to have the exact-same angle (to within one degree) for a tight seal. The valve is spun in one machine while the head is ground by a stone wheel to the desired angle.

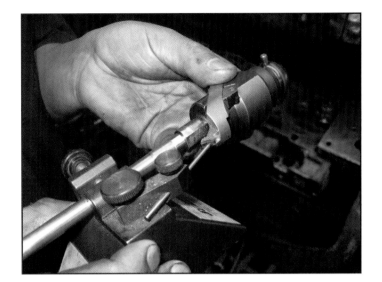

7a.12 This is one type of precision adjustable cutter used on preparing valve seats in cylinder heads.

7a.13 This is not an operation that is necessary, but it's fun. If you put a piece of Plexiglas over a combustion chamber (with valves in place), then introduce oil with a red dye from a measured burette, you can compare the reading on the burette before and after. This gives you the chamber displacement. Racers often do this to grind some chambers until they all have the exact same displacement (and thus compression ratio) for an even power stroke.

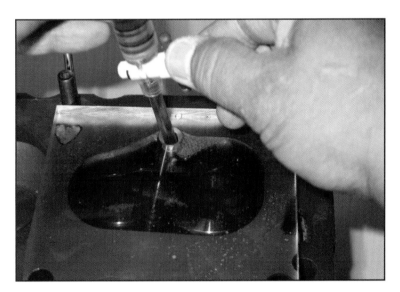

7a.14 If you are reusing your old valve springs, you must have them measured to see if they have enough pressured at a specific height. Ours were all OK, but you must check for every case, because weak springs can cause uneven running (and valve float at high engine rpms).

7a.15 Valve stem seals like these are longer-lasting than the rubber umbrella type used on your engine originally. Oil the top of the valve guide and the valve stem before installing them (most sets come with a plastic tool that allows the seal to be pushed on but not nicked by the top of the valve).

7a.16 Here are two of our freshly ground valves, along with the springs, retainers, seals and keepers. The bigger valve is for the intake.

7a.17 In order to install the valves and springs, a tool like this is used to compress one spring at a time.

7a.18 With the retainer on top of the spring, the tool compresses the spring enough to allow the two keepers to drop into the notch at the top of the valve, then the tool is slowly released.

7a.19 Once the valves are installed on the head, the installed heights can be checked. The height is measured from the base on the head to the top of the retainer. There is an allowable limit to this height specification.

7a.20 After your block has been cleaned in a pressure-wash cabinet or hot tank, it will be measured for bore wear, then the cylinders will be bored out to a little bit bigger, then fine-honed to provide a perfect fit for the new pistons. After that the block is washed with hot soapy water and thoroughly dried. Wipe the bores with lint-free towels and engine oil. When the towels come clean, oil the cylinder walls for assembly.

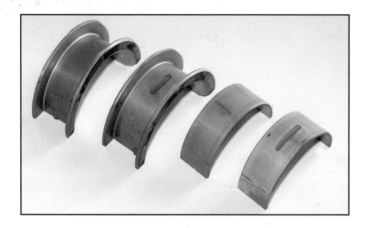

7a.21 The crankshaft is the first main component to be installed in the block. Here are some of the main bearings you will use. The flanged ones are the thrust bearings for the center-main on our 289.

7a.22 Install all the block-side (called upper main bearings) main bearings *without* any oil! We're going to check the crank clearances. The bearings on the crankshaft mains not only have a notch to line up, but the slot in the center must align with the oil hole in the block.

7a.23 The center bearing of the crankshaft is the thrust bearing (on our engine, not true for all engines) which controls the amount the crankshaft can move front to rear. The thrust bearing is installed by rocking it a bit to work it down snugly against its saddle.

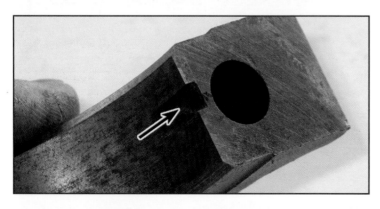

7a.24 Install the lower main bearings in the bearing caps, aligning the bearing tangs into the notches on the caps.

7a.25 The crankshaft (also not oiled) is carefully lowered into position.

7a.26 On top of each main bearing journal a small length of Plastigage is positioned.

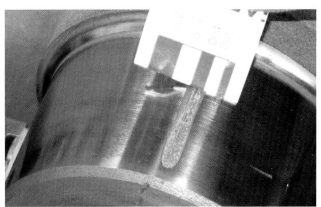

7a.27 After the crankshaft main caps have been torqued to spec, remove the bolts and inspect the crushed Plastigage by comparing the width of the plastic to the bar-guide on the Plastigage packaging. This gives us the amount of bearing clearance at each main.

7a.28 This time around, you will install an engine-assembly grease on the bearings before reinstalling the crankshaft, then you can torque the main bolts for the last time.

7a.29 Use two screwdrivers to pry the crankshaft forward and backward while taking readings of the movement with a dial-indicator (at the front here). The amount of movement is the crankshaft endplay. If yours is within specs, you can continue.

7a.30 The rear main cap also involves the rear main seal. Originals were greased rope, but today there are modern neoprene seals, shown here being lubed.

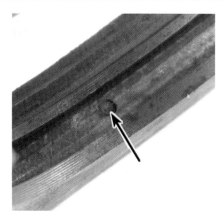

7a.31 If you choose to use a neoprene seal, you must drive out the little spike (which kept the old rope seal located) from the rear main's trough for the seal. Plug the hole with RTV sealant.

7a.32 The neoprene seal is staggered out of the groove on one side about 3/8-inch. The other piece of the seal is staggered a similar amount the other way in the main cap.

7a.33 Before final installation of the rear main cap, a small bead of RTV should be placed as shown here.

7a.34 Use an old piston to push a piston ring down in the cylinder, then measure the end-gap with feeler gauges. Check this with each cylinder. If the measurement is any wider than the maximum, you'll have to buy a set of gappable rings which you can file-to-fit.

7a.35 You should check all of your rod bolts by examining them with a magnifier. Note that the one on the left here has a pinched area that indicates the bolt was stretched, compared to the new bolt at right. If you find one bad one, replace all of them.

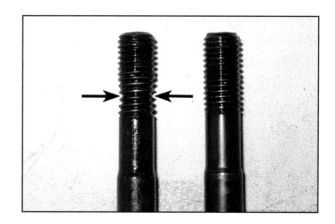

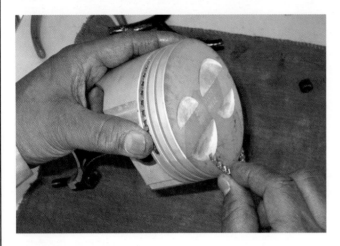

7a.36 An engine shop can install the pistons onto the connecting rods for you, which requires a special tool. Oil a piston and start installing the rings. The oil ring goes first . . .

7a.37 . . . then the side rails above and below the oil ring keeps everything in place. Stagger the placement of the spacer end gaps (see the Haynes Mustang Repair Manual).

7a.38 This is how the oil ring combo should look. Where the ends of the oil ring butt together, they should not stick out.

7a.39 The two upper rings are the compression rings, and they should not be installed by hand, but rather with a ring expander tool like this which spread the rings open only enough to install them. They can break if mishandled, and then you may have to buy another whole set just to replace that one ring. The lower compression ring goes on first, making note of the markings to indicate which side faces UP.

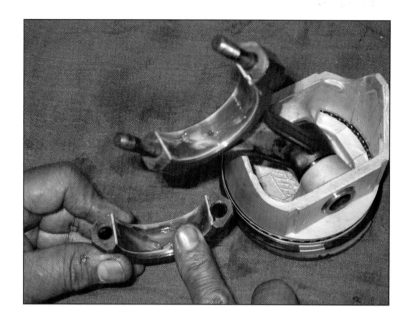

7a.40 With all the rings in place, you can begin installing the pistons/rods. Press the bearings in place and lubricate them. The upper goes in the rod, the lower in the rod cap. Make sure you have the matching cap for each rod.

7a.41 A ratcheting piston ring compressor like this can be rented at a tool supply. Tighten the compressor until it firmly squeezes against the piston and forces the rings into their grooves.

7a.42 Cut two lengths of rubber hose and put them over the rod bolts. This will prevent the rod bolts from scratching the crankshaft during piston/rod installation.

7a.43 Insert the piston and rod in the cylinder it is marked for, until the ring compressor touches the block. Tap the top of the piston with a plastic hammer handle to drive it into its bore. If there is any resistance, stop and find out why.

7a.44 Install the rod caps and nuts once the piston is down as far as it can go. Make sure the rod and the cap have the same stamped numbers (cylinder #7 here), and that the numbers face the side of the block this cylinder is on. This #7 should face the left side of the block.

7a.45 The pistons have a notch or arrow to indicate that this part of the piston should point toward the front of the engine.

7a.46 When all the rods/pistons are installed and the rod nuts torqued, you can turn the engine over on the engine stand to work on the bottom. Shown here is the oil pump pushrod. There is a stop-ring (indicated) that must go toward the distributor.

7a.47 Place a new oil pump gasket on the block.

7a.48 Guide the oil pump shaft into the oil pump and once the pump meets the block, install the two mounting bolts.

7a.49 Lubricate the camshaft thoroughly with engine assembly lube and install it in the block. Use a long bolt or threaded stock of the proper size and thread pitch screwed into the front of the camshaft to act as a handle while inserting the camshaft. You don't want to nick the cam or the bearings during installation.

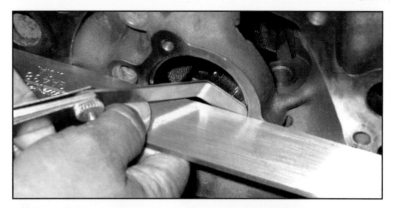

7a.50 At the front of the block, measure the spacing of the front bearing for the camshaft. Put a straightedge across the block while inserting feeler gauges between the bearing and the straightedge. The clearance should be from 0.005 to 0.020-inch.

7a.51 Bolt on the camshaft retainer plate and tap in a new pin if the camshaft didn't come with one.

7a.52 Rotate the engine so that piston #1 is at the top of the block. Slip the timing chain and camshaft sprocket on. You may have to rotate the camshaft a little (using the sprocket) so that the two alignment marks are on a straight line from crank to cam.

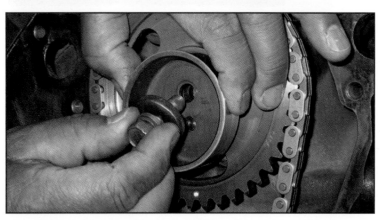

7a.53 Now you can install the fuel pump eccentric, bolting it through the cam sprocket into the camshaft. Use a small dab of blue threadlock compound on the bolt.

7a.54 Our engine front cover has been thoroughly cleaned before installation.

7a.55 Place a 2x4 under the area of the crank hole. Apply a little RTV around the seal and squarely drive the seal into the cover.

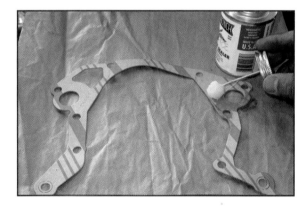

7a.56 The gasket for the front cover is coated with clear gasket glue and applied to the block, then the out-facing side is coated also.

7a.57 The cover can now be bolted on. Oil the crankshaft seal first, and make sure you have all the correct bolts, because there are various lengths. Lube the engine-side of the crankshaft damper and install it by tightening it with the bolt while the engine flywheel is held by a stop-tool.

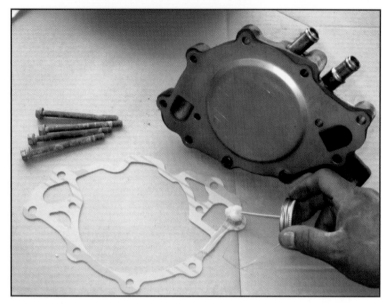

7a.58 A new water pump will not have the backplate on it, so you will need to reuse your old one. Use the clear gasket glue on the new water pump gasket and install it.

7a.59 Bolt the new water pump on the engine, keeping track of the correct bolt lengths. Some may be studs, used to secure a bracket for the alternator or other accessory, depending on the year and engine.

7a.60 With the engine turned upside down again, you can prepare for the oil pan installation. At the front of the block, apply a little RTV where the front cover meets the block.

7a.61 The cork side gaskets are glued to the block on each side. The gaskets have tabs that fit into the rubber front and rear pan seals.

7a.62 Push the new rubber seals into the grooves in the front cover and the rear main cap, then apply a little RTV where the side and end gaskets meet.

7a.63 Apply gasket sealant to the oil pan flange, then install the pan and torque the bolts to specs. Note that there are two sizes of bolts; the corners at front and rear have 5/16-inch bolts, the rest are 1/4-inch.

7a.64 Clean the top surface of the block with lacquer thinner and install the new head gaskets. This is the left side of the engine, where you will put the gasket on with the UP side UP, so that the coolant holes at the back of the block line up.

7a.65 On the right side of the engine, and this is a peculiarity with gaskets for small-block Fords, install the gasket with the UP against the *block*, and double-check that the coolant holes at the rear of the block line up with the holes in the gasket.

7a.66 With both the heads installed, your engine is starting to look pretty complete. Lubricate the lifter bores in the engine valley and install the new lifters. Never install new lifters with a used camshaft.

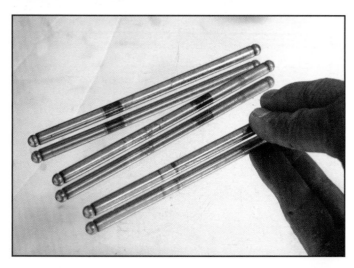

7a.67 Thoroughly clean the pushrods of any accumulated sludge and blow them clean with an air hose through the end holes. Check them for straightness by rolling them on a piece of glass. If they flop, they're bent and should be replaced.

7a.68 With a pushrod in place for every lifter, the rocker arms can be installed. Follow the procedure in the Haynes repair manual for adjusting hydraulic lifters, going from one cylinder to the next in the engine firing order.

7a.69 As insurance against water leaks, apply RTV sealant around the front and rear water passages in the cylinder heads. Most old engines like ours will have pitting in this area, and the RTV will fill in the imperfections.

7a.70 Install the side intake gaskets on the cylinder heads, and apply a little RTV at the mating points of the head and block.

7a.71 The intake manifold end gaskets are cork, and are glued to the ends of the valley. You'll notice that a tab on each side gasket fits into a slot in the end gaskets. The upper surface of the end gaskets should be treated with a thin layer of RTV sealant.

7a.72 You will find innumerable uses for this kind of wire-brush tool, driven by an electric or pneumatic drill. Here the intake manifold is being cleaned to bare metal in preparation for primer and paint.

7a.73 This important tag on your intake manifold should be removed and gently cleaned and perhaps coated with clear lacquer before reinstalling it. It identifies your engine.

7a.74 There are core plugs in both the engine block and the cylinder heads. To install them, clean the holes, apply a little core plug sealant around the hole and the plug . . .

7a.75 . . . then use an extension and a half-inch-drive socket that fits inside the core plug and drive the plug in with a hammer, just until the plug is flush.

7a.76 There are great little abrasive discs like these that can remove dirt and paint without marring the sheetmetal.

7a.77 Tape off all of the openings to prep for paint. The oil pan and valve covers were treated to a coat of primer first.

7a.78 The primered valve covers are used here to keep dirt out of the cylinder heads, in preparation for installing the engine in the car. Yeah!

7a.79 Time to install our re-coated exhaust manifolds. The manifolds are installed with the end bolts holding them in place, then the new gaskets are slid between the manifold and head

7a.80 Note here that we used the original style exhaust manifold locking washers. After tightening the bolts, tap the tabs closed with a small hammer and punch.

7a.81 When installing the mechanical fuel pump, dab some assembly grease on the tip of the lever, then insert the pump and tighten it down with a new gasket.

7a.82 No sooner did Jamie have the engine in the car and hooked to the rebuilt transmission, but all these smaller components could be installed. Here it's the rebuilt original carburetor.

7a.83 This is what our carb looked like before it was rebuilt, but luckily it was the right two-barrel carb for our engine. You can rebuild your own carburetor using a kit that has all the replaceable parts. The hard part is getting everything cleaned thoroughly.

7a.84 The water pump pulley, fan spacer and fan are bolted on. Hoses and wires are waiting their turn for final routing and installation.

7a.85 Since we were buying new hoses and clamps anyway, we used the style of clamps that were used on the car originally.

7a.86 Our air cleaner assembly has been restored, but we need to install the weather-stripping around the inside of the top. Lay out a length of the adhesive-backed weather-stripping that is long enough to go around the groove in the air cleaner cover.

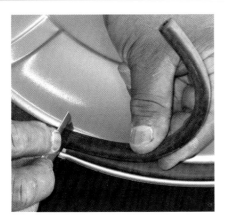

7a.87 When you get to the part where they overlap, cut it with a razor blade.

7a.88 We applied adhesive to the weather stripping and let it set up for a few minutes.

7a.89 Adhesive was also applied to the groove in the cover where the seal goes. Once the adhesive has set up a few minutes on both areas, the weather stripping can be pressed in place.

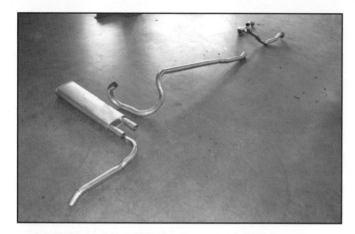

7a.90 There are several exhaust possibilities for a '65 Mustang, but since ours has the 289-2bbl. engine, we're going with the original configuration - a single-exhaust system.

7a.91 New exhaust donuts are installed at each side of the Y-pipe for a leak-free and quiet installation.

7a.92 The Y-pipe is installed first with the bolts not tightened. You are working in tight quarters here, especially on the right side where the starter also has to go in.

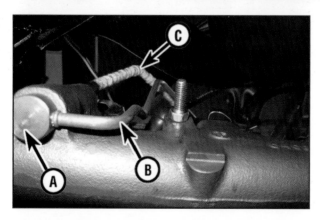

7a.93 Also on the right-side exhaust manifold, there is a system to send heat to the choke for faster warm-ups. This boss on the manifold holds a length of steel packing, capped by this fitting (A), a fresh air tube (B) connected to the carburetor and the hot air tube (C) leading to the choke.

7a.94 The use of a lift is very handy when installing driveline or exhaust components. The main pipe here is awkward to handle, but you can wire it in place with a few wire coat-hangers until the rest of the system in installed and connected.

7a.95 The crossflow muffler is mounted with a bracket with two bolts to the chassis and two bolts to the end of the muffler.

7a.96 Air cleaner snorkels for classic Mustang air cleaners are problematic because many people took them off, thinking that the engine might make more power withthout them. Now they are hard to find. We found one for ours, but the convertible's long body braces interfere with the snorkel. We're marking the interference area with a grease pencil.

7a.97 It seems a sin to cut into the snorkel we searched for, but apparently Ford sent dealers a service letter with a template for cutting a clearance notch in the snorkel for ragtops. We used an abrasive wheel to make a straight, even cut.

7a.98 Here's a reminder of what the engine compartment looked like when we bought the car and how much work awaited us.

7a.99 Here's the finished product, all detailed and ready for a show!

Transmission

There is a staggering amount of components in an automatic transmission: clutch packs, planetary gears, and the valve body and other components that shuttle transmission fluid to operate solenoids and valves and apply or release bands and other devices. Rebuilding an automatic transmission at home is a daunting enough task that most car enthusiasts just bring their transmission to a specialist, where the finished transmission has a comfortable warranty. Removing or installing the transmission, however, is easily within the capabilities of the home mechanic/ restorer with the help of a rented transmission jack. We covered the removal of our C-4 automatic in Chapter 4A.

Maintenance of your transmission is also something you can do yourself. The most important task is the changing of the fluid and the transmission fluid filter at the recommended intervals. An old pro we know at an automatic transmission shop once told us "If people just changed the fluid and filter regularly, we'd be out of business!"

There are other routine transmission repairs that can be performed at home. If you experience improper timing of shifts and clouds of white smoke coming out of your exhaust, the diaphragm inside the vacuum modulator may be cracked. This is easily checked with a vacuum gauge, and the part is easily replaceable, too.

At whatever level of your participation, the finished, rebuilt C-4 automatic will prove to be smooth, durable and efficient. Millions of these transmissions are still on the road in various Ford and Mercury vehicles. You can learn a great deal about this and other Ford automatics in the Haynes Ford Automatic Transmission Overhaul Techbook, #10355.

7b.1 Sure, it's a big, somewhat mysterious component, but with a good transmission jack and the instructions in this manual, transmission removal and installation is within the reach of most enthusiasts

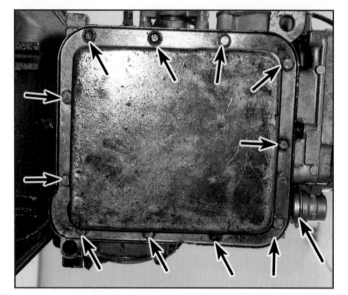

7b.2 The transmission fluid pan must be removed to drain the fluid and change the filter. Indicated is the simple vacuum modulator on the right end of the case.

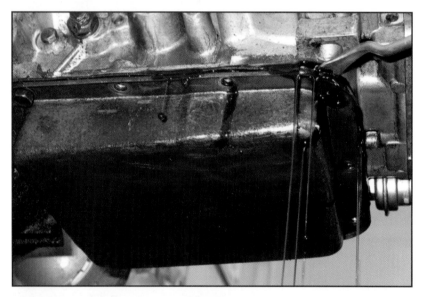

7b.3 When draining the fluid, have a wide drain pan underneath and loosen most of the pan bolts, then remove ones around the perimeter, except for the front, to tilt the pan for draining. You may have to pry the pan down to release the pan gasket. Remove the rest of the bolts.

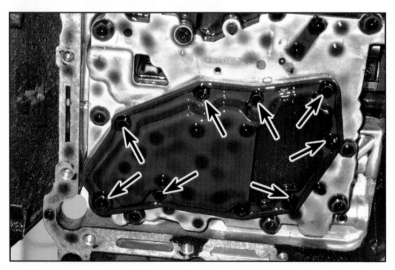

7b.4 Remove the indicated bolts securing the transmission fluid filter. Scrape the old gasket material from the case and the pan, taking care not to gouge the aluminum case. Install the new filter, which comes with a new filter seal where the filter meets the fluid pipe on the transmission.

7b.5 Remove the drain plug(s) and fully drain the converter.

7b.6 Bolted on the rear left side of the transmission is the servo unit. When the cover is removed, the springs and seals can be easily replaced in-vehicle.

7b.7 You already have your transmission out since Chapter 4A when the engine was removed, so even if yours is a known-good transmission, the least you can do is give it a thorough bath, scrubbing with engine cleaner and a hot water rinse. On a clean transmission, any beginning oil leaks can be spotted before real trouble arises.

7b.8 Like many components of our convertible, the shifter assembly has suffered from neglect, dirt and rust. We'll go through the steps to restore our shifter for maximum appearance and functionality.

7b.9 Under the car, disconnect the shift rod from the shifter, then remove the four bolts that secure the shifter assembly to the floor. Pull the assembly up from the floor. We're removing the shifter-to-floor gasket, which is waste-basket-ready.

7b.10 Turning the shifter over, you can pry out the access cover from the box.

7b.11 With the cover off, you can remove the nut that mounts the shift handle to the shifter arm.

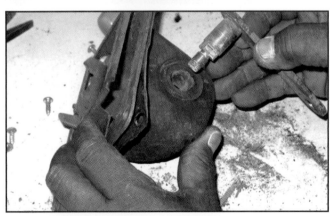

7b.12 At the other side of the box, the shifter arm is now free to be removed.

7b.13 The upper part of the assembly is composed of several layers of metal plates and plastic pieces. When you disassemble yours, lay all the pieces out in their original order and take some digital photos to identify the parts.

7b.14 All of our metal components were rusty, so they were either sanded clean, bead-blasted or for more delicate pieces, given a chemical bath to de-rust them. **Note:** *Remove the plastic parts before using chemicals or abrasive media.*

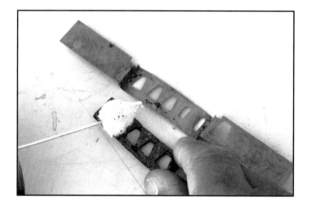

7b.15 This piece is part of the shifter-position detent function of the shifter mechanism. Its thin metal required gentle handling with rust dissolver, then it was painted with clear paint.

7b.16 The housing itself was of strong enough material to be sandblasted, then painted black.

7b.17 With proper rubber gloves, rust dissolver and a wire brush can be used to clean the housing also, which can then be washed and painted.

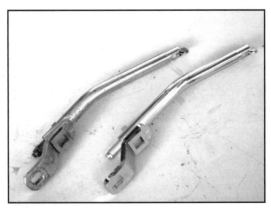

7b.18 There's more to the shift handle than looks - there is the mechanism inside that allows the pushbutton on the handle to allow the forward or rearward movement to change gears. Our handle looked OK, but not as nice as this new reproduction (right).

7b.19 Everything we needed to restore our shifter to like-new performance is available in the aftermarket, from the plastic bushings to the handle and the plastic parts of the indicator.

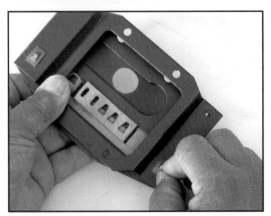

7b.20 The new colored plastic assembly is secured to the plate with two clips.

7b.21   Inside the housing, push in a new plastic bushing with its flange toward the inside.

7b.22   Another bushing is greased and installed from the outside of the housing. Now the shift arm can be installed. Rotate to check for smooth operation without binding.

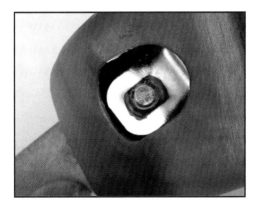

7b.23   Now the shifter can be slipped in over the "stud" end of the shift arm and a new locknut installed. Reinstall the cover over the access hole.

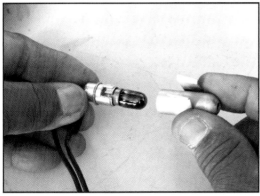

7b.24   The small bulb that lights up the shift position you're in is covered by a dome with a small hole for pinpoint lighting. Obviously, this one has expired. Install a new bulb, then reinstall the cover.

7b.25 The bulb-holder snaps into a rectangular bracket on the bottom of the shifter.

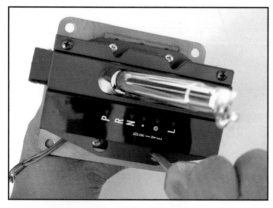

7b.26 The new shift-indicator we bought attaches to the shift housing with four screws, and it now looks showroom new!

7b.27 Position a new gasket on the floor, aligned with the four threaded holes, and install the shifter assembly.

7b.28 Bolt the shifter assembly to the floor and position the shifter in Park. From under the car, position the manual arm on the transmission in Park. Attach the shift rod to the shifter arm and tighten the control rod retaining nut.

Driveline assembly

When we use the term driveline in this book, we are referring to the driveshaft and the rear axle assembly, also called the final drive. These are not glamorous components, and are seldom seen under normal circumstances. However, it is precisely because these components are not seen regularly that they are rarely thought of. In some cases routine lubrication is overlooked for too long. The driveshaft and rear axle assembly can be a source of noisy operation and eventually more costly damage when neglected.

The lubrication is performed with a hand-held grease gun on the U-joint grease fittings. If this is done about once a year, the driveshaft and joints will last a very long time.

The rear axle assembly is a housing for the differential and the rear axles. The axles rarely give trouble, except for an axle bearing failure after perhaps 100,000 or 200,000 miles. If you follow the driveline rebuild in this Chapter, you will have no trouble whatsoever from the driveline, assuming you

lubricate the U-joints, check the differential lubricant level once a year, and drain and refill the differential every 30,000 miles.

Some of the procedures illustrated here require tools you will not likely have at home, such as a hydraulic press, but you can bring your axles to a shop for bearing replacement work.

The type of differential used on V8-powered Ford products up through the Seventies features a removable carrier, which is also referred to as a pumpkin. They are very rugged and run forever with little more attention than lubricant changes. They are a little more tricky to set up and adjust, especially if you are installing a new ring-and-pinion set and don't have a magnetic dial-indicator. However, once the carrier is removed from the vehicle, you can take it to a rear-end specialist to have them adjust the bearings and the contact-pattern of the gears.

7c.1 Our rear axles are going to receive new bearings - they'll be good for another 125,000 miles or so!

If you want to change the gear ratio in your Mustang, either for more performance or for more highway economy, unbolt your carrier and bolt in one with the desired ratio. There are eight-inch and nine-inch rear ends (the diameter of the ring gear) available. There are subtle differences between carriers you have to be aware of. On some models, there is both a drain plug and a fill plug for lubricant in the carrier, while others have a drain and fill plug in the housing, not the carrier. If your housing does not have drain/fill plugs, you must be sure the new carrier does have the plugs, otherwise you can't drain or fill the lubricant.

Six-cylinder Mustangs have an integral carrier rear end. On these rear ends, the differential does not come out of the housing. For anything other than routine lubricant changes, the rear end should be removed for repairs or adjustment, or if you have access to a vehicle lift, adjustments or changing gear ratios can be done in-car. The axle bearing and axle seal replacement procedures are the same as for the removable carrier rear ends.

7c.2 To replace the rear U-joint on the driveshaft, slip off the two bearing cups that secure the driveshaft to the rear axle assembly.

7c.3 Use a screwdriver and small hammer to tap out the retaining clips on the other ends of the U-joint cross.

7c.4 If the clip turns around on you while you're trying to remove it, tap it from the opposite side.

7c.5 We are replacing the U-joint, so the old U-joint cross can be rested on the top of the vise while a brass hammer is used to tap on the shaft's ear to drive the bearing cup out of the driveshaft. Once it is sticking out, you can wiggle the cup out with locking pliers.

7c.6 Another method is to drive the two cups out enough to allow the cross to be removed, then the cups can be popped out.

7c.7 A snap-type prick-punch should be used at the front of the driveshaft to mark the relative position of the yoke and shaft, so that the driveshaft will retain its factory balance.

7c.8 At the front of our driveshaft, the U-joint connects the driveshaft to the front yoke, which is splined to slide into the back of the transmission. With the driveshaft ears again resting on the vise, use the brass hammer as before until you can remove the cups.

7c.9 We're using a length of 4-inch ABS pipe to give our driveshaft a bath. We plugged one end and made the pipe a bit longer than our rusty old driveshaft.

7c.10 Jamie wired the pipe to our shop shelving and, using a piece of coat-hanger, lowered the driveshaft into the pipe.

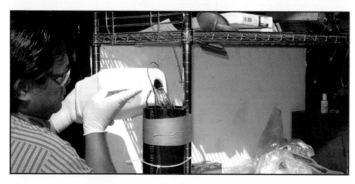

7c.11 Five quarts of Metal Ready (from POR-15) were poured into the tube. Follow the manufacturer's guidelines for safe use of the product.

7c.12 We also soaked the front driveshaft yoke in the same chemical bath.

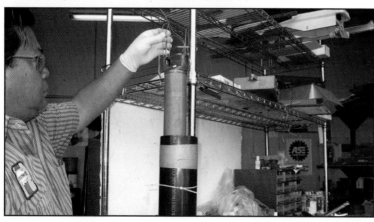

7c.13 Three hours later we withdrew the driveshaft from the solution and it looked brand new! The yoke also looked like a new part.

7c.14 To maintain that factory-new look, we painted the driveshaft and yoke with flat clear from rattle cans. New U-joints were installed and lubricated (refer to the Haynes Mustang Repair Manual).

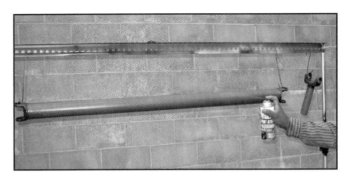

7c.15 After removing the carrier from the rear axle housing, scrape off all traces of old gasket material.

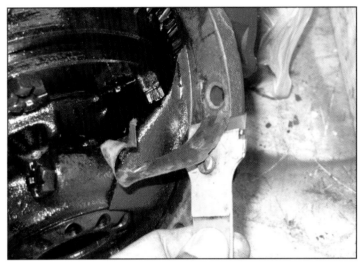

7c.16 After cleaning the differential and priming it, we painted the case with Rustoleum Ruddy Brown primer which closely matches the original color on Ford carriers.

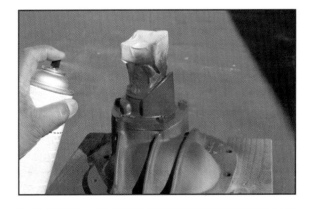

7c.17 Use a fiber disc in a drill to thoroughly clean the mounting surface of the differential to ensure there will be no leaks. Nothing stinks more than used rear end lubricant!

7c.18 Differential specialists adjust the pinion shaft with shims and tiny movements to the bearing adjustment nuts. White grease is used on the teeth and the differential is rotated to check for the contact pattern between the ring gear and the pinion. The goal is to achieve a contact pattern that is very centered. Learn more in the Mustang Repair Manual.

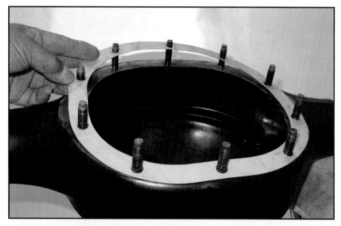

7c.19 The housing's mounting surface should be very clean before installing the new gasket. Use a die on the housing studs to clean off any sealant or dirt in the threads to make consistent torque when tightening the nuts.

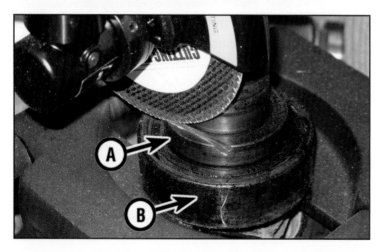

7c.20 To replace the axle bearing (B), you must first remove the inner retainer ring (A). It can be removed with a press, but most shops prefer to simply cut through the retainer. In this case a cutoff tool is used to take off part of the retainer. ** **Warning:** *Use gloves, a full-face safety mask and a long-sleeved shop coat or shirt to protect against burns from sparks.*

7c.21 Drive a chisel between the retainer ring and the axle bearing and the retainer should pop off.

7c.22 A setup like this is used to grip below the axle bearing and pull the bearing off.

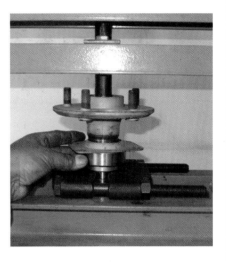

7c.23 After thoroughly cleaning the axle, set the axle and the tooling on a hydraulic press. Once the bearing is fully-seated, the new retainer ring can be pressed on.

7c.24 Scrape the bearing retainer plate, then use an abrasive pad to clean dirt and rust from the plate to make a good seal when the axle is reinstalled.

7c.25 Glue a new gasket to the inner side of the bearing retainer plate.

7c.26 Scrape the end of the axle housing, then use abrasive pads to achieve a clean mounting surface.

7c.27 The axle seal can be difficult to remove, but if you can borrow or rent a slide-hammer tool with a toggle piece on the end, you can poke past the bearing, then use the slide-hammer to pull the seal out.

7c.28 The new axle seal must be driven in squarely, using a seal driver of the correct size.

7c.29 Once the seal is all the way in and seated, apply a coat of white grease to the inner lip of the seal.

7c.30 Slide the axle through the brake backing plate, then install the T-bolts through the backing plate. **Note:** *Install the axles very straight so the splined area doesn't nick the axle seal.*

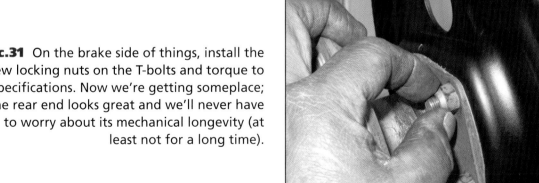

7c.31 On the brake side of things, install the new locking nuts on the T-bolts and torque to specifications. Now we're getting someplace; the rear end looks great and we'll never have to worry about its mechanical longevity (at least not for a long time).

7c.32 The parking-brake cables can now be installed on the backing plates. The little prongs will expand once the cable is pushed through. See Chapter 7D for more details on suspension and brakes.

7c.33 We're installing the wheel cylinders at this time, so foreign material can't enter the brake hard lines.

7c.34 Both rear hard lines run to this brass block that also incorporates a breather fitting and the flexible brake hose to the chassis.

Suspension and Brakes Assembly

While suspension and brake components don't carry the glamour of a fresh paint job, new chrome bumpers or new upholstery, they are hardly optional on your restoration list. Of course, there *are* true gearheads and show judges who actually look under your car to see if you did things correctly!

The true payoff of the work described and illustrated in this Chapter is the peace of mind that comes from knowing all your suspension and brake components are as good as you can make them without resorting to non-stock handling packages. How your car drives, corners and holds the road, and even how quiet it is depends on the tedious preparation of many under-car components. If your Mustang is of '67 or later vintage, it probably came equipped with front disc brakes. Follow our sequence on brakes here, since your drum rear brakes are the same as ours, and if you need information on disc brakes, go to your Haynes Mustang Repair Manual #36048.

If your Mustang is typical of most and you have driven the car for some time in an unrestored state, someone could put you in the car blindfolded after the suspension and brakes are renewed, drive you around and you wouldn't know it was the same vehicle. The final touch for most restorations is a set of new tires. The project may have been sitting on old "roll-around" tires for several years. When you drive your finished project to the tire store and they put on a new set, you won't believe the difference in driving on the way home. Tires deteriorate even when not being used, and the rubber also gets harder with time. The new ones will be supple. So, even though the tasks in this Chapter are laborious, just keep in mind that the reward of a restored chassis will pay you back every time you and your family go out for a drive in your "new" Mustang.

7d.1 Restored suspension and brakes will make your Mustang handle and stop like a new car.

Front suspension

7d.2 Most new suspension parts come with a waxy coating, designed to keep bare metal parts from rusting on the shelf, but after a couple of years of driving your Mustang with the parts left as is will result in rust under your car. All the suspension and brake parts should be coated with some type of paint. We had our rear end housing and backing plates powder-coated for durability.

7d.3 Our spindles were sprayed with "bare metal" paint, so these components will remain looking new for many years. Before spraying any new parts, use brake system cleaner to clean the waxy coating off first.

7d.4 Our Mustang lower control arms are a little tricky. From the (Ford) factory, about two-thirds of the arm is painted chassis-black like most suspension parts. However, the area indicated here as the "no-paint zone" was left bare of paint. To duplicate the factory look, mask off the arm and spray the chassis-black paint. When dry, re-tape it and spray the "bare metal" paint.

7d.5 The upper control arm here is stripped of its replaceable components. With new balljoints and shaft bushings, it will work like a new part.

7d.6 The lower spring seat acts like a rocker on top of the upper control arm. We're going to install the big bushing for the spring seat in a hydraulic press. You can also buy the rocker new with a bushing already in it. If you do use a press, you must cut a half-circle of tubing just the length to fit inside the flanges, which will prevent the press from distorting the spring seat.

7d.7 The spring seat is secured to the upper A-arm with two studs. We chose to drive them into the bushing shaft with a brass hammer and the part positioned on top of the vise, not clamped in the vise.

7d.8 Position the new balljoint to align with the four mounting bolt holes. Slip the new rubber boot over the stud.

7d.9 You can purchase new A-arms with balljoints installed. We're using a kit that has a bolt-on balljoint. The balljoint kit should give you the proper torque on the mounting bolts. Install the boot retaining ring before installing the mounting bolts.

7d.10 Don't overlook the grease fitting. It can be installed through this hole in the upper control arm. By all means, pump some chassis grease in before moving on to the next steps so you don't forget.

7d.11 We cut a length of aluminum angle stock just the length of the inside of the A-arm. The new shaft bushings have to be tightened onto the ends of the shaft, but not so much that they change the inside dimension of the arm. The aluminum piece prevents this.

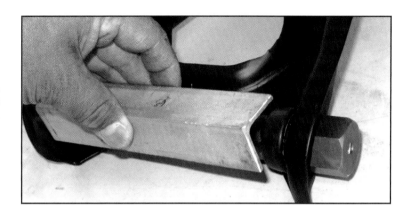

7d.12 Install a grease fitting at each bushing, but make sure they are 90-degree fittings, not straight, or you'll never be able to grease them. Now the control arm shaft can be bolted to the body. Use the same number of shims behind each spot on the shaft as you removed when you disassembled the suspension, then tighten the bolts.

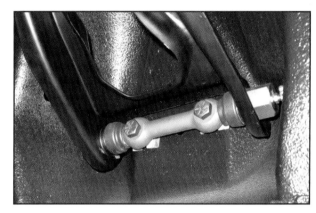

7d.13 The lower control arm balljoint is attached with rivets, rather than bolts. Drill out the old rivets (if you haven't already done so). New lower control arms are available with the balljoint already riveted on if you want to go the easy route.

7d.14 If you do choose to install rivets with a press, you will find it difficult to keep the rivet straight while pressing. We cut several lengths of plastic from a dried-up marker to position over the rivets.

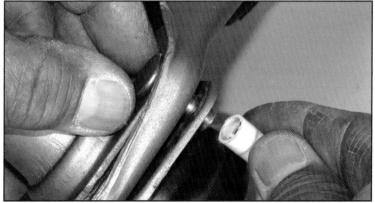

7d.15 In the press, the plastic kept the rivet aligned and squashed down in the end like a flat washer.

7d.16 Slip the balljoint boot over the top of the balljoint.

7d.17 The boot is kept in place by bolting this plate over it to the lower control arm.

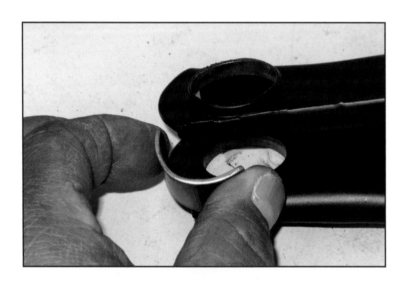

7d.18 To install the new bushing in the inner end of the lower control arm, we used a length of half-round pipe just the right length to support the A-arm while the bushing is installed.

7d.19 This is how things stacked up in the press. The bushing is pushed through from the top with an appropriate-sized socket (a quality tool, not a cheapo), while the other side of the arm is on top of another socket below that is larger than the bushing.

7d.20 Finally, we can insert the original bolt securing the inner end of the lower arm to the body. The two arms seem poised to be joined with a spindle to complete their mission.

7d.21 Connecting the spindle to both the upper and lower balljoints gives us an assembly that can be raised or lowered with a floor jack to facilitate spring installation. Tighten the balljoint nuts and install new cotter pins.

7d.22 This is the same spring compressor we used during disassembly of the front suspension (Chapter 4C).

7d.23 Push the tool and spring up into the upper spring seat, using a floor jack to raise the lower control arm.

7d.24 At the top of each suspension tower in the engine compartment, insert the three carriage bolts into their slots. They will retain the upper front shock absorber mount.

7d.25 With the spring located in the spring seats at each end and a jack in place below the lower control arm, you can remove the spring compressor components from the spring. ****Warning:** *The floor jack must remain in position until the shock absorber is installed.*

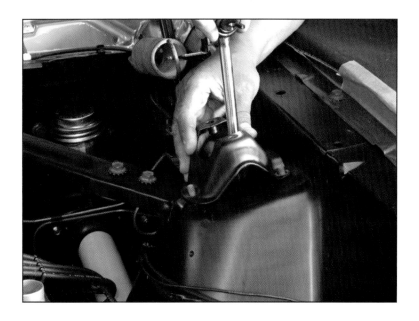

7d.26 Extend the shock absorber to its full length, position the shock bracket over the top of the shock absorber and drop the shock absorber down through the bracket to the lower mounting. Install nuts on the three carriage bolts and tighten them.

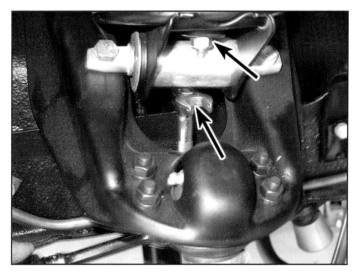

7d.27 Two studs on the bottom of the shock absorber fit into holes in the lower spring seat. The outside nut is easy to reach, but the rear nut may require a crows-foot wrench to tighten.

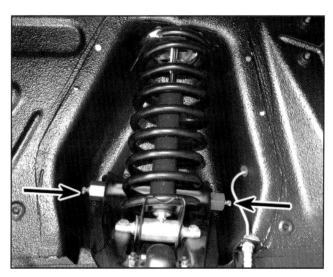

7d.28 Here you can clearly see why the grease fittings (indicated) on the upper control arm have to be 90-degree type and facing outward in order to get a grease gun on them for periodic lubrication.

7d.29 Two bolts secure the upper end of the shock absorber to the shock bracket.

7d.30 Apply some rubber lubricant to the strut rod bushing and squeeze the bushing into it with large pliers.

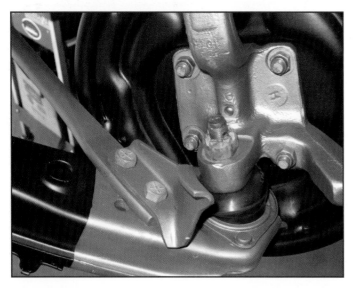

7d.31 On models with caster adjusting nuts, thread one large nut down the rod, then a dished washer on the front end and push the rod through the bushing. On other models, install the dished washer and bushing. At the other end, install and tighten the mounting bolts securing the strut rod to the lower control arm. Install the other bushing, washer and nut on the other side of the chassis bracket.

Steering components

7d.32 We used a wire wheel to clean all the rust and grime from our steering column. After it was down to bare metal, we sanded with 320-grit sandpaper, followed up with successively finer grades, ultimately wet-sanding with 1000-grit. No more pits!

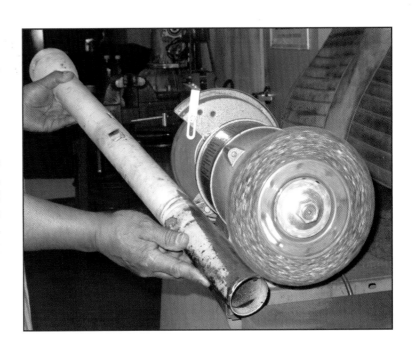

7d.33 The column was cleaned with paint pre-cleaner and two coats of primer were applied. When thoroughly dry, the column was cleaned again and two coats of our interior white lacquer were applied. It was quite a makeover for the little effort involved.

7d.34 The steering box on '65 and '66 Mustangs has an integral shaft, so when installing it, you have to feed the shaft through the firewall. Have someone inside the car to guide the shaft where it won't do any damage. The column can now be slid down over the shaft and the seal at the firewall installed. On later Mustangs, the shaft can be separated from the steering box.

7d.35 Briefly install the steering wheel so you can center the steering box, then install the Pitman arm. It should align with the splines at only one or two places. Install the lockwasher and Pitman arm nut.

7d.36 The steering idler arm bolts to the right side of the chassis with the arm pointing forward. The drag link connects the Pitman arm on one side and the idler arm on the other side.

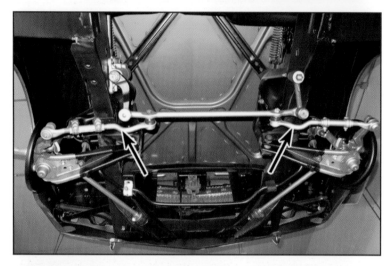

7d.37 The tie-rods connect the spindles with the drag link, completing the steering linkage. Tighten all tie-rod ends and install new cotter pins.

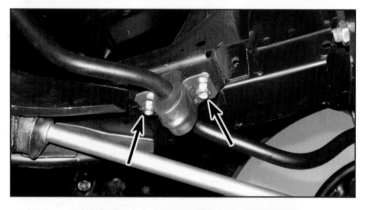

7d.38 Position the new rubber bushings over the front stabilizer bar and install the clamps with the bolts somewhat loose. Slide the stabilizer left-and-right until it is centered on the body, then tighten the clamp bolts.

7d.39 Insert one of the long bolts for the stabilizer bar links, with washers and rubber bushings as shown, through the eyes at the end of the stabilizer bar.

7d.40 With one washer and one rubber bushing on the bottom end of the tube, insert the bottom of the bolt through the lower control arm, then install the lower bushing, washer and nut.

Rear suspension

7d.41 The rear suspension on our favorite years of Mustangs is simplistic but effective. There are two parallel leaf springs (usually sagging on unrestored Mustangs), each with a bushing at the front end and a moveable shackle at the rear. That, the rear axle and two shock absorbers constitute the extent of rear suspension on early Mustangs.

7d.42 Lubricate the rubber bushings with WD-40 and squeeze them into the two rear subframe rails with a large C-clamp. One bushing goes through from each side.

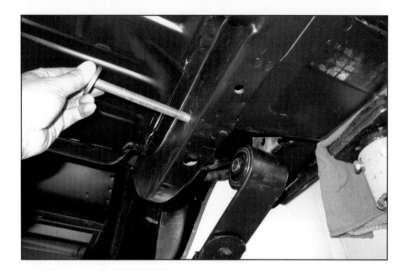

7d.43 A long bolt goes through the subframe rail and the forward spring eye.

7d.44 Use a new locknut to secure the front spring-eye bolts. Remember it's the spring end with the bigger eye of the spring that goes forward.

7d.45 Disassemble the new spring shackle kits and install two bushings of the four into the pocket in the rear subframe rail. With the other two bushings installed in the rear spring eye, you can push the two studs on the shackle plate through the spring and the rail at the same time. Finish the installation by installing the locknuts.

7d.46 This is a considerable landmark in your restoration progress. You could actually put the rear wheels on and set the back half on the floor, but let's not get too far ahead of ourselves.

7d.47 The last items to install on the rear suspension are the shock absorbers. On most models, the access holes for the upper shock fasteners are at the front of the trunk, but on convertibles the access holes are here behind the rear seat.

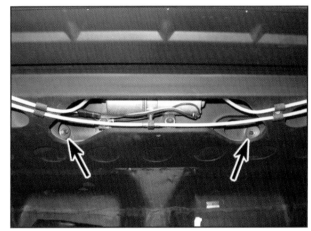

7d.48 On the new shock absorber, install one cup washer and one rubber bushing, then push up from below until the stud is visible through the access hole.

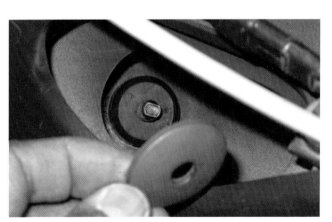

7d.49 With a helper holding the shock from below, place the other rubber bushing and washer on the stud and get the nut started on the shock stud.

7d.50 Tighten the upper shock stud nuts and reinstall the plastic access covers for the shocks.

7d.51 The bottom of the rear shock is simply bolted to the tab on the plate under the leaf spring. Install the rubber bushings and washers on each side and install the retaining nut.

Brakes

Front brakes

7d.52 Taking the approach we have in other aspects of our restoration, most of our brake parts are being replaced with new ones. Our front drums were shot and the wheel studs were no better. The drum and hub are pressed together and must be separated the same way. With a thick-wall tube or socket positioned under the wheel stud/drum, the press pushes down on the stud.

7d.53 Rust notwithstanding, we separated the hub from the drum. The hub was then cleaned of rust and painted, while the drums were tossed for recycling.

7d.54 The hub carries both the inner and outer wheel bearing races and bearings. Toss the old bearings, then use a hammer and a blunt punch from the other side to drive the bearing race out of the hub. When one race is removed, flip the hub over and drive out the race for the other bearing.

7d.55 New races must be driven into the hub, one for the inner bearing and one for the outer bearing. Here you must use a bearing driver, not a punch.

7d.56 A driver of the correct diameter does a perfect job of squarely installing the bearing races, using a hammer on the shaft. Drive the race in until it bottoms at the ledge.

7d.57 To combine the hub and the new drum, the two are aligned in a press by pushing the new wheel studs squarely in each hole. The stud must be kept straight during the procedure. **Note:** *Six-cylinder Mustangs have only four lug-studs per wheel, while V-8 models have five.*

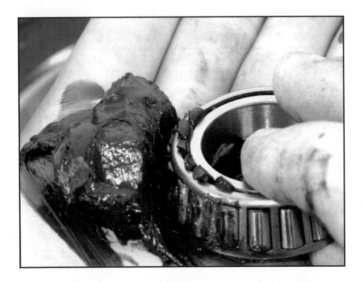

7d.58 Wear latex gloves while packing the wheel bearings with wheel bearing grease. Fill your palm with grease, then drag the bearing over the grease in a wiping motion, until you see the grease coming up through the bearing. Do this all around the bearing. Inexpensive bearing packer tools are readily available in auto parts stores that make the job less messy.

7d.59 Smear grease on the outside of the inner bearing and install it in the hub. Make sure you don't get any grease on the hub or the inside of the drum, as this could ruin the new brake shoes you are going to install.

7d.60 Lubricate the inner race with grease, then install the inner wheel bearing

7d.61 You can install the inner grease seal by tapping a piece of 2x4 over the seal (keeping the seal from rocking), but a seal driver will do a better job without damage to the seal.

7d.62 Don't bother trying to rebuild your old wheel cylinders. Here is a new front wheel cylinder that will provide you with many miles of confidence in your brakes, along with two pushrods and the mounting bolts.

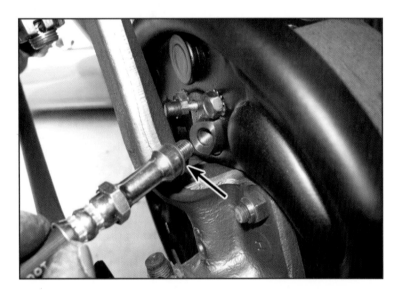

7d.63 Before installing a new flexible front brake hose, place a new copper sealing washer over the threads on the hose fitting.

7d.64 The other end of the brake hose is attached to a chassis bracket with a steel U-clip. If you aren't ready to connect a new steel brake line here, install a plug in the hose to keep out dirt or contaminants.

7d.65 Insert the two pushrods into the boots on the wheel cylinder and you're ready to assemble your front brakes. Buy or borrow the few brake tools needed, such as brake pliers, brake spring hold-down tool and a "spoon" brake adjuster tool.

7d.66 The rear (or secondary) brake shoe can be identified by having a longer brake lining than on the front (or primary) brake shoe. The shoe is first attached by slipping the upper part into the slot-end of the wheel cylinder pushrod and installing the hold-down spring.

7d.67 Next, install the front (primary) brake shoe.

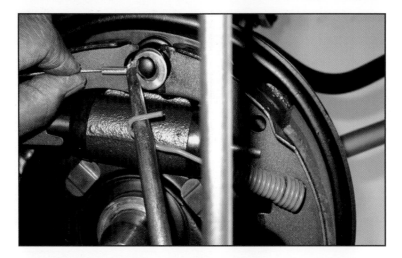

7d.68 The cable eye for the self-adjuster mechanism slips over the anchor pin on the backing plate, then the shoe-to-anchor springs can be installed, starting with the primary spring. The brake tool has a notch in the end to stay on the anchor pin while stretching the spring.

7d.69 Before installing the secondary shoe spring (yellow), position cable guide in the hole in the shoe, then insert the end of the spring into the hole and use the spring tool to stretch the other end over the anchor pin.

7d.70 Here's one complete front brake assembly. Note the way the brake adjusting lever cable and spring are connected between the two shoes at the bottom.

7d.71 Our new drum and restored hub can now be installed over the completed brake assembly. The drums are painted with cast-iron grey paint to keep them from rusting.

7d.72 The greased outer wheel bearing is slipped in place, the big washer is installed, followed by the spindle nut.

7d.73 Gradually tighten the spindle nut to seat the bearings and remove all play, then back it off and tighten just a little more than hand-tight. The drum should rotate smoothly and with no wobble. Too loose or too tight and the bearings (and tires) won't last long. Follow the specs and procedure in the Haynes Mustang Repair Manual #36048.

7d.74 Slip the nut lock over the spindle nut and see if any holes align with the hole in the spindle. If so, install a new cotter pin and bend the ends over. If the cotter holes don't align, remove the nut lock and turn it a little for cotter pin installation.

7d.75 The final step for this drum brake assembly is tapping the dust cover into the hub to keep out dirt and moisture.

Rear brakes

7d.76 Position the new wheel cylinder into the opening in the backing plate, but don't install the mounting bolts yet.

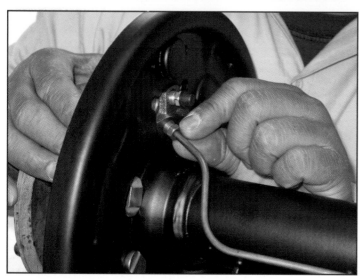

7d.77 With the cylinder loose, your can align the fitting from the hard brake line so that it threads in properly. Once the fitting is in enough threads to ensure it won't cross-thread, you can install the two wheel cylinder mounting bolts.

7d.78 Just as with the front brakes, insert the pushrods with the slots aligned to accept the brake shoes.

7d.79 Here are all the new components of the rear brakes. Consider them all to be critically important.

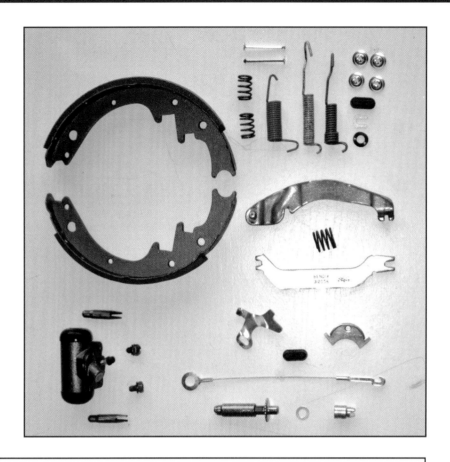

7d.80 Before installing your new brake shoes, apply a small dab of brake grease to the flat shoe support areas on the backing plate.

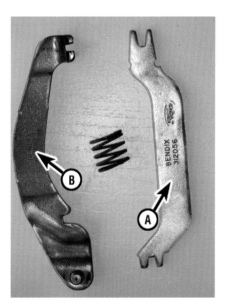

7d.81 These two pieces last almost forever, the link bar (A) and the parking brake lever (B). A brake rebuild kit will include the new spring for the link bar, and a new retaining clip for the secondary brake shoe-to-parking brake lever.

7d.82 Apply a small amount of brake grease to the stud on the parking brake lever's stud before joining it to the secondary brake shoe.

7d.83 Place a new spring-washer over the stud and push the new clip in place. Use pliers to squeeze the clip securely.

7d.84 Install the secondary (rearmost) brake shoe and keep it in place by installing the hold-down spring and cup, with the head of the pin 90-degrees to the slot in the cup.

7d.85 Install the link bar with a spring at one end. The bar should fit between the notches on each brake shoe.

7d.86 The primary shoe is installed now with the pushrod engaged to the wheel cylinder, the link bar in place, and the shoe return spring hooked to the shoe.

7d.87   Push the adjuster cable eye over the anchor pin and install the primary shoe return spring to the anchor pin, then install the secondary shoe return spring also.

7d.88   The brake adjuster mechanism is threaded into one side, while the unthreaded end has a cap over it. Lubricate the threads and the cap with brake grease, then install a thin washer and the cap.

7d.89   The adjuster fits between the two shoes at the bottom. To know which way to install the adjuster, make sure the star-wheel is aligned with the adjuster hole in the backing plate. The end of the parking brake cable fits into a U-bent portion of the parking brake lever on the rear shoe. **Note:** *Left-hand-threaded adjusters have a single groove near the primary shoe end, and are only for the left side. Don't mix up right and left adjusters.*

7d.90 Slip the hook-end of the adjuster cable into the hole in the adjuster bracket .

7d.91 One of the last details on the rear brakes is to install the spring (blue here) for the adjuster. The multi-function brake spring tool can be used to stretch the spring from the adjuster primary shoe until it hooks into the hole in the adjuster bracket.

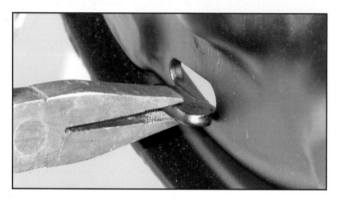

7d.92 If your backing plates do not have an opening at the bottom for using a brake adjuster tool through the slot, your brakes may never have been adjusted properly! The metal plug shown here should have been knocked out with a hammer and punch decades ago. Once the hole is open just get a package of four rubber plugs; they keep out water and dirt.

7d.93 Inspect your wheels carefully before mounting new tires. Look for dings or scrapes, bent edges, and deep pitting. The area on the rim where the tire bead fits should be sanded smooth and free of rust. Prime the wheels twice and wet-sand before painting them black. Bring the wheels to a tire shop and have them check the bare wheels for runout or instability on their balancing machine.

7d.94 The standard steel wheels have a "date code" stamped into them. We had two correct wheels but had to search out two more. The "5 M f" is correct for our '65 convertible. It doesn't matter much because with the hubcaps on, only you will know if they are right or not.

Heating, cooling, air conditioning systems

The comfort of heated air when it's cold and cooled air when it's hot is a pleasure we take for granted with our modern cars, so much so that dealers almost give away cars that the manufacturer has shipped them without climate control.

In 1965, this was not the case. Luxury cars like Cadillacs, Lincolns, Buicks and Oldsmobiles were usually very well-equipped, including air conditioning, but that latter option was seldom ordered at the other end of the marketplace. Thus, many buyers found the A/C option an expensive one on the $2,300 Mustang. But when you're 18 and just bought a red Mustang coupe on a payment plan, you don't mind opening your fresh air vents and rolling down your windows when it's hot.

Today's collectors are no longer 18 and in fact most of us who graduated from high school when the Mustang made its debut are now well over 60, and we like our comforts. Finding a car with the original under-dash A/C is getting harder, and even when you have it, it is an expensive system to restore. Our modern cars all have the environmentally-friend-

lier R-134A refrigerant, which our modern compressors, condensers, O-rings and other components are designed for, while cars more than 15 years old used the R-12 refrigerant that their equipment was designed to handle. The R-12 is practically ordered out of existence, and is very expensive when you find it. There are substitutes, but they don't perform as efficiently. Most air conditioning shops can change the O-rings and put R-134a into your system, but it is usually not as effective as the original system.

The dilemma for the restorer of a Sixties-era car is: update your original system and have reduced cooling performance, or replace the compressor with a modern unit and not have it look original in your engine compartment. There are several high-performance aftermarket kits available for all years of collectible Mustangs. Some kits have an under-dash A/C unit that looks almost stock, while some kits have a combined heat/AC unit that tucks up under the instrument panel, so there are several options to weigh.

Restoration of the stock heater/HVAC components is not complicated (HVAC stands for "Heating, Ventilation, and Air Conditioning"). As with most everything else on collectible Mustangs, new parts are readily available, from clips to heater cores and blower motors. Not surprisingly, our system turned out to be rusty. Before working on the system, have the A/C system (if equipped) discharged and recovered by a licensed technician, then drain and flush the radiator and cut the heater hoses off at the firewall.

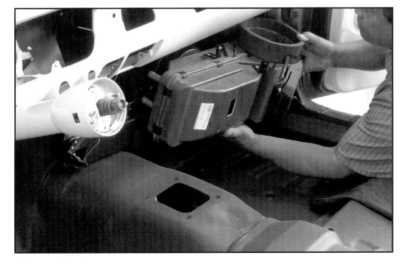

7e.1 Tucked tightly up under the dash, the heater housing is something you rarely see. You'll appreciate a refurbished heater unit when the weather turns cold, though!

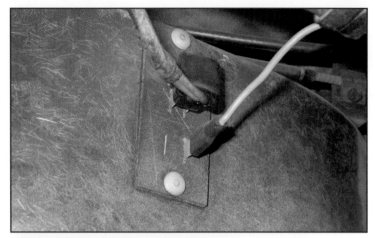

7e.2 You can begin your removal of the heater unit by disconnecting the two wiring plugs from the blower motor resistor on the interior side of the case.

7e.3 Disconnect the heater cable, using side-cutter pliers to remove the little pressed-metal clip. Slide the inner cable end from the lever, then remove the bolt securing the outer cable.

7e.4 Perform the same steps with the temperature cable, which is mounted closer to the firewall edge of the housing.

7e.5 The last cable to disconnect is the defrost cable, which controls a flapper inside the defroster plenum. You will notice here that there is a chunk of plenum missing; the originals were made of pressed cardboard and heavy moisture or a sharp blow could easily render them damaged.

7e.6 Remove the four nuts securing the blower mounting on the engine side of the firewall. From inside the car, remove the mounting nuts for the heater housing.

7e.7 If your Mustang has the original air conditioning unit, you must remove it from the car to fully access the heater housing for removal. ****Warning:** *Do not crack open the A/C refrigerant fittings to bleed the system, it is dangerous to your skin, your eyes and the environment. Have the refrigerant recovered by an air conditioning shop. If you have old R-12 in there, it's worth money also.*

7e.8 Remove the large round seal that connects the heater housing to the cowl fresh air. We purchased a complete heater housing seal kit (not very expensive) that extracts maximum performance from the heater.

7e.9 Unbolt the blower motor from the housing and remove it. Test it with a 12-volt jumper and a ground wire. Ours was in good working condition, requiring only cosmetic renewal and new mounting plate seals.

7e.10 To remove the rusty blower wheel, use a long Allen wrench to go through the cage and loosen the set-screw. It may take a little penetrating oil and some patience to wrestle the cage off. Take your time and don't damage the cage.

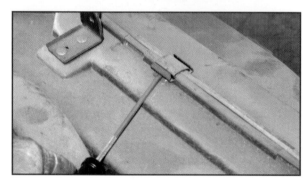

7e.11 The two halves of the heater housing are held together with these clips around the flanges of the housing. Pry the clips off, but try not to lose any. New clips are around $4 each.

7e.12 We've gotten used to seeing new horrors during the disassembly of our convertible, but the inside of the heater case was as ugly as it could possibly be. The heater core is almost unrecognizable, and any steel parts inside were thoroughly rusted.

7e.13 Once we started delving into the heater housing with a plan to de-rust the metal parts and paint them, we were disappointed to find the doors rusted right through.

7e.14 If the doors don't seal well, the whole heat/defrost system will not work as engineered.

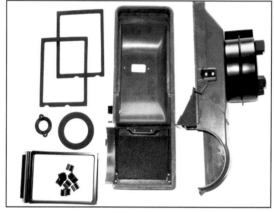

7e.15 We purchased a new heater housing, with the metal doors mounted and with all the foam and other sealing materials required.

7e.16 Install all of the foam gaskets and seals. Their job is preventing air from going around the core instead of through the core as it should. When you first take your Mustang out on a frosty fall day you'll be glad your heater assembly has had this treatment.

7e.17 The heater core itself is the main item in the system. They are not very expensive and will last a very long time as long as you keep the proper amount of antifreeze in your cooling system.

7e.18 The new heater core pops right into the bed prepared for it. Make sure none of the sealing materials are pinched or torn in the process.

7e.19 When reassembling the housing, keep the blower half of the case down on the bench (with the heater core facing up) while settling the upper half over the heater half. Install some of the case-clips to hold everything together.

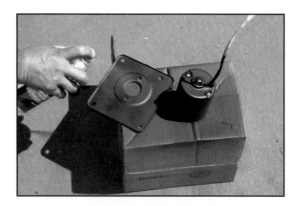

7e.20 Remove the mounting plate from the blower motor, so you can clean, prime and paint the motor and the mounting plate.

7e.21 The side of the mounting plate that faces the motor has a gasket that must be replaced with a new one. Sealing well around the blower motor is important. There are both 2-speed and three-speed blower motors.

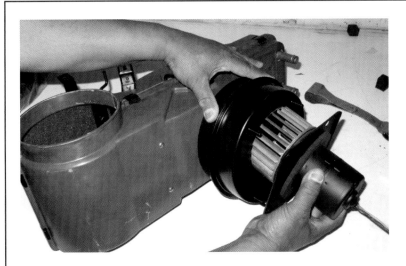

7e.22 If you have bead-blasted your blower fan and painted it to prevent future rust, install the mounting plate, then install the fan and tighten the Allen set-screw. Position a new seal between the blower mounting plate and the blower housing on the heater case, push the plate over the studs and secure with nuts.

7e.23 Apply a small bead of weatherstrip adhesive on the plate, close to the motor but not on the motor.

7e.24 Push a new firewall seal over the blower motor and seat it firmly into the adhesive.

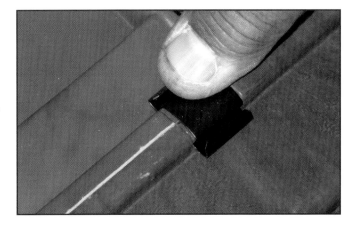

7e.25 Install the remaining heater housing clips.

7e.26 We had a very nicely-restored heating system up to this point, except for the broken cardboard defroster plenum. We replaced that with a new plastic unit that is much sturdier.

7e.27 The new plenum snaps onto the blower housing just like the original, but also attaches with several screws for additional strength.

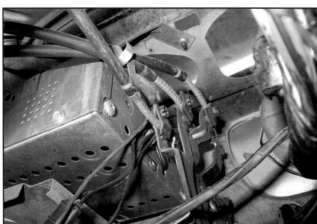

7e.28 Here is our original control unit before restoration, just to indicate how little room there is to work on the controls behind the dash.

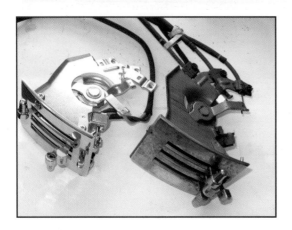

7e.29 With the heating box assembly secured to the firewall with the four nuts, we turned our attention to the controls. We have a new control unit, to which we transferred the switch wiring.

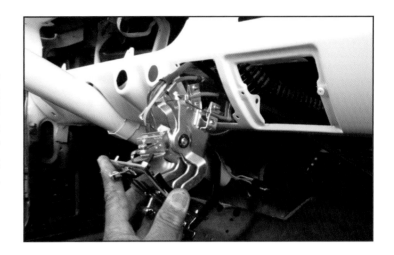

7e.30 With the old and new controls side-by-side, you can transfer one cable-end at a time to the new controls. When they are all connected, route the cables under the dash to their destinations at the heater/defroster housing. Try to keep the same adjustment length as the old ones.

7e.31 The ventilation system in early Mustangs is very simple to fix. The one-piece tubular plastic unit under each end of the dashboard just bolts in place and its only moving part is a hand-operated rod that either opens or closes the vent.

7e-32 This compressor is typical of the Ford and York compressors used on early Mustangs. When converted to modern R-134A refrigerant and used with new O-rings, they will work, but not as efficiently as modern compressors made for R-134A.

7e-33 There are several very complete A/C and A/C-heat kits available from the aftermarket. The most common compressor in these kits is the Sanden (shown) which is compact, but not original-looking.

8 Interior and convertible top

Interior

One of the aspects of restoring any collector automobile that frightens most owners is the interior. Generally, the materials are expensive, and the labor is even more expensive. Good auto upholsterers make good money and are always in demand. They usually have a waiting list, which means you don't have access to work on your project as long as it sits in a shop waiting.

Once again, the restoration of a classic Mustang puts you in a much better situation than someone restoring a Packard, LaSalle, Studebaker, etc. The sheer number of Mustang owners represents a substantial marketplace, and thus everything you need for your interior is readily available, with factory-like quality and at reasonable prices.

The availability of complete interior packages that include padding, carpeting, upholstery, arm rests, door panels and sun visors probably costs less than one or two days work at a custom upholsterer! What we installed in our Mustang, never having done it before, came out like new.

You'll be surprised as to what you can do yourself. Follow all of our steps and take your time. Go through this Chapter several times if necessary, and comparing your own Mustang to our photos will answer a lot of your questions. Fixing up the interior is one of the biggest appearance changes you can make, aside from a new paint job. There are a few specialized tools for installing new upholstery: a narrow sharp pair of scissors, hog-ring pliers (get the longer-handled ones), hog rings (sometimes included with whole interior packages), an upholstery pin or two (safer for your hands than an awl when poking through material to find a hole), some spray glue, cotton padding, strips of jute padding, and burlap material. An upholstery supply shop should have all of these items, or you could search online for them.

One design element common to almost all automotive upholstery is what are called listing wires. Just hog-ringing a piece of vinyl to a seat frame will probably tear the material over time because the pressure is just on the half-dozen or so hog-rings in that area. Upholstery is made with cloth sleeves called listing in which there are steel wires in the OEM seat. You will be removing the listing wires from your old seat to reuse with the new uphol-

8a.1 Modern vehicles are nice, comfortable and functional, but they can't match the style of a freshly restored '60's-era Mustang. Beautiful!

stery, and you must cut through all of the hog-rings with side-cutter pliers to get the old upholstery off. Some kits come with new listing wires.

When a section of upholstery is fastened to the seat frame with a listing wire, the load is spread all along the wire. Before you do a thing to your seats, take digital photos of the underside to see how the upholstery was originally attached. Remove the listing wires and identify with tape where they came from.

Today's car seating has progressed a long way in comfort and style, with electric heaters, power lumbar supports, six-way power movements, and even a computer that stores all the parameters of your favorite seating position. However comfortable the new cars are, one thing their seats don't have is that cool factor like the classic 1965 to 1970 Mustangs. When these cars were seen in the Ford showrooms of their day, people actually said "Wow!" They may say it when they see your Mustang tomorrow.

Carpeting

8a.2 The padding and carpeting are installed before the seats or other interior components, but the drain holes in the floorpan must be sealed. Smear a little seam-sealer around the openings.

8a.3 Also apply a bead of seam-sealer on the floorpan side of the metal caps, then install the caps and secure them with their screws.

8a.4 Most of the padding is cut so that it's very obvious where each piece goes and how it's oriented to the floorpan. The padding is to make the floor more comfortable for your feet and to dampen road noise. On convertibles like ours, the center reinforcement is almost entirely under the seats, so padding isn't needed there.

8a.5 The carpeting comes in sections and most sets are molded to fit well against the floor. When you put one in it just seems to go right where it's supposed to. Keep the carpet centered in the car. You can put down some newspaper on the carpet and position some heavy weights to keep the carpet centered during installation.

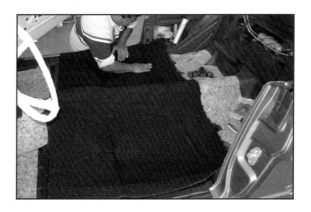

8a.6 In the rear section of the carpet, find the seat belt bolt holes with an upholstery pin or awl and cut matching holes in the carpet. Once the seat belts are bolted back in, the carpet can't move out of place.

8a.7 The front carpet section overlaps the middle and the relationship is secured when you find the seat track mounting holes. Locate with an awl from above.

8a.8 Use chalk to mark the spots, then use very sharp and slender scissors to snip out the bolt holes in the carpet. Do not use a drill – it will quickly wind up the carpet strands and possibly ruin the carpet. A hobby knife works well, or you can make clean holes by placing a piece of 2x4 under the carpet and using a small hammer and a gasket punch of the appropriate size.

8a.9 Go slowly and carefully when cutting the hole to fit over the headlight dimmer switch on the driver's side. Most carpet kits come with this grommet you can push through the hole.

8a.10 After all this time with the Mustang in pieces and in various colors and finishes, it's a pleasure to add the carpet and other interior details. The repainted kick panels can now be installed, as they keep the carpet in position up front. You'll have to push hard on the panel to depress the new carpet, then install the kick panel mounting screws.

8a.11 In the center of the car, remove the four shifter mounting bolts and lift the shifter up, so that you can mark the carpet for four holes to be made. Tuck the carpet under the shifter.

8a.12 Locate one or two of the door sill trim cover holes and install screws finger-tight, then align the rest of the screw-holes and install the remaining screws. When all screws are in place, tighten them. The sill cover secures the carpeting to the door sill.

Console

8a.13 Our console was missing several parts and had numerous cracks, so we started off with a new repro unit to save time over restoring our old one.

8a.14 Because reproduction consoles have to fit several different floor pans, there are a few places scribed on the plastic to indicate the sections to be removed to fit different body styles. A coping saw is being used here to cut along the line on a section marked for convertibles. You could also cut the plastic using a utility knife with a new blade, but be careful.

8a.15 The new console comes in black only, like a Model T. Jamie has cleaned the surface of our console and is applying non-filler primer here. Do not sand the console; it has the correct grained texture to match other interior components.

8a.16 The primer was followed by a spray-can application of the correct lacquer interior color, which is white in our case.

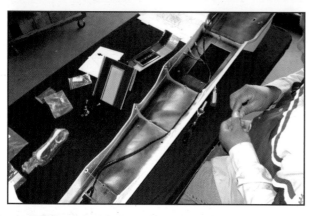

8a.17 The console wiring harness is quite simple, and is laid out by following the orginal routing.

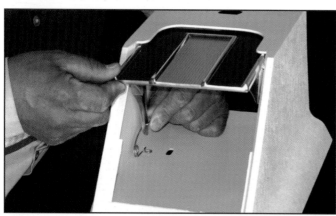

8a.18 Fitting the new console door is a little tricky, and you'll need some small needle-nose pliers to install the door hinge springs.

8a.19 A screw secures the spring and also is a destination for a ground wire.

8a.20 The two black decorative strips have studs that fit into holes in the console. They really look good against the white console.

8a.21 The strips are secured from underneath, using the supplied speed-nuts. Do not tighten these any more than is necessary to secure the trim strips.

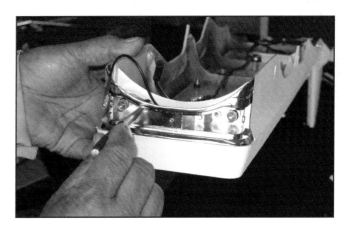

8a.22 Our console required two holes to be drilled to secure the courtesy light housing. Here the housing is held in place while marking through the screw holes in the housing. Mount the console to the floor using an awl to find the original screw holes.

Convertible interior quarter trim

8a.23 We enlisted a professional upholsterer to install the padding and pre-sewn vinyl upholstery over our rear seat interior quarter trim panels. He said our repair to the panel was strong, but he sanded that area for better adhesion of his upholstery glue.

8a.24 There is a thin foam padding that is glued on before the upholstery, as our old padding crumbled away when the upholstery was removed.

8a.25 The vinyl is carefully pulled to align with the edge. At this point the only backside glue is in that area. The glue upholsterers use is very sticky, but is formulated so that you can lift up a glued area, stretch the vinyl and stick it back down.

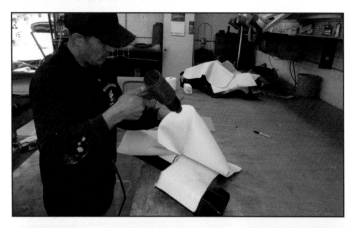

8a.26 Another weapon in the upholsterer's arsenal is a heat gun. He can direct it, as here, just to the area near the stitched seam, allowing a little more stretching of the vinyl.

8a.27 The short length of material that covers the ashtray area is pulled back snugly and glued down. When you pull one direction, this can create a wrinkle somewhere else, which is why this kind of work can't be rushed.

8a.28 Once the seam is glued down without wrinkles, the rest of the material can be applied, one side at a time. He lifts up the material, sprays the panel, sticks the material down, then smoothes out any wrinkles. When the wrinkles are gone, he presses down with his hand to ensure even glue contact.

8a.29 The remainder of the work is to cut the excess vinyl around all the edges, leaving about an inch border that can be glued to the backside of the panel.

8a.30 It takes a practiced hand to make slits in the excess material without going too far (which might show later on the good side). The slits also have to be made so that there are no bunched-up spots around the perimeter. He's at the first go-round here.

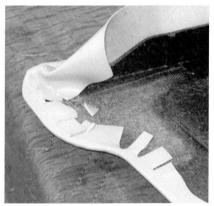

8a.31 On straight edges, the process is simple and there are few slits to be made, but it becomes more difficult when you go around corners. You have to cut triangular pieces out to avoid bunching.

8a.32 To cut out material at an opening, make a center cut with a razor, then make a second cut that forms an X. This leaves four flaps to pull back and glue around the underside of our rear ashtray opening.

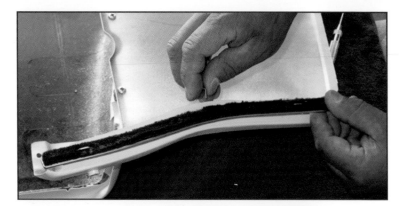

8a.33 A weatherstrip is attached to the backside of the quarter trim. Mark through the holes in the strip to align it with the panel. If no holes are present, drill some with a very small bit.

8a.34 Push the staple through the strip and into the holes.

8a.35 Use pliers to bend the staples down to the panel. The panel is done, just be careful when installing it not to nick the material, especially when installing screws and the snaps for the top boot.

8a.36 Here's our quarter trim panel looking like it just came off the 1965 Mustang assembly line.

Rear seat upholstery

8a.37 The rear seats are simpler to re-cover than the bucket seats, but you'll get the hang of the methods doing the backseat back and backseat bottom. The hog-ring pliers seem archaic as a fastening system, but that's how it's done. When the ring is kept in the grooved jaws of the hog-ring pliers, you put the ring over the items you want to fasten together and squeeze the pliers, which forms a closed ring.

8a.38 Most backseat cushions have a listing wire at the front, back and sides. Our seat also has a U-shaped listing wire in the center, seen here being fed through the listing sleeve in the new upholstery.

8a.39 Unroll some cotton padding on a clean bench covered with clean towels, cardboard or butcher paper. Cut the padding to be bigger all around than the seat bottom.

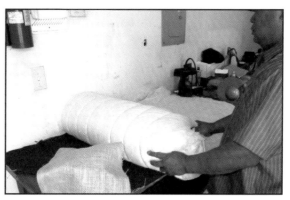

8a.40 During the disassembly of our Mustang, we had cleaned the rust from the front and rear seat frames, then painted them with black Rustoleum. The rear seat bottom is laid upside down over the padding and burlap.

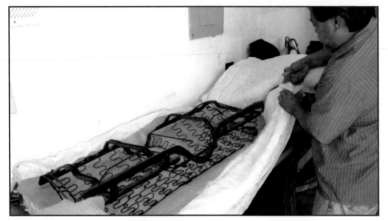

8a.41 The padding and burlap can be trimmed down to a tighter fit with the frame, leaving more material at the sides and front, and less at the rear. The padding makes the seat more comfortable, but also has the aesthetic purpose of preventing the frame from showing itself through the upholstery.

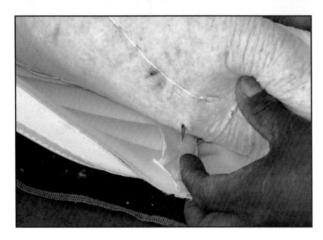

8a.42 The point of the scissors is pushed through the cotton padding to indicate where the listing starts. Cut a long slit in the padding so that the listing wire can be hog-ringed to the middle of the seat frame.

8a.43 More trimming around the seat frame is required now that the upholstery cover is upside-down under the seat frame. The back padding can be trimmed without much overlap at the frame.

8a.44 To make sure that the jute and burlap materials stay put around the front side of the seat, several hog-rings will keep it there.

8a.45 Now carefully install several hog-rings at the front, attaching the front listing wire to the seat frame. When you install a hog-ring, make sure there are no wrinkles in the vinyl before installing the next hog-ring.

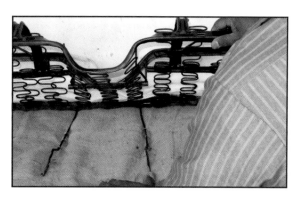

8a.46 In our seat bottom, these two rods in the frame are released at the front end, laid down on the burlap and hog-ringed in several places along their length.

8a.47 Don't push down too hard while hog-ringing the two rods or you could puncture the upholstery.

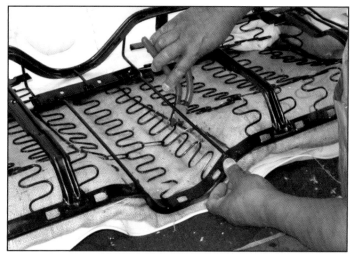

8a.48 Here the padding has been temporarily secured to the back edge of the frame, while the new cover is tugged into position over the padding and frame.

8a.49 With the listing wire in place, the front of the cover can be fastened to the frame, then the sides, using the side listing wires, if applicable.

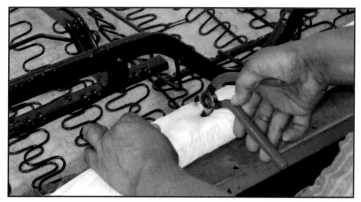

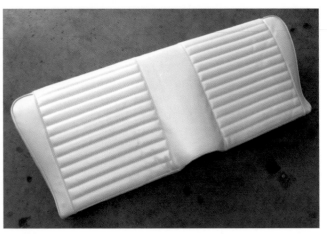

8a.50 When the front and sides are all clipped in place and no wrinkles are evident, finish attaching the rear listing wire to the square holes in the seat frame. Use one ring for each square hole, no extra rings are required.

8a.51 Once this seat bottom is back in its place in the '65 convertible, it's going to look factory-fresh and no one will know by looking if we did it ourselves or not. Definitely no eating in the car!

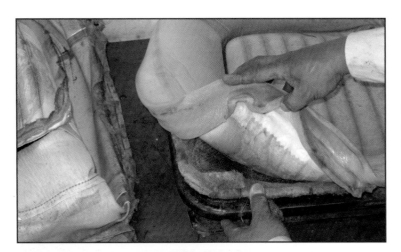

Bucket front seats

8a.52 What we found after stripping the old upholstery from our front seats was pretty ugly. We cleaned and painted the seat frames and set them aside. We chose to replace the bottom and back seat foam with new foam.

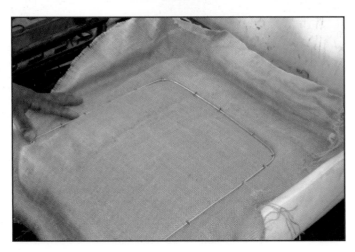

8a.53 The backside of the seat bottom was covered with burlap to protect the foam from direct contact with the metal frame.

8a.54 The seat frame is attached to the foam by hog-ringing the frame to the listing wire and the burlap.

8a.55 Hog-ring a few of the springs to the listing wire to further unitize the seat components.

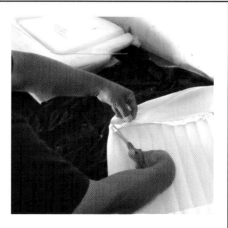

8a.56 The cloth listing is sewn closed, so use scissors to snip open the ends of the listing.

8a.57 Insert the new wire in the cloth listing that gives the seat the sewn-in look when the seat is finished.

8a.58 The U-shaped wire is inserted in the cloth listing sleeve and worked around the seat bottom upholstery.

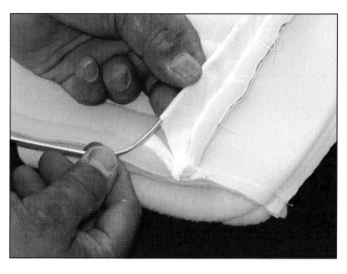

8a.59 Locate the listing wire in the deep groove in the seat foam. Don't use a heat gun (or a hair dryer) at this point unless you have previous experience. The simplest treatment is to lay the upholstery panel out in the sun until the vinyl is warm and pliable.

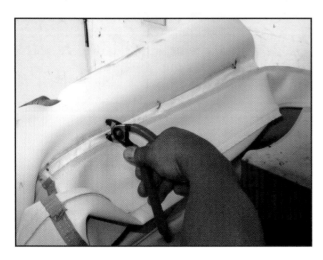

8a.60 Push the foam from one side while pushing the vinyl down in the groove and hog-ringing the listing wire. ****Warning:** *Make sure you keep your fingers offset from the spot you are attaching. The hog-rings wouldn't look very stylish clipped into one of your fingers.*

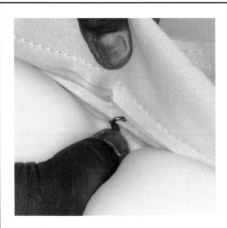

8a.61 We're pulling the out side part of the foam so you can see how the listing is secured to the seat.

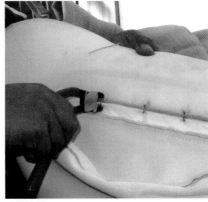

8a.62 Don't scrimp on the rings. They should be spaced evenly around the seat. Check the photos you took during the seat assembly for a guide to how may to use in any one area.

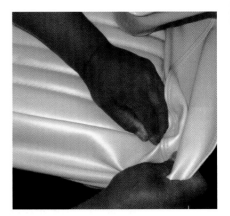

8a.63 At this point you'll have to wrestle the new vinyl onto the seat, making sure that the foam underneath keeps its shape and doesn't bunch up.

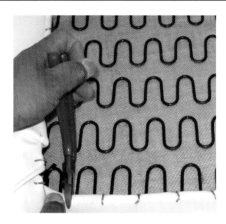

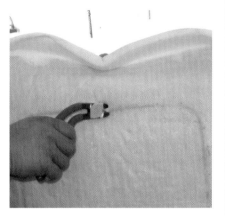

8a.64 Begin pulling the vinyl towards the seat frame all around, and stagger the points at which you install hog-rings by criss-crossing from side-to-side and front-to-back.

8a.65 Where the seat back mounting post is located, use a hobby knife to cut just enough of a hole to allow the post to come through. Push the vinyl down around the post, and carefully trim off any excess vinyl.

8a.66 The operations to restore the seat-back are much the same as for the seat bottom, beginning with securing the listing wire that establishes the same U-shaped pull on the vinyl.

8a.67 Burlap is cut to fit the back of the seat-back and is secured to the seat foam with an extra listing wire on this side.

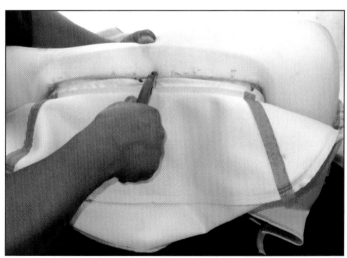

8a.68 With the vinyl warm, begin to go around the listing wire with hog-rings, again being careful to keep your hands out of the way.

8a.69 The frame for the seat-back should be secured to the material with hog-rings, so no shifting can take place during the vinyl installation.

8a.70 Keep looking all around the seat-back to be sure that none of the foam has become bunched. If it has, smooth out the foam with your hand and hog-ring that section.

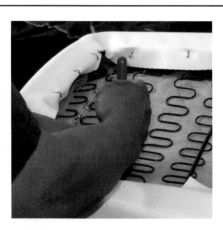

8a.71 Install hog-rings at the center of the top, bottom and sides, then install additional rings while ensuring there are no wrinkles in the upholstery.

8a.72 Carefully pulling the vinyl and attaching it to the seat-back is handled just as on the seat-bottom.

8a.73 If you attach the top first, attach the bottom of the vinyl next, then one side and the other, always looking for wrinkles or pinched foam as you go.

8a.74 One major difference with the seat-back is the frame. There are a number of holes in the frame that are not used to ring vinyl to directly, but are for attaching to rear cover, which is a fiberboard panel already covered with vinyl.

8a.75 These upholstery clips fit into rectangular openings in the fiberboard, and are designed to have enough room for the clips to be moved around to align with the clip holes in the seat-back frame.

8a.76 With the all of the clips attached to the back cover, compare the locations to the holes in the frame. All the clips have to align with holes in the frame.

8a.77 Start along one side, pushing the clips into the holes, then push in the upper and lower clips, finishing with the last row of clips on the unattached side.

8a.78 The seat-back looks like a pro did it, and yours will too. Don't forget to install the seat-back adjuster pad on the seat-bottom, and the seat adjuster bolt into the bottom of the seat-back.

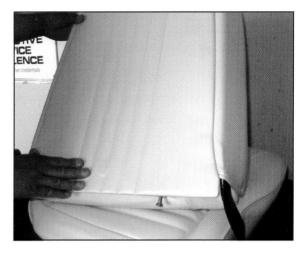

Dash pad installation

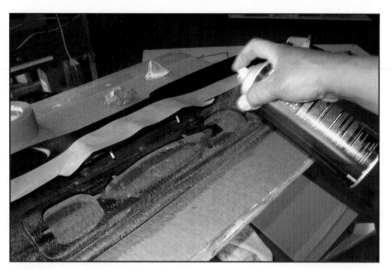

8a.79 With the new dash pad out of the car, clean the backside with lacquer thinner, wipe it dry and spray a light coat of contact adhesive on the pad. Do this outdoors preferably and without any wind.

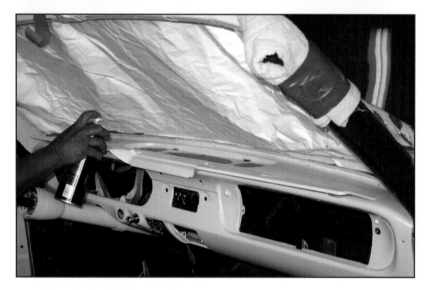

8a.80 Mask off the windshield and the radio speaker grille area, and spray a light coat of adhesive along the dashboard. If you're working inside, wear a very good face mask to avoid inhaling any of the airborne glue.

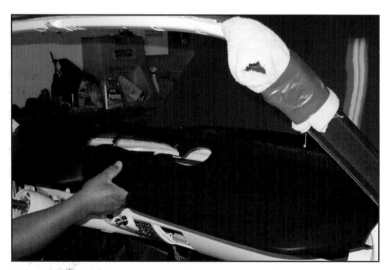

8a.81 Slip the new dash pad over the dashboard, and begin installing the nuts behind the radio, the trim strips over the instrument cluster and the glove box, the speaker, the defroster ducts, the speaker grille, and the trim strip and screws near the base of the windshield. That's it!

Convertible top

If you have followed the other Chapters in this book, you may have ventured into trying new tasks, and perhaps discovered skills you didn't know you had. One of those areas of restoration that you might have been hesitant to try would have been the interior of your Mustang. If you had started with the carpeting and new door panels, you may have surprised yourself and received a bit of confidence in how it turned out.

Next up would have been upholstering the seats, which is more work than the carpet, but we're sure you did just fine on the seats also. Now we'll deal with the restoration of the convertible top mechanical components and the installation of a new top. On our project, we chose to dismantle the whole mechanism, have it powder-coated then reassembled with white grease on all the pins and other moving parts. The original Ford shop manual (reprints available at Mustang suppliers) has a section on the top with drawings you may find helpful. **Note:** *Do your research before you begin this installation, and make sure you have all the supplies and materials that will be required. Almost everything except glue and staples will come with the aftermarket convertible top kit, and if you mess up*

8b.1 In a perfect world, this is how a convertible top would *always* be - retracted and covered by the boot! It's important to have a well-functioning top for when conditions are less than perfect, though.

one of the tack-strips, new ones can be purchased separately, as can a number of other hard and soft parts.

By now, you have hopefully learned to work at a slow and even pace, without rushing anything. The convertible top is somewhat more difficult, even frustrating at times, but mostly it is a job of tedious precision. The top is not what you would call a bolt-on component of the Mustang. The rear window may have to be installed and removed quite a few times to get it just right if this is your first top installation. If you are patient and follow through our photos and captions, you can do this yourself. After driving your Mustang for years with an old tattered top, the finished, installed new top will make your car look like another car entirely!

8b.2 It's always a good idea to install new bushings at all pivot points to ensure smooth operation.

8b.3 There are two hydraulic cylinders, one on either side of the rear seat well. Clean and lubricate the bolts that secure the top frame to the cylinders, and lubricate all pivoting components.

8b.4 When connecting the top frame to the top of the cylinders, two pegs on the cylinder (fitted with nylon sleeves) fit into this frame-end and are kept there by the two bolts shown here.

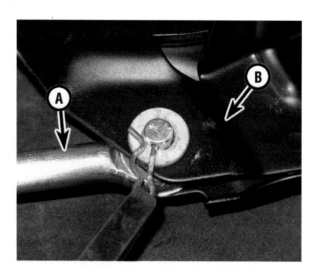

8b.5 Move the top frame until you can line up the eye on the lift cylinder rod (A) (counter-balance rod on models with manual tops) with the frame, and insert a lubricated pin through the frame arm (B).

8b.6 Slip the cylinder and frame assembly down into the quarter-panel well. Bolt the top assembly in with the original bolts, securing one side loosely, then when all bolts are started, tighten them.

8b.7 Assemble the remainder of the top mechanism, using new bushings and lubricating the pivot points, then pull top mechanism up and forward until it reaches the windshield.

8b.8 Try moving the mechanism forward and rearward. If it is at all stiff, go back and check that all pins, pivot points and riveted joints have been cleaned and lubed with white grease.

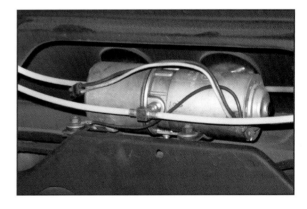

8b.9 The hydraulic pump is centered behind the rear seat lower cushion. Bolt it down and connect the electrical connector.

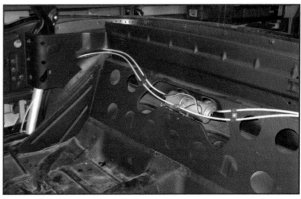

8b.10 Plastic lines are connected to each of the two lift cylinders in this routing. Don't allow the lines to be chafed where they pass near chassis components. If necessary, cut some pieces of rubber tubing and slit them lengthwise and install them over the lines to prevent abrasion (you definitely don't want hydraulic fluid all over your interior!).

8b.11 One fitting in the center of the pump feeds both cylinders. Do not overtighten.

8b.12 With the top mechanism UP, position some newspaper or rags below the compressor. Remove the fluid fill plug with a screwdriver, and check the fluid, which should be less than a 1/4-inch lower than the filler plug hole. Add fluid if necessary and reinstall the plug.

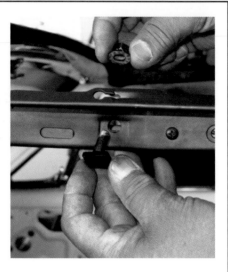

8b.13 Install the fasteners that connect the front bow to the top frame. Start with one of these T-bolts on each side of the #1 bow.

8b.14 Install one of the front alignment pins in either side of the front bow.

8b.15 Install the screws securing the two latches that lock the front bow to the windshield. If you have any difficulty installing the screws and you had powder-coated your frame, you may have to use a tap to clean out the threaded holes.

8b.16 Install the greased washer and this large round-head bolt, one on each side, then install the nuts and tighten securely. The latch is now secure.

8b.17 Use a pair of pliers to install the latch tension spring that returns the latch after opening.

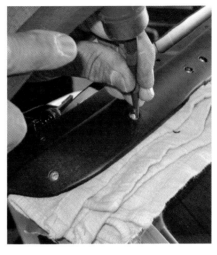

8b.18 Use a drill to remove the rivets on the #1 bow. Lingering remnants of rivet heads can be removed with a hammer and small punch.

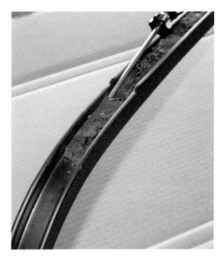

8b.19 If you haven't already done so, remove any residue from the old tack-strip material from all of the top bows.

8b.20 Make yourself wooden templates from 1/2-inch plywood or OSB to ensure the bows are in their rightful positions before you attach anything to them. The dimensions are in the original shop manual and are also included in some kits.

8b.21 Apply glue to the groove in the #1 bow. Press the tack-strip material into the groove and protect it with masking tape, both to keep glue from being transferred to clean areas of the top and to keep pressure on the tack-strip.

8b.22 Install top bows #2 and #3 at this time. You should have two templates, one for each side. Clamp or tape the template to the bows, which will stay in their proper relationship during the top installation.

8b.23 Glue a double-layer of tack-strip in Bow #2 and Bow #3, then use clamps to secure them. Allow these bows to dry overnight before attaching anything to the tack strips.

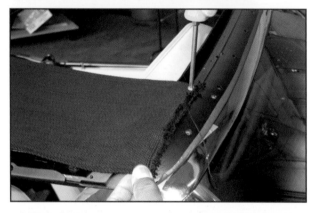

8b.24 The side pads are secured to the front bow with screws. Use the rearmost set of holes in the bow. Locate the screw holes with an awl.

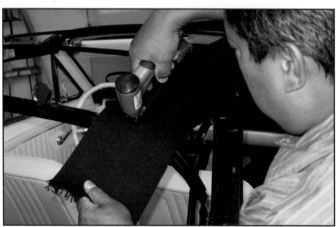

8b.25 The side pads are secured to the other bows with staples into the tack-strips.

8b.26 Use a sharp hobby knife or utility blade to trim the excess material ahead of the screws on the front bow.

8b.27 Gorilla® tape is applied over the screw heads on the front bow so they don't wind up showing through the vinyl.

8b.28 Thin foam padding is stapled down over the side pads. Trim off any excess foam around the edges.

8b.29 Before installing the top well material, remove the rear seat bottom if it's in place.

8b.30 Also remove the seat back, since our next move is to apply the covering for the top well, and we don't want anything to get on our pristine new white seats! The quarter trim panels also should either be masked off or removed.

8b.31 Spray glue on the front side of the seatback panel, being careful with masking for overspray.

8b.32 The piece that goes over the forward-most sheetmetal is coated with glue on the white strip you see here, pressed in place on the seat side, then glued down in the rearward side of the panel.

8b.33 Measure the width of bow #3 and mark the center of that bow. Taking pains to be accurate, measure again from one side to the mark, then compare with the other side. If the measurement is the same, you marked the center.

8b.34 Lay out the plastic rear window. If you're working in your garage in the winter, turn on the heater to help the plastic to lay down flat. Find and mark the centerpoint at the top and bottom of the rear window.

8b.35 Bring the rear window up to bow #3 and align the center mark on the window to the center-mark on the bow and install one or two staples, no more. You may have to remove staples and readjust the window several times, so accumulated stapling could damage the tacking strips and the material.

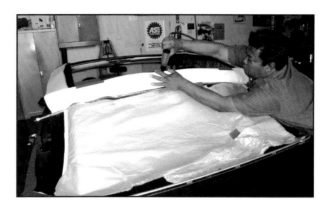

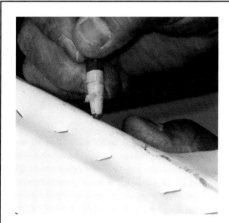

8b.36 Pull the material tight and install more staples if the window fits right and doesn't have wrinkles anywhere. Use a grease pencil to mark the material and the excess to remove.

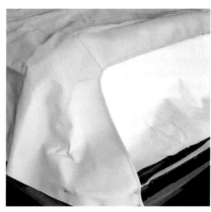

8b.37 Finally, you can lay the actual top material on the bows! Pull the rear corners down a bit on each side and install several temporary staples. If you had four helpers that could hold all the corners while you stapled, the job would go quicker, but you would still wind up stapling and removing staples quite a few times before you're done.

8b.38 Pull the front corners tight at bow #1 and install a few temporary staples. Do not use glue at this point. You should now have a rough-looking fac-simile of a top, although one that still needs a lot of work.

8b.39 To install the ten-sion wire, use a straight-ened coat hanger with a hook formed on one end to fish the wire through the sleeve in the top material. Wrap a little electrical tape over the tip of the hanger and the junction of hanger and tension wire to prevent tearing the top material.

8b.40 Raise the top a foot or two and you can reach the end of the tension wire.

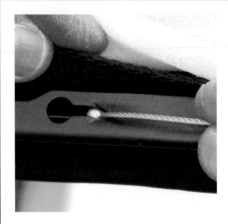  

8b.41 Position the ball-end of the tension wire into the slot in the top frame. Other models have a tension wire that hooks over a stud at the front of the top frame and end in a threaded rod that goes through a bracket at the rear, so the tension is adjustable.

8b.42 Lift the padding a little at the rear of the top and connect the spring to the wire and to the hook on the top frame. Repeat for the other side and lower the top back down.

8b.43 To continue in the battle with the rear window, you are now going to begin attaching the rest of the rear corner material. Attach the side tack strips to the rear tack strip by drilling through both pieces and installing screws.

8b.44 The original tack strips are attached to the body with screws, however, the screw holes were getting worn out during several rear window installation-and-removal episodes, so Jamie drilled a few of the holes to a larger size and installed threaded inserts that could take repeated usage without stripping.

8b.45 Rivet the rear side tack-strips to the main rear tack-strip, then install a few tack-strip screws on the side strips. The rear corners of the top can now be pulled down and stapled (not fully), working out any wrinkles by pulling to the side and stapling.

8b.46 Lower the top and reattach the front corners by stapling, following the alignment marks you made earlier.

8b.47 When gluing the top to bow #1, you may have to snip out some small triangles of excess material when it bunches up at the corner, but do so cautiously. If you snip too far, the cut could open up under the pressure of repeated top operations.

8b.48 Over all the staples and material at bow #1, a final touch is to staple down the front cushion strip to prevent air and rain from coming in over the windshield.

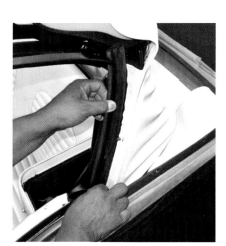

8b.49 Glue the weatherstripping into the channels on the sides of the top. The rear quarter glass weatherstrip is attached with small screws to the top frame.

8b.50 Along the back of the top, a decorative strip is stapled over the seam. The strip is called a hide-em strip, because you open the strip, staple inside as you go, then push the strip together to hide the screws or staples.

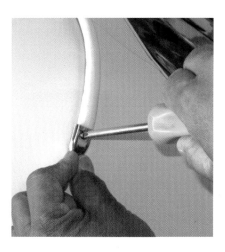

8b.51 Finishing off the hide-em strip are classic little metal ends. Push the end in place and use an awl to make a hole to get the retaining screw started.

8b.52 The well liner dust boot attaches to the rear tack strip. Drill small holes for the special screws, which have a very large head that require an Allen bit to install.

8b.53 Here the well liner dust boot is installed, ready to accept a folded top on a trip to the beach, the mountains, or any of your favorite destinations.

8b.54 The last detail on the top assembly is reinstalling the chromed rear trim. We'd recommend using masking tape over the paint in the area of the moldings to avoid the slightest chance of ruining the new paint job.

8b.55 It's often necessary to iron-out wrinkles with a blow dryer, or sometimes things will smooth-out once the car sits out in the warm sun for awhile. Or like we said before, it might take a few attempts to complete the installation just how you want it. But there's no denying the finished white top really pops on our Twilight Turquoise convertible! Who gets the keys first?

Headliner

Headliner replacement is one of the more daunting tasks for novices in interior restoration because it is labor intensive and requires close attention to detail. The key to success isn't so much talent, but patience. You want to be very methodical in your execution and take your time. Don't be in a hurry. You're going to need a can of 3M Super Trim Adhesive. No other type of spray trim-adhesive works as well as 3M. You will also need a razor blade and several feet of windlace to hold the headliner in place until you can reinstall the windshield and rear window. You're also going to need a heat gun or hairdryer to massage out wrinkles. And for your own safety, wear a dust mask and eye protection.

Headliner replacement cannot be performed properly with the windshield and rear window installed, both must be removed and contact surfaces must be free of all sealer and gasket. When Ford built the Mustangs, the interior was installed before the windshield and rear window. The headliner material was glued along the top edge of the window openings, where it would be locked in securely once the glass was installed. We have seen amateur headliner installations that tried the shortcut method, which is to leave some of the front and rear of the headliner, apply some glue, and stuff the extra material behind the windshield and rear window rubber. It never lasts very long before the material comes out. When you order a headliner kit, also purchase some windlace and new weatherstripping for the front and rear glass.

Your first step is to line up a good glass shop that can carefully remove and store your windshield and rear window. Now you get the thrill of driving home with no windshield. Wear some goggles, pray it doesn't rain, and enjoy the experience!

Remove the windlace around the door openings, then the coat hooks, sun visors, package tray and dome light, and store them in a safe place. Use a solvent like lacquer thinner to remove windshield sealer. When you remove the old headliner, take note of each headliner bow's location and its color code. Apply tape to each bow and mark the tape to indicate the location. Also note right and left orientation of the bow ends. All bows must go back in the same location, though there are a variety of bow mounting holes to help you with headliner tension and adjustment.

Begin headliner installation with a good sound-deadening package against the roof to keep out noise, heat, and cold. There are some excellent peel-

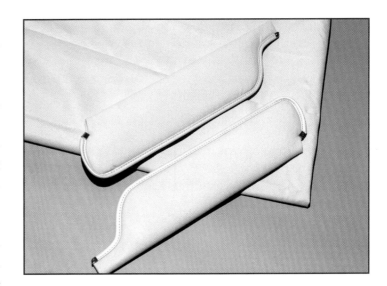

8c.1 Complete TMI Products headliner kits for classic Mustangs in all original colors are available from Mustangs Plus and other major suppliers. Sun visors, windlace, and related hardware are extra, but worth the expense. If your headliner was bad enough to replace, most likely your sun visors have also seen better days.

and-stick products that keep out heat and dampen noise. You won't get another chance to insulate the roof. If you discover any rust under the roof, paint the inside of the roof with Rustoleum rusty-metal primer before applying the sound deadener.

Headliner installation begins with orienting the new headliner from front to rear, marking with a pencil where the center of the headliner is at the front and rear, then sliding it onto each of the bows. You're going to have to carefully slit each end of the listing sleeves (like the ones used in seat upholstery, see Chapter 8A) to get the wrinkles out, but don't cut too far - you'll ruin the headliner.

The main thing to remember is to keep good tension on the headliner as you work from rear to front and from side to side. Always begin pulling and securing from the rear forward for best results. The headliner kit itself is not very expensive, so if you aren't happy with your first headliner installation, bite the bullet and buy another kit for a pro to install while you still have the glass out.

8c.2 Headliner bows are color coded to their proper location. Take note of these locations when you remove the old headliner. New sound-deadener/insulation has been glued to the inside of the roof.

8c.3 Headliner bows are carefully inserted into the new headliner. Do this in order from front to rear and orient the headliner.

8c.4 Begin installation with the first bow in front and work back. It can become overwhelming because it hangs in your field of vision. Get all bows installed, and then work from rear to front securing the headliner.

8c.5 This tensioner wire secures the rear bow to provide tension to the headliner.

8c.6 The rear bow is secured to the tensioner wire as shown here.

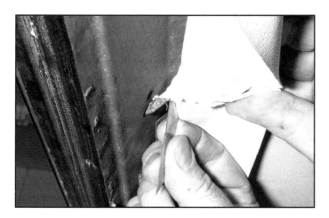

8c.7 This is where you must be careful about cutting. Each side of the headliner is pulled tight to give the headliner tension. As you pull to get tension, you're going to have to carefully slit the headliner sleeves until wrinkles are removed. Slit too far and you have a throwaway. It is easier to cut a little at a time until you get it right than cut too far and have a ruined headliner.

8c.8 Trim adhesive is sprayed on both surfaces and allowed to get sticky. This takes about five minutes. Wear latex gloves while working with a clean new headliner, or at least make sure your hands are clean.

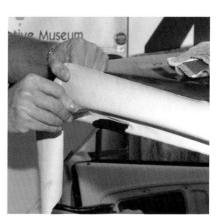

8c.9 The reason 3M Super Trim Adhesive is sprayed on both surfaces and allowed to become tacky is for better adhesion. Mate the surfaces when it is wet and you won't get adhesion; it must be sticky and nearly dry before it is effective. Make sure any painted surfaces around the window openings are masked off before spraying glue.

8c.10 When the adhesive has become tacky, you're ready for installation. Pull the headliner good and tight to where most wrinkles are gone and you have good tension. Secure the headliner by pushing on short pieces of windlace as shown here. Leave them in place until you are ready to install the windshield and rear window.

8c.11 Once the headliner is secure, carefully trim off the excess material with a razor blade.

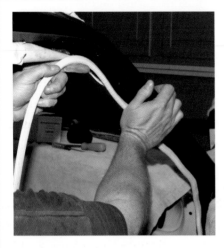

8c.12 The sides are pulled tight and secured last with windlace.

8c.13 A heat gun is used carefully to work out wrinkles. A hairdryer or steamer is also quite effective. Bend back the prongs at each side of the package tray, then roll some of the excess headliner material around the cardboard strip, push it behind the prongs and bend down the prongs when the material is wrinkle-free. Reinstall the package tray.

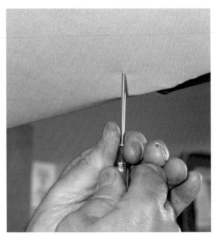

8c.14 Carefully use an awl to locate the screw holes for the sun visors and rearview mirror.

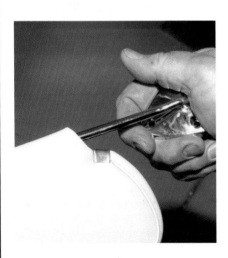

8c.15 Insert the sun visor brackets. This is tricky because these things tend to be tight. Wipe some upholstery cleaner on the shaft to help things along.

8c.16 Polish up your rearview mirror and install it with the original screws.

8c.17 The headliner has been trimmed away from the dome light bulb and socket. The lens and bezel are installed at this time. Take your last ride without a windshield and get your front and back glass installed!

Instrument panel

Most Mustang restorers have their own prioritized list of when and how each aspect of their project will be addressed. For some it might be engine first, others the suspension, some the bodywork. One thing you can bank on, whatever your plan, is that visitors who come to check on your progress or those lucky enough to be invited for a ride in your project focus on one thing, the interior and the instrument panel. If you don't believe us, watch spectators at a car show. After having admired the great paint job, within ten seconds a spectator will bend at the waist to see inside a car's interior! That's how important your interior and dash will be to yourself and other enthusiasts. You want the instrument panel to be done to a high standard, since you will be staring at the dash for many years to come, and you don't want to look back at some part of the dash that you feel you could have finished better. There is always that temptation to tell yourself during a lengthy project, "This is good enough, I've got to move on to the next phase of restoration." There are many details to the restoration of a vehicle that require a lot of work, like the suspension, and yet only you know what a change you made. The work you put into the instrument panel is something everyone will see and appreciate.

In this book, we refer to the whole instrument panel as what stretches from one windshield post to the other. We refer to the instrument cluster as that portion of the instrument panel that contains the gauges and warning lights. We also sometimes use the word "dash" or "dashboard" as the more commonly-used name for the instrument panel. We're certain that many Chapters in this book have been helpful to you with information, advice and step-by-step photos. This Chapter will do the same for your instrument panel, and you'll smile every time you get behind the wheel!

We have also included in this Chapter some tips on restoring two brake-related items. The brake pedal and its chassis mounting bracket are mounted below the instrument cluster, between the firewall and the front edge of the instrument panel. Also below the instrument cluster, the parking brake handle on Mustangs is often cracked if not broken completely. After decades of use, a cracked plastic handle can snap while your hand is twisting it and you can find your left hand wrapped around a jagged hunk of plastic. Replace the handle before this happens. Both the pedal assembly and the parking brake are easier to restore before you install your instrument cluster, which is why these items are in this Chapter instead of with the other brake-related tasks.

8d.1 We can hardly wait to get on the road and test our restored instrument cluster.

Glove box

8d.2 Consider our newly painted white instrument panel as the canvas upon which we will display all the other pieces that had been removed during the car's restoration.

8d.3 This is the before photo of our instrument panel. We removed the glove box long ago, which made for better access when working behind the instrument panel.

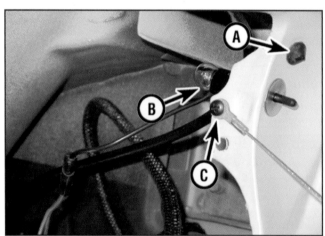

8d.4 To remove the heater and defroster assembly under the instrument panel, the cardboard glove box has to be removed, so it was designed to fold up for easy removal. Before the box can be installed and screwed in place, several other related items have to go in first, such as the rubber bumpers (A), the glove box light (B), and the eye that secures the door restraint cable (C).

8d.5 Push the cardboard glove box into the dash opening, taking care not to tear the fragile cardboard.

8d.6 Push the glove box sides outward until they snap into place, then secure the box to the opening in the dash with the original screws taken from the old glove box.

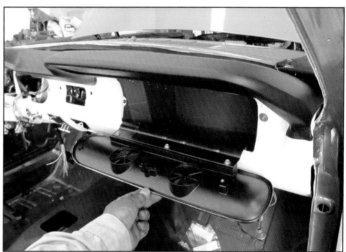

8d.7 Barring an accident, the door to the glove box seldom needs any work other than to clean and paint it. Clean the chromed rim and the Mustang emblem, mask them off and spray the bulk of the door with semi-flat black spray paint. There are some years and models with different finishes, even wood-grained.

8d.8 Now looking as good as it did in '65, the only thing left to do is mount the lock.

8d.9 Of course, the glove box lock won't work until the latch is mounted inside at the top. Don't tighten the screws all the way until you have adjusted the latch forward or rearward so the glove box door latches just right, neither loose nor tight.

8d.10 This is a good point to take care of a few details before rushing into instrument cluster installation. Organize the wiring behind the cluster area and mask off the lower edge of the cluster opening so the new white paint isn't scratched during cluster installation.

8d.11 The cluster opening allows easier access to the defroster hoses, so this is a good time to attach them to the ducts in the center/top of the dashpad.

Instrument Cluster

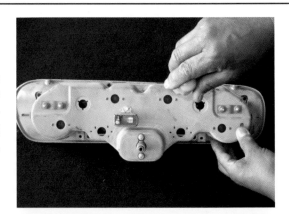

8d.13 Remove the screws on the backside of the instrument cluster to begin separating the layers of the cluster.

8d.12 We purchased several items to renew the look of our instrument cluster. At the top is our new plastic lens. After forty years or more, the old plastic is hard to see through! The new bezel (center here) will really add some flash.

8d.14 Gently separate the housing from the front panels.

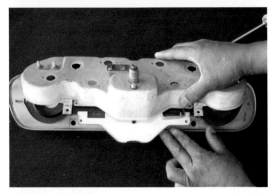

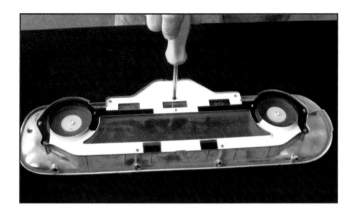

8d.15 Remove this one screw and you can separate the metal plate and the plastic lens over the instruments.

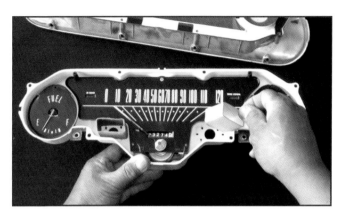

8d.16 Once the lens has been removed, you must work carefully, as the gauges are fragile. If you break off one of the needles, that gauge will have to be sent to an instrument shop to be fixed, or you will have to find another good instrument cluster to restore.

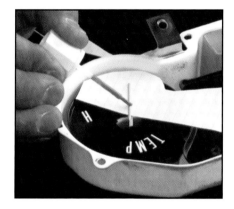

8d.17 There is little that can be done with the gauges (if they don't work, have them fixed or replaced), but the needles can be refreshed with fluorescent orange paint. Apply the paint to the needles with a very small brush, and slip a piece of paper below the needle so as not to get any paint on your gauge faces.

8d.18 The speedometer needle is much longer, but is painted with the same technique. Allow plenty of time for the paint to dry before handling the instrument cluster.

8d.19 Before sealing up the cluster with the new plastic lens, make sure the interior of the cluster is perfectly clean. Use a lint-free micro-fiber cloth to eliminate any dust being trapped in there.

8d.20 You don't want to touch anything inside the cluster, especially the black cardboard behind the gauges, since they are probably older than you are and can be soiled by sweaty fingerprints. Here canned air (find it at computer and camera stores) is being used to dust off the cluster.

8d.21 Once it is as clean as you can get it, it's time to install the new plastic lens. Make sure the two little rectangular cardboard lamp shrouds are where they're supposed to be (they direct the light through the ALT and TEMP warning lights).

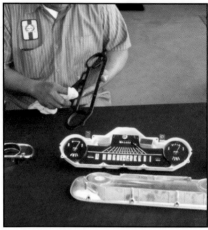

8d.22 Using the screws removed during disassembly, install the metal plate that goes over the plastic.

8d.23 Gently position the housing over the front of the instrument cluster, settle the two sections together and install the screws.

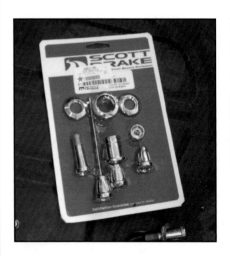

8d.24 This is a good time to install the new knobs and bezels for instrument panel switches that we purchased.

8d.25 You will have to perch the instrument cluster in this position while you are connecting all the wires to the back of the cluster. Squirt some speedo cable lubricant down the speedometer cable housing and reconnect the cable to the speedometer.

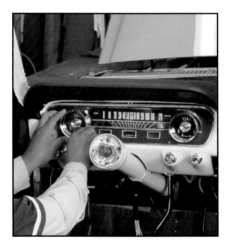

8d.26 Installing the cluster and the last four mounting screws is very satisfying after everything you've done leading up to this point. If you did all of this yourself, you've done something to be proud of.

Brake/Clutch Pedals

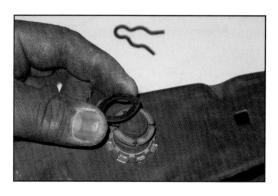

8d.27 Unbolt the pedal assembly from the cowl and the back of the dash and remove it from the car. Our components were as rusty as the rest of the car had been, but the pedal assembly had been removed before the media-blasting and painting. Pull the clip, then remove the washer. Ours has only a brake pedal, but if your Mustang is a manual, you'll be removing the clutch pedal, too.

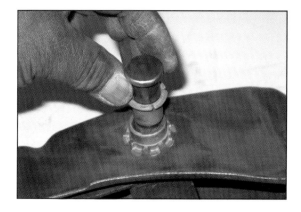

8d.28 Remove the pedal shaft and plastic bushings from the pedal support bracket. Rust or dirt in this assembly can cause rough pedal action or even dragging brakes.

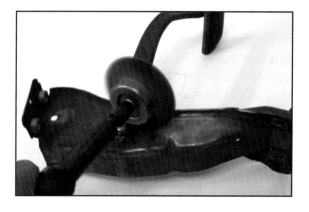

8d.29 Our bracket required some wire-brushing to get the worst of the rust off. **Caution:** *Be very careful using a wire brush in an electric drill. The brush can catch on something and spin the drill, grabbing your clothes or worse, skin!*

8d.30 We have successfully used Metal-Ready™ from the makers of POR-15 to clean rust from steel parts. We soaked the pedal support in a gallon container (one half at a time) for half an hour. You can see the untreated part at top here and the fresh steel coming out of the solution. We then put the unrestored end of the support in the chemical.

8d.31 Some items are hard to get into a gallon bucket and reach all sides, so the brake pedal was suspended on a coat hanger while Metal-Ready™ was applied with a spray bottle.

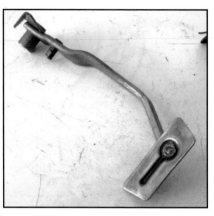

8d.32 A light going-over with steel wool and our pedal looks shiny and new! Remember to also clean the pedal shaft.

8d.33 Our brake pedal parts were cleaned with lacquer thinner and painted with spray paint. When dry, we installed new plastic bushings with some chassis grease, reattached the pedal to the support with the pedal shaft, and installed the washer and clip.

Parking Brake Handle

8d.34 The mechanism unbolts from the firewall end with two nuts; the end that mounts to the instrument panel is mounted with two screws. Drop the assembly down, and release the ball on the cable end from the shaft.

8d.35 We stripped our parking brake assembly to check for rust and to apply some white grease for lubrication. This roll-pin must be driven out of the shaft so the shaft can be slid out of the housing.

8d.36 Remove the clip and the clevis pin to remove the roller for the cable.

8d.37 After powder-coating the outer housing chassis black, the inside shaft was lubed and installed in the housing, the cable ball was connected to the bottom of the inside shaft and a new roll-pin was used to retain the shaft.

8d.38 The parking brake handle is attached to the shaft with a serrated pin. If you are replacing an old handle, drive the pin out and remove the old handle. When installing the new handle, use only as much force as it takes to drive the serrated pin in until it is flush, using light taps with a small hammer and punch.

8d.39 Our completed assembly isn't exciting, but it is one more component of the car that we won't have to worry about. Plus, no gouges in our left hand from a broken handle!

9 Detailing

In the past few decades, average new-car prices have risen almost ten-fold. For example, a new Ford Mustang could have been purchased in 1965 for under $2,300; while today a new base model 2012 Mustang would cost $23,100.

Why is there a Chapter on Detailing in this book? You may have just finished a nice, long-term restoration and you love your Mustang! It's nice to receive waves and compliments from everyone who sees your car. However, without proper detailing, that glow is inevitably going to fade - unless you never take the car cover off to drive the car, and what fun is that? E v e n for a brand new car, proper preparation for taking care of the finish will involve some elbow grease on a regular basis. On a car even a year old that hasn't been meticulously maintained, some definite effort is necessary at the start. What you are trying to do is establish what we'll call a detailing baseline. Once the effort has been invested to bring your vehicle to that baseline, only regular maintenance will be required thereafter. The important factor is obtaining a paint job that is clean, undamaged, and glossy and then protecting that finish with a good wax. When you've achieved that attractive baseline the rest is easy, and how hard it is to get there depends strictly on the condition of your existing paint.

The basics of washing

Every professional detailer will tell you the most common mistake made by average motorists in cleaning their cars is the soap they use. Never use common household cleaners, whether laundry soaps, dish soaps or even hand soaps to wash your car! There are some household products that have a place in some areas of detailing, but washing isn't one of those areas. Household soaps are much too strong for your paint finish, rubber and chrome, and can dull paint and leave light-colored streaks. Always wash with specific car-washing soaps. These can be purchased in any auto supply store or discount chain store. They clean your car gently and can be purchased in quantity sizes that make them economical to use as well.

The second most common mistake is washing the car outside on a sunny day. Even in areas where the tap water isn't particularly hard, you will get unsightly, hard-to-remove water spots all over the paint job when your wash water dries instantly on the hot sheetmetal, chrome and glass. In areas of the country where water is hard (has high mineral content), these water spots can be very difficult to remove and may require abrasive paint cleaners which you don't want to use if you can help it.

Start with the roof, hood and trunk lid, then work your way down the sides, followed by front end and rear end. Do not use hard hand pressure on your wash mitt. If there are really stubborn spots or stains, you can take care of them later with the proper product, but during the wash phase you don't want to use the mitt as if it were a buffer; this will drag dirt around and scratch the paint.

Once you have the car clean, it's time to rinse it off. You must make sure to get any soapy water solution off of the finish as quickly as possible. Even the specialized car-washing soaps can have a dulling effect on paint if left to dry on the finish. Also, the soaps dry with a slightly sticky surface, and any place on your car left sticky will become a dirt magnet. Use common sense. The areas that are hardest to clean will also wind up being the areas where dirt and moisture can collect over time to create paint or chrome problems, even body rust. So when rinsing, be thorough.

While a strong spray from your garden hose nozzle was helpful at the beginning to loosen dirt, now that you are rinsing you want to use the hose without a nozzle. Detailers say that the next phase, drying the car, can be performed a lot quicker if you get more water off the surface. They use a low-pressure flow from the hose, held close to the car, to flood areas of the sheetmetal. Try this! It makes the water come off in sheets, leaving much less water on the car's surface. When you use a hard spray to rinse the car, the overspray keeps getting on other areas of the car, and you never get all of it off, so consequently you use a lot of towels for drying.

Another pro's tip for drying the car is to use a squeegee, but *not* the kind that has a windshield-wiper-type rubber. Those would be much too hard for your paint job. There are drying squeegees made with a soft rubber which work great at getting large flat areas of glass and sheetmetal clear of 90% of the water.

Now you start in with either a natural or artificial chamois. There actually is an animal called the chamois, described in the dictionary as "a small, goat-like antelope of Europe and the Caucasus," and the secondary definition is "a soft, pliant leather made from the skin of the chamois or sheepskin." We would call a natural chamois for car drying one made from some kind of animal. They have been used for as long as there have been automobiles, with some of the best natural chamois coming from Great Britain. They are as soft as a baby's skin when you first buy them, but once used for drying water off your car they dry up into something like the stiffness of cardboard.

Once you wet it again, it comes back to life and is soft once more. They work like a very fine version of a sponge, absorbing water from paint, glass and chrome, without either abrading the surface (like a true sponge would do when it is unlubricated by soap) or leaving any streaks behind. The latter benefit makes a chamois the perfect tool for drying glass.

A car can be dried completely with chamois, but there will be a lot of wrist-bending wringing-out when you get down to the last beads of water. Most pros use terrycloth towels for final drying. Such towels should be 100% cotton, and you should buy and set aside towels just for the drying phase of your detailing. Never use a towel for other aspects of detailing, such as waxing, polishing or wheel-cleaning, and expect to wash that towel out and use it some other time for car-drying.

Cleaning paint

Chances are, if this is your first serious detailing effort on your car, your paint will need some kind of cleaning. Not just washing, but cleaning. We'll stress a very important point here which applies to most aspects of detailing. What we're all after is a car that really shines in all areas of paint, glass, chrome and wheels. The shine of a surface, or reflectivity to be more scientific, is a factor of that surface's flatness.

You probably noticed while rinsing your car off how

shiny it looks with a sheet of clear water all over it, and you may have thought to yourself "If I could only get the car to look that good all the time." You can, and that's what detailing is all about, making the maximum of what you've got. The water in our example is acting as a surface covering which is temporarily filling in the minute scratches in your paint. The techniques and products we'll demonstrate in this Chapter show you how to achieve that wet look gloss and keep it protected. The basic plan is to wash the vehicle until it is as clean as it will ever get, surface the paint to make it as flat as possible, then protect that gloss with clear, durable wax that will enhance that shine and guard the surface from dirt, contaminants and the other paint disasters we have mentioned. Once the surface is clean and flat and you keep up a good wax protection, future detailing will be only a matter of an hour or two per week. In a later part of this Chapter, we will deal with flattening a really faded or damaged paint job, but for now we'll assume you have a car in typically good shape and proceed with our initial detailing.

Like sandpaper, paint cleaning products come in varying degrees of abrasiveness, from rough compounds that are used only when machine-buffing a new, wet-sanded two-stage paint job, to polishing compounds that are good for getting off stubborn spots or treating really faded paint, to fine polishes and paint cleaners. The latter are very fine abrasives often mixed with wax and labeled "cleaner-wax" for a one-step procedure. The condition of your paint surface determines how abrasive a treatment you need to achieve the flatness we're looking for. The more abrasive the product, the more actual paint you will remove in the process of achieving flatness, and you want to remove as little paint as possible. When restoring an old, faded paint job, it can be difficult not to polish through the paint and down to the metal!

Most cars that have been cared for somewhat, garaged often or that are nearly new should still have plenty of paint on the surface, making the kind of paint flattening we're addressing here quite safe for the paint. There is one caveat, however. Many new cars in the past decade feature a two-stage paint, also called basecoat/clearcoat. In this process, a base color coat is applied, and then a protective coat of clear paint is applied to protect and add gloss to the base paint. They are in many cases easier to care for and maintain a shine longer than factory paint jobs of the past, but some precautions are in order.

The main problem in polishing a car with a clearcoat is that you don't necessarily know when to stop since you can't see the oxidized clearcoat particles accumulating on your polishing cloth as you would with a conventional paint where your cloth right away starts to show the color of the paint you're cleaning. Since the scratches and surface imperfections we are trying to remove in obtaining

a flat finish are so tiny, it wouldn't hurt at all to examine the paint close up with a strong magnifying glass in good lighting. You want to clean the surface only enough to get rid of the scratches and imperfections. Going any further may only remove more protective clearcoat.

The surface you'll see with the magnifying glass will amaze you! You'll see lots of scratches you never saw before. On conventional paint jobs (non-clearcoat), the pigmented (color) layer is usually deep enough to withstand the polishing-out of most scratches. Clearcoats are another story, and here's where yet another type of product comes into use: sealer and glaze. Each of these detailing products has its own uses, but the function with each type is to help fill in the minute valleys in your paint, almost like the sheets of water temporarily did when you were rinsing the just-washed vehicle.

Buffing

Sealers and glazes require buffing to achieve their effect, and then they must be waxed over right away or the sun and atmosphere will immediately start to dull them down. There is considerable elbow grease involved in using them, but they are the stock-in-trade of the top professional detailers and show-car owners. There is a bewildering array of them on the market, including combination glaze/sealers, and many detailers have their personal favorites that they use exclusively. For most readers, one of the national brands in the least aggressive form would be fine, especially if you are trying to do this by hand.

As with any paint cleaner or protectant, it's best to work one small area at a time when using sealers and glazes, and they

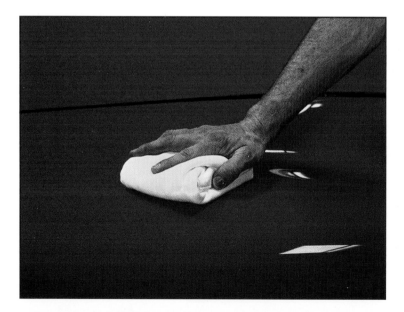

must be used in the shade on a cool painted surface. Whether working by hand or with a machine, handle an area no bigger than half the hood size of the average vehicle. The pro detailers, who must work fairly quickly and efficiently to make a living, use professional buffers whenever possible, but some of the products available can be used by hand if the directions are followed closely.

Hand buffing today, especially on sensitive clearcoats, requires that you use only the cleanest and softest, all-cotton, non-abrasive cloths. These should not be mixed with the cleanup towels. Professional cotton polishing cloths are available at automotive paint stores, and many detailers also swear by using cloth baby diapers. To really carry the polishing product well, a very open weave in the material is best. With a tight weave, sometimes the polishing material and dead paint can become balled up and you drag this around as you polish, putting in minute scratches instead of taking them out. The amateur's biggest mistake, other than using too aggressive a polish, is using the polishing cloth after it has become dirty and clogged with paint and dried polish. You must turn the cloth over frequently to constantly expose clean cloth to the area you are working on; don't let dried material and dirt on your cloth defeat what you are trying to do, which is to achieve clean, flat paint. If the polishing cloth doesn't come clean after washing with normal detergent in your washer, it's time to toss that

cloth or relegate it to some other detailing function like wheel or engine cleaning.

To get back to using sealers and glazes, it's vitally important that you read the directions on the product before use. Of course, like any detailing product, they should be used only on cool surfaces, preferably in the shade or indoors, but with plenty of lighting so you can really see where the minute scratches are and how well you're doing on evenly glossing the surface. Most of the glazes and combination glaze/sealer products must be buffed off before they fully dry. They often contain resins that help them fill in swirl marks left by previous polishing or compounding. Using a back-and-forth motion with your cloth to apply the product, let dry only to a semi-haze; then buff with the same motion, not a circular motion. Buff until there is a high gloss. Some of the many glazes and sealers are very tough to buff out to a gloss if you let them dry fully before buffing, so do it in the shade and make sure your phone's answering machine is on when you start the project. You'll love the results of the glaze or glaze/sealer. This may be the shiniest you've ever seen your car!

Waxing

Wax is the final line of defense in your effort to shine and protect your car's paint, and its importance can't be overstated. All of the preparation work you've invested up to this point is lost if you don't wax the vehicle thoroughly and immediately. Everything we've suggested so far is aimed at getting a clean, smooth painted surface free of scratches, tar, bug stains or any other imperfections. Now you can use a good wax to protect all that effort.

Wax products are among the most ubiquitous detailing products in national advertising, and scores of brands vie for space on the shelves at your auto supply store or retail chain. The key buzzword in wax has always been carnauba, a substance derived from South American plants. It is a natural wax that is very hard and can withstand high temperatures, like on the hood of your car on a hot day. Carnauba in pure form is fairly expensive, and you'll find that generally the more expensive waxes have more carnauba in them. The substance has enough mystique about it that it is the marketing ingredient for car-care products, and you'll find the word carnauba used on products that contain very little natural carnauba wax. Always check the label for specific contents.

Those products that have high levels of carnauba will most likely give you the best shine and the longest protection, up to as long as 3-6 months. Their labels will most likely state that these waxes are intended only for use on cleaned, polished paint. It would be a waste of time to apply good carnauba over a dirty or dull paint.

If you have followed through with us so far on washing and polishing your paint, then we recommend that you not wimp out on elbow grease at this final stage of waxing. Use a carnauba paste wax. The carnauba has to be thinned considerably to be put into spray-waxes and liquid waxes. Obviously, the liquids and sprays are faster and easier to apply, but generally offer less protection and may not have the deep gloss of buffed carnauba wax. Apply the wax of your choice following the manufacturer's directions, usually with a back-and-forth motion with a slightly-dampened cotton terry cloth. Many detailers also use cloth baby diapers cut into small sections for applying wax, and some use cheesecloth because it carries so much product when applying wax. Some waxes come with a foam applicator in the can, or you can buy separate small sponges or foam pads specifically designed for applying wax. These other products are only for applying wax, not buffing it - cloth is still the proper material for hand buffing.

Most wax manufacturers recommend two light coats rather than one thick application. A thick coat of wax is very difficult to buff off properly, especially if it's carnauba. If you have already done the glaze/sealer process, you have filled in the minute scratches in the finish, and probably only need one coat of wax to protect it all. The sealers, glazes and waxes all contain resins and oils to feed the paint and keep it from drying out and oxidizing. Think of detailing as skin care for

your car. If you thought it was important to wash your Mustang out of direct sunlight, this is even more important when applying carnauba wax.

When waxing around areas such as chrome trim, fender emblems, antenna, etc., you should be cautious not to build up too much wax in the joints of mating surfaces. It may attract dirt later on and also can be hard to remove from detailed areas of trim without tedious work.

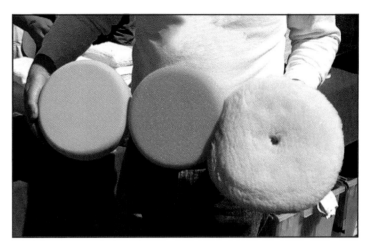

The end result is going to be a finish that you'll find well worth all the efforts you've expended. During all of the foregoing detailing procedures, there is considerable hand labor involved. You have to block out plenty of time to complete these steps, and the products you use and the effort you put in is going to depend on just how sharp you want the vehicle to look. Some busy people prefer to do the whole procedure only on one section of the car at a time, like the top surfaces one weekend, and the sides and front and rear the next weekend. Use whatever schedule works for you, but remember that an area that is washed, cleaned and glazed needs to be waxed right away. If you wait until the next weekend for the waxing, the environment will have already affected the finish and you may have to start over again to be ready for waxing.

Only you can determine how much time is worth the effort. What we have described above is a procedure for really premium gloss and protection. You may be too busy for that, or maybe you're not keeping the car very long. There are much easier products to use when you want a simple wash'n'wax - you would skip the cleaning, polishing or glazing of the paint, and their attendant buffing, and just use a cleaner/wax after washing. This will offer some protection of the paint and a reasonable shine. Easiest of all detailing products to use are the liquid cleaner/waxes, which are both easy to apply and easy to buff off. The result will look good, but the shine will not be as deep. Most of the scratches and imperfections will still be there, and the wax protection won't last long.

It's easy to tell how much wax protection you have when you are washing your vehicle. How the rinse water looks on the surface of the car tells you a lot about the presence of waxes and resins protecting the paint. If the water beads up all over the finish, then it is still protected against the elements. However, if the water runs off easily in flat sheets, you don't have enough protection and it's time to re-wax the vehicle. How long the protection lasts depends on the weather and the amount and type of detailing, particularly the final waxing. If your initial preparation to achieve the baseline finish is successful, you won't have to expend this much effort on the finish for at least six months or longer if your Mustang isn't driven regularly.

The finish baseline is the most important aspect of detailing, but there are many other products and techniques that clean and protect other areas, such as the interior vinyl, wheel and tires, and inside and outside chrome. Common sense tells us that if you keep up on detailing these items, a simple dusting and you'll always be prepared to go to a car event.

9.1 You won't need a trunk full of chemical products to detail your car. A basic kit would include a good car-washing soap, polish, wax and a vinyl protectant. You can use any of a variety of brands, finding out what works best for you, but most enthusiasts and detailers stick with one line of supplies for the sake of compatibility between products.

9.2 A large, soft sponge can be used to wash your vehicle, but detailers prefer to use a sheepskin mitt. They are soft, have two sides to work with and will absorb and disperse a lot of soapy water, which means fewer trips back and forth to the wash bucket.

9.3 The most common car-care mistake is using the wrong kind of soap. Each product has its own properties, but the function with each type is to remove contaminants and dirt from the paint. Instead of strong household soaps, use dedicated car-washing soaps, of which you'll find an ample array available at your auto supply store.

9.4 Road tar deposits can be removed easily and safely with household kerosene lamp fluid. It's basically just scented kerosene, but doesn't leave your hands or rags smelling like straight kerosene.

9.5 Don't wait for your regularly scheduled car-washing to take care of bird splatters like this. The bird stuff can eat into your paint if left too long. When you see such a deposit, soften it first with a spritz of water, let that soak, then take the mess off with a paper towel. When dry, follow with a local application of a cleaner-wax or five-minute detailer product to ensure the paint is clean.

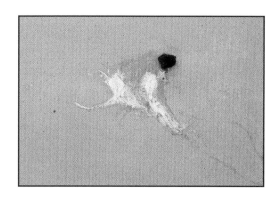

9.6 Many pro detailers rinse a car by removing the spray nozzle and just flushing the surface with a large volume of water rather than a hard spray. There's less contamination of the other sections, and the surfaces dry quicker with less spotting.

9.7 Natural chamois will dry up and harden after use and will have to be softened with clean water before the next use, but the artificial ones don't attract mildew and can be stored slightly damp in their original airtight containers so they can be ready anytime.

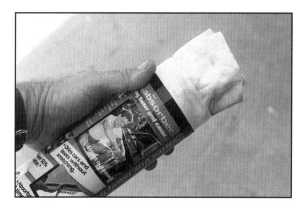

9.8 Many detailers use only clean cotton toweling for drying cars, feeling they are better able to get into nooks and crevices than with a chamois, and they save time by not having to constantly wring out a chamois. They use small towels and use lots of them, so they usually have a commercial laundry service supply them.

9.9 The One Grand line of vehicle care products has been around since 1933, mostly serving the detailing professionals and owners of specialty show cars. Some paint and detail shops sell the line as well as use it, and they can be purchased by mail in consumer-size quantities. The detailers purchase most of their products in gallon containers for convenience and economy.

9.10 Use two cloths when buffing off your wax. One covers your other hand when you rest it on the car while rubbing the wax off with the main cloth. This prevents hand oils and acids from imprinting the surface when you rest your hand on the just-buffed surface.

9.11 Pro detailers and showcar owners like to use soft cotton diapers to polish and wax very expensive paint jobs such as this. Keeping the cloth folded to about half-inch thickness at all times prevents the shape of your hand and fingers from causing uneven pressure on the paint when rubbing.

9.12 Only the right side of this paint section had been properly treated with quality carnauba wax, which is why the water is beading up there, indicating that the paint is well-protected. The true carnauba paste waxes are admittedly a little more work to apply but offer the longest-lasting protection.

9.13 At right here is a standard sheepskin buffing pad, while to its left are the newer foam buffing pads. Varying densities of the foam give these pads different characteristics: a hard one for compounding, softer ones for fine polish and waxes.

9.14 When using aggressive products, even with an orbital polisher, swirl marks can still show up if you use too much pressure on the surface. The orbital's manufacturer recommends letting the weight of the machine provide all the pressure against the paint. Even so, the orbital marks are easily removed with machine or hand-buffed glaze and final wax.

9.15 Terrycloth pad covers come with most orbital machines. The ones with sealed backings are for applying products; the softer, unbacked ones are for buffing off dried products. The covers are washable.

9.16 Household cotton swabs should be in everyone's detail bag. They are perfect for cleaning in tight areas or applying small amounts of protectant to rubber trim that is next to paint or chrome.

9.17 Weather stripping needs an occasional treatment with vinyl dressing to keep it from drying out and deteriorating.

9.18 At car shows and concours events, you'll see plenty of toothpicks in evidence, as they are quite useful for picking out tiny pieces of dirt or wax residue in places like around this antenna trim.

9.19 Old-fashioned method of newspaper and vinegar/water solution still does a good job of glass cleaning without leaving lint. Do not get the vinegar/water solution on painted surfaces, though.

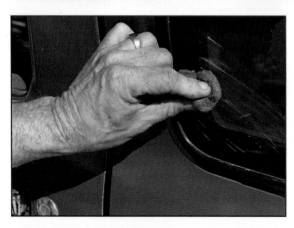

9.20 Stubborn hard-water spots can be removed from glass with fine steel wool soaked in glass cleaner.

9.21 With a cloth top, wet down during your basic washing treatment, sponge the top with suds from a dedicated car-washing soap only. Using a soft sponge or mitt, gently go over the plastic back window at the same time. Vinyl convertible tops are easier to clean.

9.22 Few areas of a car are as fragile as the plastic rear window in a convertible, but they can be kept looking very new with frequent polishing with dedicated plastic polish. Most brands suggest considerable shaking of the contents before applying the milky plastic polish, which has tiny abrasives in suspension.

9.23 Pro Motorcar Products markets this paint thickness gauge, which can be useful in determining how thick your paint actually is before doing any buffing or other paint repairs. If the paint is too thin, repairs may cut through to your primer, at which point the panel will need complete repainting. It also helps if you're evaluating a Mustang to buy, it can tell you where excessive filler may be hidden under the paint.

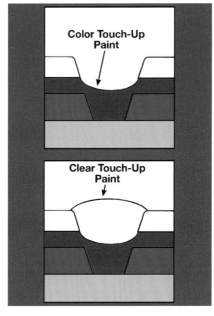

Color Touch-Up Paint

Clear Touch-Up Paint

9.24 Under great magnification, your paint damage looks like a crater or ravine. The most invisible repair means coloring that crater, then bringing it up to above surface level with clear, protective lacquer.

9.25 Dirty ashtrays can contribute to a lingering smell inside a car, even if the current owner doesn't smoke. Serious cleaning with soap-and-water and a short detail brush gets most of the gunk out of the ashtray.

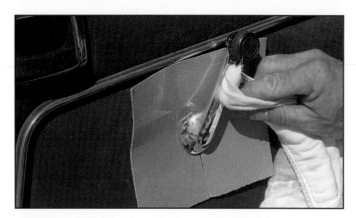

9.26 A cardboard mask is very helpful when you have chrome door handles up against cloth interior panels. When cleaning a chrome handle, the mask protects the upholstery around it. Keep one of these in your trunk for the future.

9.27 For the most basic engine cleanup, start by covering the distributor, coil and carburetor with aluminum foil, plastic baggies or plastic wrap. Spray the engine compartment with engine cleaner and let it soak, working in tight areas with throwaway paintbrushes to loosen the grime. Tough areas may require a second spray.

9.28 Your garden hose with a spray nozzle won't have the power of a steam-cleaner, but directed properly it will do the job. Make sure painted or aluminum components are particularly-well rinsed.

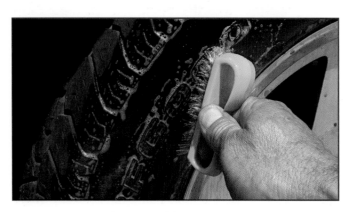

9.29 Start tire detailing with just a thorough washing with soap and water, using a short-bristled brush to scrub oxidized dead rubber from the tires, especially around the lettering. Don't use the brush on the wheels.

9.30 Eagle One suggests making a cardboard disc and covering it with duct tape, to use as a mask when cleaning tires and wheels. Holding the disc up to your wheel while you apply tire cleaners or dressings masks the already-cleaned wheel perfectly.

10 Now what?

Now that you have finished your Mustang restoration to the point where you are comfortable with it and proud of your work, what do you plan to do with it? Scenic drives to the beach, the lake and the mountains are reason enough to have a fun car to drive. Just going out for breakfast on a Sunday morning in your Mustang is more fun than driving a little white import like everyone else. The practical little cars serve their purpose, but no one comes over to you and says "What is that, a 2008 Hyundai, and did you paint it yourself? How fast does it go?"

If you finished your project car and after six months of enjoying it you've lost the initial rush of accomplishment, you may find yourself getting a little bored with it. You're wondering if this is all there is to owning a classic car. This hap-pens often, no matter how big or expensive the project was. You need to introduce yourself and your Mustang to other people who share your interest.

Car clubs

You don't have to wait until your Mustang is finished or even driveable; joining a Mustang club will introduce you to some other fine folks who share a passion for vintage Mustangs. There are a number of benefits to being a member of a club. You will get to see other people's projects, in or out of their garage, finished or in-progress, and the other members will be very helpful with advice they have picked up on restoration matters. They can recommend good shops for services such as chrome-plating, media-blasting, bodywork and painting. Steering you away from shops that have not been helpful could save you thousands of dollars. There is a national organization, the Mustang Club of America, with 170 chapters, and there are plenty of regional clubs, including probably one in your area. A number of regional clubs are listed in Appendix A at the end of this book. The Mustang Club of America website is regularly updated with listings of events around the country.

Clubs usually have regular meetings, ranging from casual meeting for donuts every other Saturday morning or organized monthly meetings in some local public building. Depending on the weather, not everyone brings their old car to every gathering, especially since there are always a number of members with their cars up on jackstands for restoration work.

10.1 Showtime!

10.2 Your first trip to a Mustang event will be educational and fun. Soon you'll know all the differences between the years and the special collectible options and models. Some car owners, if asked politely and sincerely, will let you sit behind the wheel to see which cars suit you.

10.3 You may even find your dream car for sale at an event, although this nearly finished and highly collectible 1970 Boss 302 might be a little outside your budget at over $40K!

Another group of events are called Fun Ford Sundays, which are open to all Fords with Ford engines (no Deuce roadsters with Chevy engines!). There will be many Mustangs there from '65 to present day models with 412hp and 26 mpg, but also some fine restored Falcons, Comets, Fairlanes, Galaxies and collectible Ford pickups and vans. Some of these events are on fairgrounds and others at drag strips, where you can watch 'em run like they did in the Sixties, and the winner is always a Ford! Just check the Web for event listings.

More adventure

Speaking of tracks, this is another avenue for Mustang fun: racing! You will find that many of the Mustangs that come to shows are not completely stock, with modifications from headers and a four-barrel carb to stroker motors, turbochargers and everything in between. The guys who pile on the engine goodies are obviously interested in more performance than their Mustang had when new, and often try their car out at events held at drag strips. In most cases you need only a minimum of safety equipment to run, such as seats belts, a helmet and a driveshaft safety strap (to prevent the driveshaft from hitting the track if a U-joint fails). However, we recommend a complete package of safety equipment that is up to current maximum standards.

10.4 This red-on-red '65 convertible really got us going.

10.5 The Shelby-American Mustangs are a draw wherever they appear. Driving one puts you right back in the heyday of the muscle cars. They have also been a very good investment over the last 20 years.

10.6 As long as they have the pony spirit, everyone has a great time at Mustang events, whether they currently have a Mustang or are looking for one.

There is another group of Mustangers who also enjoy horsepower but whose primary emphasis is on handling. There are a lot of different aftermarket chassis kits for levels of handling from better-than-stock to ready-to-race. People who enjoy the challenges and thrills of racing attend events usually held on road-racing courses, usually SCCA (Sports Car Club of America) venues. A group will get together to rent the track for a weekend and may even combine with another club such as a Porsche or Ferrari club, in order to keep the per-entry cost of the insurance down. There are also SCCA autocross events with tightly-pyloned courses where time and driving finesse is more important than horsepower.

As a less strenuous kind of driving experience, most clubs have cruises. They are often a weekend activity where everyone books rooms at a scenic spot, near the beach, in the mountains, anyplace where the scenery is fresh and the destination has something to please everyone.

An event you can have closer to home is a poker run. You line up with other drivers and leave from the first stop, where you draw a playing card from a paper grocery bag, and the person at that stop writes down what card you drew. This is repeated over a half-hour or hour drive through interesting areas, following the map and drawing a card until you have a full hand. At most of these events, you pay $5 or something at the start of the run, and if you have the best poker hand at the end, you receive half the money, and the sponsoring club keeps the other half for their expenses.

10.7 American Mustang Supply (Sacramento, CA) was on hand at this show to help with tech questions and support the needs of their local customer base.

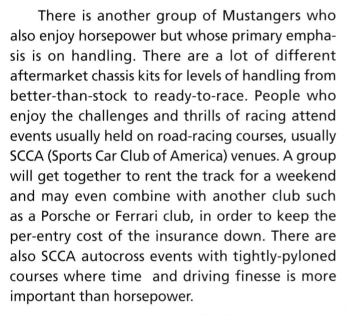

10.8 Many exhibiting Mustang owners will have a scrapbook on hand to illustrate the condition the Mustang was in when purchased, and the progress photos of the restoration.

book and camera to collect reference notes. You will find when asking some restoration questions that it sometimes depends on who you ask. One person will say "No, that part should be painted body color, not chassis black," and another will tell you the opposite. When you can pin one down, ask a judge.

Showing off

Some shows are casual, community-based events with raffle prizes and a few trophies, while others are on a large scale and have judges inspecting the cars. In most Mustang shows you can enter your Mustang in whatever condition it's in, ranging from first time out driving on the road or at the end of your restoration. They often have separate categories for the different years such as '65 to '66, '67 to '68 and '69 to '71, and in each of these year categories, there are Mustangs entered that are beautifully restored to original, plus cars that are listed as "modified."

Not only are such events fun to attend, but very educational. During the time that your project car is in progress, looking at lots of restored Mustangs can be very helpful. Everyone there knows a lot about Mustangs and can answer many of your questions. Bring a note-

Insurance

All this discussion about participating in car events brings up the unglamorous but essential subject of insurance. Your large basic insurance company that you may have for your house and everyday car insurance may not be the best carrier for your restored Mustang. There are a number of insurance companies that specialize in handling policies designed strictly for antique and collectible cars - you will find their advertisements in most of the car magazines. There is so much to consider when buying insurance of any kind, so you must do your research diligently, not just to find the lowest rate, but to find a policy that suites your requirements.

10.9 One owner was proud to show how far he had taken his restoration. A photo of the car on a rotating spit shows he went the most serious and labor intensive route possible.

10.10 Maybe you would enjoy a more animated event, such as the drag races at a Fun Ford Sunday at Sacramento Raceway (CA). A hot Mustang side-by-side with a big-block Galaxie fastback takes us right back to the Sixties! You can watch and/or race.

It used to be that insurance companies would not underwrite for vintage cars that were used for more than 1,500 miles a year, or driven more than going to and from recognized shows and events, which is quite restrictive. Remember that insurance companies don't make money by taking on risks. The specialty insurers have features such as coverage for cars that have been modified, something other insurers won't touch.

You must read your policy very carefully before you sign. There may be language in there that says you must stay close to your vehicle when at car events, which seems quite unreasonable. Another limitation most companies have is how many miles a year you can drive your collector car. For some it's 1000 miles, others 2,500, and one we found allowed 10,000 miles per year.

Among the many technicalities of insuring your car, is what happens if your car is vandalized, destroyed or stolen while it is in a restoration shop. Never assume

10.11 Mustang suppliers Mustang Plus have raced several Mustangs on road courses for fun and continually evaluate their handling packages.

that the shop has its own coverage, because it generally covers the shop, not your car. The only way you could get any payment is if the shop was found negligent in some way. See what the policies you are considering have to say on this. A body/paint shop has all kinds of flammable materials on hand, so make sure your coverage includes being in a shop.

One universal issue with insurance companies is that you cannot race your car in any way. If you carefully read your existing life insurance policy, you will probably find a clause prohibiting racing there also. There may be companies who might accept you as a client despite your amateur racing, but the coverage would probably be very expensive, even if your racing is limited to one or two events a year.

10.12 Maybe a poker run or cruise is more your style, but any time and place you go with a car you restored yourself is like automotive therapy.

10.13 Now what should we do with our Mustang?

11 Mustang resources

ABS Power Brake, Inc.
233 North Lemon St.
Orange, CA 92866
714-771-6549
www.abspowerbrake.com

Acme Auto Headlining Company
550 West 16th
Long Beach, CA 90813
562-437-0061
www.acmeautoheadlining.com

Affordable Classics
19010 Hawthrone Blvd.
Torrance, CA 90503
310-542-5824
www.affordableclassics.com

Accurate Auto Trim & Upholstery, Inc.
402 East Lincoln Way
Ames, IA 50010
800-367-7228
515-232-2060
www.accurateautotrim.com

All Classics Restoration, LLC
704-239-7581
www.allclassicsrestoration.com

American Mustang Parts
11315 Folsom Blvd.
Rancho Cordova, CA 95742
916-635-7271
www.american-mustang.com

AMK Products
(Fasteners)
800 Airport Rd.
Winchester, VA 22602
540-662-7820
www.amkproducts.com

Atlas Auto Trim
732-985-6800
www.atlasautotrim.com

Auto Custom Carpets
1429 Noble St.
Anniston, AL 36202
800-352-8216
www.accmats.com

Auto Data VIN Labels

631-831-7427

autodata9@aol.com

Borgeson Universal

(Steering Gears, Components)

91 Technology Park Dr.

Torrington, CT 06790

860-482-8283

www.borgeson.com

Branda Shelby & Mustang Parts

800-458-3477

814-942-1869

www.cobranda.com

BRUT

4680 Alabama Avenue S.W.

Navarre, Ohio 44662

888-533-2693

www.brutmfg.com

California Mustang Parts and Accessories

19400 San Jose Ave.

City of Industry, CA 91748

800-775-0101

www.cal-mustang.com

Carolina Machine Engines

171 Lee St.

Johnston, SC 29832

800-903-6446

www.comengines.com

CJ Pony Parts

7164 Allentown Blvd.

Harrisburg, PA 17112

800-888-6473

717-657-9252

www.cjponyparts.com

Classic Auto Parts

8701 South Interstate 35

Oklahoma City, OK 73149

800-654-3247

405-631-3933

www.classicautoparts.com

Classic Mustang

24 Robert Porter Rd., Unit A

Southington, CT 06489

860-276-9704

www.classicmustang.com

Classic Tube

80 Rotech Dr.

Lancaster, NY 14086

716-759-1800

www.classictube.com

Cobra Automotive

37 Warehouse Point Rd.

Wallingford, CT 06492

203-284-3863

www.cobraautomotive.com

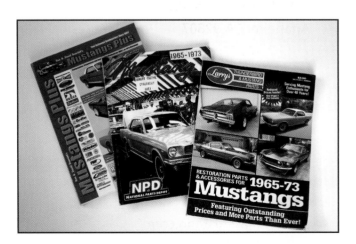

Cobra Restorers Ltd.
770-427-0020
www.cobrarestorers.com

Coker Tire (California)
5468 East Lamona
Fresno, CA
559-453-3278
www.cokertire.com

Coker Tire (worldwide)
1317 Chestnut Street
Chattanooga, TN
866-513-2744
423-265-6368
www.cokertire.com

Collectors Auto Supply
888-772-7848
www.collectorsautosupply.com

Comp Cams
3406 Democrat Rd.
Memphis, TN 38118
800-999-0853
901-795-2400
www.compcams.com

Complete Radiator
407-422-6007
clynchcomplete@aol.com

Concept One Pulley Systems
6320 Highway 400 North
Cumming, GA 30028
877-337-0688
770-889-5900
www.C1pulleys.com

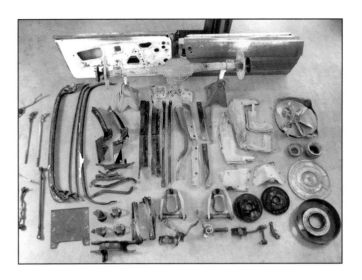

Convertible Top Guys
M & T Manufacturing
30 Hopkins Lane
South Kingstown, RI 02879
800-999-2892
401-789-7720
www.convertibletopguys.com

Crane Cams
1640 Mason Ave.
Daytona Beach, FL 32117
866-388-5120
386-310-4875
www.cranecams.com

Currie Enterprises
1480 North Tustin Ave.
Anaheim, CA 92807
714-528-6957
www.currieenterprises.com

Dallas Mustang
10720 Sandhill Rd.
Dallas, TX 75238
800-687-8264
214-349-0991
www.dallasmustang.com

Dearborn Classics
5200 South Washington Ave.
Titusville, FL 32780
800-252-7427
541-318-7471
www.dearbornclassics.com

Eastwood
(Restoration tools and supplies)
263 Shoemaker Road
Pottstown, PA 19464
800-343-9353
www.eastwood.com

Factory Muscle Parts
352-583-2212
www.factorymuscleparts.com

Federal-Mogul Corporation
(Fel-Pro Gaskets, Speed Pro Engine Parts)
248-354-7700
www.federal-mogul.com

Flaming River
800 Poertner Dr.
Berea, OH 44017
800-648-8022
440-826-4488
www.flamingriver.com

Ford Muscle
www.fordmuscle.com

Ford Racing Performance Parts
800-FORD-788
www.fordracingparts.com

FrameOff Equipment Company
P.O. Box 320396
Los Gatos, CA 95032
866-350-0045
www.frameoff.com

Gateway Classic Mustang
(Complete Restorations)
10461 North Service Rd.
Bourbon, MO 65441
800-396-6488
573-732-3541
www.gatewayclassicmustang.com

Harbor Freight Tools
3491 Mission Oaks Blvd.
Camarillo, CA 93011-5034
800-423-2567
www.harborfreight.com

Hydro-E-Lectric
(Convertible Top Parts)
800-343-4261
www.hydroe.com

Ididit
610 South Maumee St.
Tecumseh, MI 49286
517-424-0577
www.ididitinc.com

Inland Empire Driveline Service
4035 East Guasti Rd., Suite 301
Ontario, CA 91761
909-390-3030
www.iedls.com

Inline Tube
15066 Technology Dr.
Shelby Township, MI 48315
800-385-9452
586-532-1338
www.inlinetube.com

In Search of Mustangs
www.insearchofmustangs.org

JGM Performance Engineering
(Engine builder, specializes in Ford)
28130 Avenue Crocker, Ste. 331
Valencia, CA 91355
661-257-0101

JJ's Classic Mustang Parts
6413 Bonnie Oaks Dr.
Chattanooga, TN 37416
423-894-2068
www.jjsmustangparts.com

John's Mustang
5234 Glenmont Drive
Houston, TX 77081
800-869-6894
713-668-5646
www.johnsmustang.com

Just Rear Ends
(Specializes in Ford rear axles)
295 Gentry Way, #21
Reno, NV 89502
775-826-8448
www.justrearends.com

K.A.R. Auto Group - The Mustang People
1166 Cleveland Avenue
Columbus, OH 43201
800-341-5949
614-294-4433
www.karmustang.com

Kelsey Tire
1190 East Highway 54
Camdenton, MO 65020
800-325-0091
573-346-2506
www.kelseytire.com

Larry's Mustang & Thunderbird
1180 California Ave. #B
Corona, CA 92881
800-854-0393
951-270-3223
www.larrystbird.com

Laurel Mountain Mustang
113 Mustang Lane
Ruffsdale, PA 15679
888-925-7669
www.laurelmountainmustang.com

Lokar Performance Products

10924 Murdock Dr.

Knoxville, TN 37932

877-469-7440

865-966-2269

www.lokar.com

Marti Auto Works

(Concours Restoration Parts, Ford Data Base,
The Marti Report)

12007 W. Peoria Ave.

El Mirage, AZ 85335

623-935-2558

www.martiauto.com

Master Power Brakes

888-351-8785

www.mpbrakes.com

MCE Engines

(Engine Builders specializing in Ford)

323-731-0421

MCEEngines@aol.com

Mid-America Mustang

444 Little Hills Blvd.

St. Charles, MO 63301

636-946-4444

www.midamericamustang.com

Mr. Hi-Po

931-698-1261

www.Mr-Hi-Po.com

Mr. Mustang

800-543-9195

www.mrmustang.com

Mustang Club of America

4051 Barrancas Avenue PMB 102

Pensacola, FL 32507

850-438-0626

www.mustang.org

Mustang Decoder Online

Classic Mustang dataplate decoder

www.mustangdecoder.com

Mustang Depot

2510 Sunset Rd., #3

Las Vegas, NV 89120

702-262-0011

www.mustangdepot.com

MUSTANG Magazine

877-279-3010

863-701-2707

www.mustangmagazineonline.com

Mustang Monthly Magazine

www.mustangmonthly.com

**Mustang Owners Club
of California**

Craig Cunningham, President

P.O. Box 8261

Van Nuys, CA 91409

818-785-1180

www.mustangownersofca.org

Mustang Parts House
3124 Spengler Way
Turlock, CA 95380
800-956-8782
www.mustangpartshouse.com

Mustang Village
605 Oak Court
San Bernardino, CA 92410
909-383-5444
mustangvill@msn.com

Mustangs Etc.
(Parts & Restoration, Service, New Old Stock)
14843 Bessemer St.
Van Nuys, CA 91411
818-787-7634
www.mustangsetc.com

Mustangs & Fast Fords OC
(Parts & Restoration, Service)
3001 S. Main St.
Santa Ana, CA 92707
714-850-1500
www.mustangsandfastfordsoc.com

Mustangs Plus
2353 North Wilson Way
Stockton, CA 95205
800-999-4289 (ordering)
209-944-9977 (info)
www.mustangsplus.com

Mustangs Unlimited
www.mustangsunlimited.com
info@mustangsunlimited.com

Mustangs Unlimited (Connecticut)
440 Adams Street
Manchester, CT 06042
860-647-1965
888-398-9898

Mustangs Unlimited (Georgia)
2505 Newpoint Parkway
Lawrenceville, GA 30043
770-446-1965
888-229-2929

National Parts Depot (NPD)
www.autocraftinvestments.com

NPD California
1376 Walter St. #1
Ventura, CA 93003
800-235-3445
805-654-0468

NPD Florida
900 S.W. 38th Ave.
Ocala, FL 34474
800-874-7595
352-861-8700

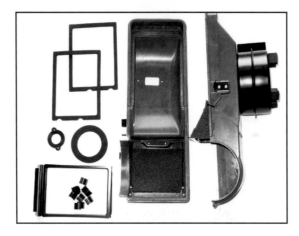

NPD Michigan
2435 S. Haggerty Rd.
Canton, MI 48188
800-521-6104
734-397-4569

NPD North Carolina
7000 MacFarlane Blvd.
Charlotte, NC 28262
800-368-6451
704-331-0900

Painless Performance Products
2501 Ludelle St.
Fort Worth, TX 76105
817-244-6212
www.painlessperformance.com

Performance Suspension Technology (PST)
877-226-4101
www.p-s-t.com

Premium Pony Parts
866-430-7669
www.premiumponyparts.com

Randall's Rack
(Rack & Pinion Conversions)
877-500-RACK
www.randallsrack.com

Restore Mustangs
888-592-2502
www.restoremustangs.com

Sacramento Mustang
4631 Auburn Blvd.
Sacramento, CA 95841-4215
800-442-8333
916-484-3434
www.sacramento-mustang.com

Scott Drake Reproductions

Drake Automotive Group
130 Cassia Way
Henderson, NV 89014
800-999-0289
702-853-2060
www.scottdrake.net
www.drakeautomotivegroup.com

Smeding Performance
(Crate Engines)
210-338-8585
www.smedingperformance.com

Stainless Steel Brakes
800-448-7722
www.ssbrakes.com

Summit Racing Equipment
800-230-3030
330-630-3030
www.summitracing.com

Superior Mustang Parts
4221 W. Eisenhower Blvd. Suite #1
Loveland, CO 80538
888-MY-STANG (697-8264)
www.superiormustangparts.com

Survival Motorsports

(Specializing in Ford Power)

248-366-3309

248-931-0358

www.survivalmotorsports.com

Texas Mustang Parts, Inc.

5774 South University Parks Drive

Waco, TX 76706

800-527-1588

254-662-2893

www.texasmustang.com

The Auto Bolt Co.

216-881-3913

www.autobolt.net

The Restomod Shop

(Restorations, Car Projects)

209-942-3013

www.therestomodshop.com

Total Control Products

A Division of Chris Alston's Chassisworks

8661 Younger Creek Drive

Sacramento, CA 95828

888-388-0298

www.totalcontrolproducts.com

TP Tools

705 State Route 446

P.O. Box 649

Canfield, OH 44406

800-321-9260

www.tptools.com

Trans Am Racing

310-323-5417

taracing@earthlink.com

Vintage Mustang Owners Association

P.O. Box 5772

San Jose, CA 95150

www.vintagemustang.org

Virginia Classic Mustang

195 West Lee St.

Broadway, VA 22815

540-896-2695

www.virginiamustang.com

YearOne

(Restoration parts and supplies)

800-932-7663

706-658-2140

www.yearone.com

VIN/Data Plate Information

If you want to make sure you are taking your Mustang back to true original condition, you have to do some homework. These cars are old enough now that it is likely that most of them have been repainted at least once, and, since Mustangs lend themselves well to modifications, many may have non-original drivetrains or other appointments. That's ok, but for a true showroom-like restoration, that's not going to cut it.

You'll need to locate the data plate, also known as the "patent plate" or "warranty plate." This plate is located on the end of the driver's door and is stamped aluminum on 1969 and earlier models. On 1970 and later models it's a vinyl-covered paper sticker. This plate contains information regarding how the vehicle was equipped when it was built, such as the body style, paint color, interior trim type, build date, district (or destination) code, axle type and engine type. It also contains the Vehicle Identification Number (VIN), which should match the VIN stamped on the left-front inner fender apron (1967 and earlier models) or on a tag affixed to the left front corner of the instrument panel, visible through the windshield (1968 and later models). Always verify that the VIN on the data plate matches the VIN on the chassis; it's possible that somewhere in the life of the vehicle the driver's door may have been replaced, and the information on the data plate won't truly reflect the car it is on now.

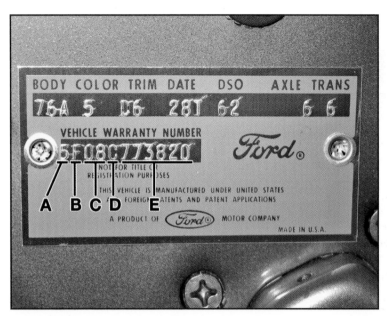

The data plate contains important details about your Mustang. This one is from our 1965 convertible. Other model years have slightly different configurations, but the plate is clearly marked as to what is what. The string of numbers and letters in the Vehicle Warranty Number (or Vehicle identification Number) is broken down like this:

A Last digit of model year

B Assembly plant

C Body serial code

D Engine code

E Chassis number

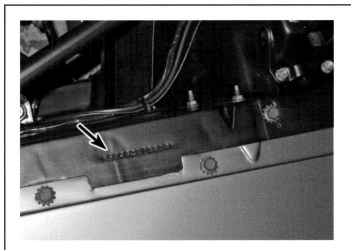

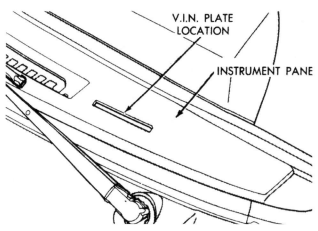

The Vehicle Identification Number (VIN) on 1967 and earlier models is stamped into the left-front inner fender apron

The Vehicle Identification Number (VIN) on 1968 and later models is located at the left-front corner of the instrument panel

There are many very handy resource available on the internet, such as www.mustangdecoder.com. You can simply enter your data plate information on the simulated data plate, click on "Decode," and all of the pertinent information for your Mustang will appear. Additionally, reproduction data plates are available (based on your VIN) through various vendors in the event that yours is missing, doesn't match your VIN, or is in bad shape.

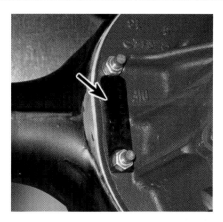

The engine identification tag is located on the right side of the intake manifold, ahead of the carburetor

The transmission identification tag can appear in various places, depending on transmission type and year, but usually it will be found on the left side or rear of the transmission

The rear axle identification tag is secured to the differential carrier by one of the mounting nuts

Data Plate Decoder

Body Style

	1965	1966	1967	1968	1969	1970
Fastback	63	63	63	63		
Hardtop	65	65	65	65	65	65
Convertible	76	76	76	76	76	76
Sportsroof					63	63

Seats

(Letter following Body Style code (example: 76A would be a convertible with standard seats)

	65	66	67	68	69	70
Standard	A	A	A	A	A	A
Luxury	B	B	B	B	B	B
Special					E+	E+
Bench Seats	C	C	C	C/D*	C/D*	C/D*

*Deluxe

+Grande

Paint Color

Code	1964-1/2	1965	1966	1967	1968	1969	1970
A	Raven Black	Raven Black	Raven Black	Raven Black	Raven Black	Raven Black	Raven Black
B	Pagoda Green	Midnight Turquoise		Frost Turquoise	Royal Maroon	Royal Maroon	
C		Honey Gold				Black Jade	Dark Ivy Green Metallic
D	Dynasty Green	Dynasty Green		Acapulco Blue	Acapulco Blue	Acapulco Blue	Yellow
E						Aztec Aqua	
F	Guardsman Blue		Light Blue	Arcadian Blue	Gulfstream Aqua	Gulfsteam Aqua	

Code	1964-1/2	1965	1966	1967	1968	1969	1970
G							Medium Lime Metallic
H	Caspian Blue	Caspian Blue	Sahara Beige	Diamond Green			
I	Champagne Beige	Champagne Beige		Lime Gold	Lime Gold	Lime Gold	
J	Rangoon Red	Rangoon Red					Grabber Blue
K	Sliversmoke Gray	Sliversmoke Gray	Nightmist Blue	Nightmist Blue			Bright Gold Metallic
L							
M	Wimbledon White	Wimbledon White	Wimbledon White	Wimbledon White	Wimbledon White	Wimbledon White	Wimbledon White
N				Diamond Blue	Diamond Blue		Pastel Blue
O	Tropical Turquoise	Tropical Turquoise			Seafoam Green		
P	Prairie Bronze	Prairie Bronze	Antique Bronze			Winter Blue	
Q		Brittany Blue	Brittany Blue	Brittany Blue			Medium Blue Metallic
R	Ivy Green	Ivy Green	Dark Green Metallic		Highland Green		
S	Cascade Green			Dusk		Champagne	Medium Gold
T			Candy apple Red	Candy apple Red	Candy apple Red	Candy apple Red	Red
U			Tahoe Turquoise		Tahoe Turquoise		Grabber Orange
V	Sunlight Yellow	Sunlight Yellow	Emberglow	Burnt Umber			
W				Clearwater Aqua	Meadowlark Yellow	Meadowlark Yellow	
X	Vintage Burgundy	Vintage Burgundy	Vintage Burgundy	Vintage Burgundy	Pres. Blue		
Y	Skylight Blue	Silver Blue	Silver Blue	Dark Moss Green	Sunlit Gold	Indian Fire	

Paint Color (continued)

Code	1964-1/2	1965	1966	1967	1968	1969	1970
Z	Chantilly Beige		Med. Sage Metallic	Sauterne Gold			Grabber Green
1							Calypso Coral
2						Lime	Light Ivy Yellow
3	Poppy Red	Poppy Red				Calypso Coral	
4			Silver Frost	Silver Frost		Silver Jade	
5	Twilight Turquoise		Signal Flare Red				
6				Pebble Beige	Pebble Beige	Pastel Gray	Silver Blue Met.
7	Phoenician Yellow						
8		Springtime Yellow	Springtime Yellow	Springtime Yellow			
Special			Medium Palomino Metallic	Playboy Pink			
			Medium Silver Metallic	Anniversary Gold			
			Ivy Green Metallic	Columbine Blue			
			Tahoe Turquoise Metallic	Aspen Gold			
			Maroon Metallic	Blue Bonnet			
			Silverblue Metallic	Timberline Green			
			Sauterne Gold Metallic	Lavender			
			Light Beige	Bright Red			

Interior Trim

1964-1/2	
42	White Vinyl with Blue Trim
45	White Vinyl with Red Trim
46	White Vinyl with Black Trim
48	White Vinyl with Ivy Gold Trim
49	White Vinyl with Palomino Trim
56	Black Vinyl and Cloth
82	Blue Vinyl with Blue Trim
85	Red Vinyl with Red Trim
86	Black Vinyl with Black Trim
89	Palomino Vinyl with Palomino Trim

1965	
22	Blue Vinyl with Blue Trim
25	Red Vinyl with Red Trim
26	Black Vinyl with Black Trim
28	Ivy Gold Vinyl with Gold Trim
29	Palomino Vinyl with Palomino Trim
32	Blue Bench
35	Red Bench
36	Black Bench
39	Palomino Bench
62	Blue and White (Luxury)
65	Red and White (Luxury)
66	Black and White (Luxury)
67	Aqua and White (Luxury)
68	Ivy Gold and White (Luxury)
69	Palomino (Luxury)
76	Black Fabric and Vinyl
79	Palomino Fabric and Vinyl

D2	White with Blue Trim
D5	White with Red Trim
D6	White with Black Trim
D8	White with Ivy Gold Trim
D9	White with Palomino Trim
F2	White with Blue Trim (Luxury)
F5	White with Red Trim (Luxury)
F6	White with Black Trim (Luxury)
F7	White with Aqua Trim (Luxury)
F8	White with Ivy Gold Trim (Luxury)
F9	White with Palomino Trim (Luxury)

1966	
22	Blue with Blue Trim
25	Red with Red Trim
26	Black with Black Trim
27	Aqua with Aqua Trim
32	Blue Bench
35	Red Bench
36	Black Bench
62	Blue and White (Luxury)
64	Emberglo and Parchment (Luxury)
65	Red (Luxury)
66	Black (Luxury)
67	Aqua and White (Luxury)
68	Ivy Gold and White (Luxury)
C2	Parchment with Blue Trim Bench
C3	Parchment with Burgundy Trim Bench
C4	Parchment with Emberglo Trim Bench
C6	Parchment with Black Trim Bench

Interior Trim (continued)

1966 (continued)	
C7	Parchment with Aqua Trim Bench
C8	Parchment with Ivy Gold Trim Bench
C9	Parchment with Palomino Trim Bench
D2	Parchment with Blue Trim
D3	Parchment with Burgundy Trim
D4	Parchment with Emberglo Trim
D6	Parchment with Black Trim
D7	Parchment with Aqua Trim
D8	Parchment with Ivy Gold Trim
D9	Parchment with Palomino Trim
F2	Parchment with Blue Trim (Luxury)
F3	Parchment with Burgundy Trim (Luxury)
F4	Parchment with Emberglo Trim (Luxury)
F6	Parchment with Black Trim (Luxury)
F7	Parchment with Aqua Trim (Luxury)
F8	Parchment with Ivy Gold Trim (Luxury)
F9	Parchment with Palomino Trim (Luxury)

1967	
2A	Black Standard/Buckets
2B	Blue Standard/Buckets
2D	Red Standard/Buckets
2F	Saddle Standard/Buckets
2G	Ivy Gold Standard/Buckets
2K	Aqua Standard/Buckets
2V	Parchment Standard/Buckets
4A	Black Bench
4V	Parchment Bench

5A	Black Comfortweave (Luxury)
5V	Parchment Comfortweave (Luxury)
6A	Black Buckets (Luxury)
6B	Blue Buckets (Luxury)
6D	Red Buckets (Luxury)
6F	Saddle Buckets (Luxury)
6G	Ivy Gold Buckets (Luxury)
6K	Aqua Buckets (Luxury)
6O	Parchment Buckets (Luxury)
7A	Black Comfortweave Buckets
7V	Parchment Comfortweave Buckets

1968	
2A-6A*	Black Vinyl Buckets
2B-6B*	Blue Vinyl Buckets
2D-6D*	Red Vinyl Buckets
2F-6F*	Saddle Vinyl Buckets
2G-6G*	Ivy Gold Vinyl Buckets
2K-6K*	Aqua Vinyl Buckets
2V-6V*	Parchment Vinyl Buckets
2Y-6Y*	Nugget Gold Vinyl Buckets
7A-5A*	Black Comfortweave Buckets
7B-5B*	Blue Comfortweave Buckets
7D-5D*	Red Comfortweave Buckets
8A-9A*	Black Comfortweave Bench
8B-9B*	Blue Comfortweave Bench
8D-9D*	Red Comfortweave Bench
8V-9V*	Parchment Comfortweave Bench
50	Parchment Comfortweave Buckets

*Used with special "decor group"

1969	
1A	Black Cloth and Vinyl (Luxury)
1B	Blue Cloth and Vinyl (Luxury)
1G	Ivy Gold Cloth and Vinyl (Luxury)
1Y	Nugget Gold Cloth and Vinyl (Luxury)
2A	Black Vinyl Buckets
2B	Blue Vinyl Buckets
2D	Red Vinyl Buckets
2G	Ivy Gold Vinyl Buckets
2Y	Nugget Gold Vinyl Buckets
3A	Black Knitted Vinyl, Mach I
3D	Red Knitted Vinyl, Mach I
3W	White Knitted Vinyl, Mach I
4A-DA*	Black Comfortweave Hi Buckets
4D-DD*	Red Comfortweave Hi Buckets
DW	White Comfortweave Hi Buckets
5A	Black Comfortweave (Luxury)
5B	Blue Comfortweave (Luxury)
5D	Red Comfortweave (Luxury)
5G	Ivy Gold Comfortweave (Luxury)
5W	White Comfortweave (Luxury)
5Y	Nugget Gold Comfortweave (Luxury)
7A	Black Convertible Deluxe Buckets
7B	Blue Convertible Deluxe Buckets
7D	Red Convertible Deluxe Buckets
7G	Ivy Gold Convertible Deluxe Buckets
7W	White Convertible Deluxe Buckets
7Y	Nugget Gold Convertible Deluxe Buckets
8A-9A*	Black Comfortweave Bench
8B-9B*	Blue Comfortweave Bench
8D-9D*	Red Comfortweave Bench
8Y-9Y*	Nugget Gold Comfortweave Bench

1970	
3A	Black Knitted Vinyl Mach I
3B	Blue Knitted Vinyl Mach I
3E	Vermillion Knitted Vinyl Mach I
3F	Ginger Knitted Vinyl Mach I
3G	Ivy Knitted Vinyl Mach I
3W	White Knitted Vinyl Mach I
AA	Black Houndstooth Cloth and Vinyl
AB	Blue Houndstooth Cloth and Vinyl
AE	Vermillion Houndstooth Cloth and Vinyl
AF	Ginger Houndstooth Cloth and Vinyl
AG	Ivy Houndstooth Cloth and Vinyl
BA	Black Vinyl
BB	Blue Vinyl
BE	Vermillion Vinyl
BF	Ginger Vinyl
BG	Ivy Vinyl
BW	White Vinyl
CE	Vermillion Blazer Stripe Cloth
CF	Ginger Blazer Stripe Cloth
EA	Black Comfortweave Vinyl
EB	Blue Comfortweave Vinyl
EG	Ivy Comfortweave Vinyl
EW	White Comfortweave Vinyl
TA	Black Comfortweave Vinyl
TB	Blue Comfortweave Vinyl
TG	Ivy Comfortweave Vinyl
TW	White Comfortweave Vinyl
VE	Vermillion Blazer Stripe Cloth
VF	Ginger Blazer Stripe Cloth

*Special Interior Decor Group

Build Date Code

1969 and earlier models: The first two numbers of the build date code denotes the day of the month the car was built; the letter following the numbers indicates the month of production.

1970 models: The build date appears in the upper left corner of the data plate and indicates the month and year the car was built, in a more conventional manner (09/70 = September 1970).

Month	1st Year Code
January	A
February	B
March	C
April	D
May	E
June	F
July	G
August	H
September	J
October	K
November	L
December	M

Month	2nd Year Code
January	N
February	P
March	Q
April	R
May	S
June	T
July	U
August	V
September	W
October	X
November	Y
December	Z

Domestic Special Order (DSO) Code (District or Destination Code)

Code	City	Code	City	Code	City
11	Boston	34	Indianapolis	62	Houston
12	Buffalo	35	Lansing	63	Memphis
13	New York	36	Louisville	64	New Orleans
14	Pittsburgh	41	Chicago	65	Oklahoma City
15	Newark	42	Fargo	71	Los Angeles
21	Atlanta	43	Rockford	72	San Jose
22	Charlotte	44	Twin Cities	73	Salt Lake City
23	Philadelphia	45	Davenport	74	Seattle
24	Jacksonville	51	Denver	81	Ford of Canada
25	Richmond	52	Des Moines	83	Government
26	Washington	53	Kansas City	84	Home Office Reserve
31	Cincinnatti	54	Omaha	85	American Red Cross
32	Cleveland	55	St. Louis	89	Transportation Service
33	Detroit	61	Dallas		Export

Axle Ratio Code

	1965	1966	1967	1968	1969	1970
1	3.00:1	3.00:1	3.00:1	2.75:1	2.50:1	
2		2.83:1	2.83:1	2.79:1	2.75:1	2.75:1
3	3.20:1	3.20:1	3.20:1		2.79:1	2.79:1
4	3.25:1	3.25:1	3.25:1	2.83:1	2.80:1	2.80:1
5	3.50:1	3.50:1	3.50:1	3.00:1	2.83:1	2.83:1
6	2.80:1	2.80:1	2.80:1	3.20:1	3.00:1	3.00:1
7	3.80:1			3.25:1	3.10:1	3.10:1
8	3.89:1	3.89:1		3.50:1	3.20:1	3.20:1
9	4.11:1			3.10:1	3.25:1	3.25:1
A	3.00:1*	3.00:1*	3.00:1*		3.50:1	3.50:1
B					3.07:1	3.07:1
C	3.20:1*	3.20:1*	3.20:1*		3.08:1	3.08:1
D	3.25:1*	3.25:1*	3.25:1*		3.91:1	
E	3.50:1*	3.50:1*	3.50:1*	3.00:1*	4.30:1	
F	2.80:1*	2.80:1*		3.20:1		2.33:1
G	3.80:1*			3.25:1*		
H	3.89:1*	3.89:1*		3.50:1*		
I	4.11:1*					
J					2.50:1*	
K					2.75:1*	2.75:1*
L		2.83:1*			2.79:1*	
M					2.80:1*	2.80:1*
N					2.83:1*	
O					3.00:1*	3.00:1*

Axle Ratio Code (continued)

	1965	1966	1967	1968	1969	1970
P					3.10:1*	
Q					3.20:1*	
R					3.25:1*	
S					3.50:1*	
T					3:07:1*	
U					3.08:1*	
V					3.91:1*	3.91:1*
W					4.30:1*	4.30:1*
X						2.33:1*

*Limited-slip differential

Transmission Code

	1965	1966	1967	1968	1969	1970
1	3-speed manual	3-speed manual	3-speed manual	3-speed manual	3-speed manual	3-speed manual
3			3-speed manual			
5	4-speed manual	4-speed manual	4-speed manual	4-speed manual	4-speed manual	4-speed manual
6	C-4 automatic	C-4 automatic			4-speed manual *	4-speed manual *
V			C-6 automatic	C-6 automatic	C-6 automatic	C-6 automatic
W			C-4 automatic	C-4 automatic	C-4 automatic	C-4 automatic
Y					FMX automatic	FMX automatic

*Close-ratio gearbox

Assembly plant

F	Dearborn, Michigan
R	San Jose, California
T	Metuchen, New Jersey

Engine code

Model	1965	1966	1967	1968	1969	1970
170 (I6)	V					
200 (I6)	T	T	T	T	T	T
250 (I6)					L	L
260 (V8)	F					
289 2V	C	C	C	C		
289 4V+	D					
289 4V	A	A	A			
289 HiPo	K	K	K			
302 2V					F	F
302 4V				J		
302 4V Boss					G	G
351 2V*					H	H
351 4V**					M	M
390 2V				Y		
390 4V			S	S	S	
427 4V				W		
428 4V				P		
428 4V CJ					O	O
428 4V SCJ					R	R
429 4V Boss					Z	Z

+ 1964-1/2 only

* Cleveland or Windsor

**Cleveland

ACURA
12020 Integra '86 thru '89 & Legend '86 thru '90
12021 Integra '90 thru '93 & Legend '91 thru '95
12050 Acura TL all models '99 thru '08

AMC
Jeep CJ - *see JEEP (50020)*
14020 Mid-size models '70 thru '83
14025 (Renault) Alliance & Encore '83 thru '87

AUDI
15020 4000 all models '80 thru '87
15025 5000 all models '77 thru '83
15026 5000 all models '84 thru '88
15030 Audi A4 '02 thru '08

AUSTIN-HEALEY
Sprite - *see MG Midget (66015)*

BMW
18020 3/5 Series '82 thru '92
18021 3-Series incl. Z3 models '92 thru '98
18022 3-Series, '99 thru '05, Z4 models
18023 3-Series, '06 thru '10
18025 320i all 4 cyl models '75 thru '83
18050 1500 thru 2002 except Turbo '59 thru '77

BUICK
19010 Buick Century '97 thru '05
Century (front-wheel drive) - *see GM (38005)*
19020 Buick, Oldsmobile & Pontiac Full-size (Front-wheel drive) '85 thru '05
Buick Electra, LeSabre and Park Avenue; Oldsmobile Delta 88 Royale, Ninety Eight and Regency; Pontiac Bonneville
19025 Buick, Oldsmobile & Pontiac Full-size (Rear wheel drive) '70 thru '90
Buick Estate, Electra, LeSabre, Limited, Oldsmobile Custom Cruiser, Delta 88, Ninety-eight, Pontiac Bonneville, Catalina, Grandville, Parisienne
19030 Mid-size Regal & Century all rear-drive models with V6, V8 and Turbo '74 thru '87
Regal - *see GENERAL MOTORS (38010)*
Riviera - *see GENERAL MOTORS (38030)*
Roadmaster - *see CHEVROLET (24046)*
Skyhawk - *see GENERAL MOTORS (38015)*
Skylark - *see GM (38020, 38025)*
Somerset - *see GENERAL MOTORS (38025)*

CADILLAC
21015 Cadillac CTS '03 thru '11
21030 Cadillac Rear Wheel Drive '70 thru '93
Cimarron - *see GENERAL MOTORS (38015)*
DeVille - *see GM (38031 & 38032)*
Eldorado - *see GM (38030 & 38031)*
Fleetwood - *see GM (38031)*
Seville - *see GM (38030, 38031 & 38032)*

CHEVROLET
10305 Chevrolet Engine Overhaul Manual
24010 Astro & GMC Safari Mini-vans '85 thru '05
24015 Camaro V8 all models '70 thru '81
24016 Camaro all models '82 thru '92
24017 Camaro & Firebird '93 thru '02
Cavalier - *see GENERAL MOTORS (38016)*
Celebrity - *see GENERAL MOTORS (38005)*

24020 Chevelle, Malibu & El Camino '69 thru '87
24024 Chevette & Pontiac T1000 '76 thru '87
Citation - *see GENERAL MOTORS (38020)*
24027 Colorado & GMC Canyon all models '04 thru '10
24032 Corsica/Beretta all models '87 thru '96
24040 Corvette all V8 models '68 thru '82
24041 Corvette all models '84 thru '96
24045 Full-size Sedans Caprice, Impala, Biscayne, Bel Air & Wagons '69 thru '90
24046 Impala SS & Caprice and Buick Roadmaster '91 thru '96
Impala - *see LUMINA (24048)*
Lumina '90 thru '94 - *see GM (38010)*
24047 Impala & Monte Carlo all models '06 thru '10
24048 Lumina & Monte Carlo '95 thru '05
Lumina APV - *see GM (38035)*
24050 Luv Pick-up all 2WD & 4WD '72 thru '82
Malibu '97 thru '00 - *see GM (38026)*
24055 Monte Carlo all models '70 thru '88
Monte Carlo '95 thru '01 - *see LUMINA (24048)*
24059 Nova all V8 models '69 thru '79
24060 Nova and Geo Prizm '85 thru '92
24064 Pick-ups '67 thru '87 - Chevrolet & GMC, all V8 & in-line 6 cyl, 2WD & 4WD '67 thru '87; Suburbans, Blazers & Jimmys '67 thru '91
24065 Pick-ups '88 thru '98 - Chevrolet & GMC, full-size pick-ups '88 thru '98, C/K Classic '99 & '00, Blazer & Jimmy '92 thru '94; Suburban '92 thru '99; Tahoe & Yukon '95 thru '99
24066 Pick-ups '99 thru '06 - Chevrolet Silverado & GMC Sierra '99 thru '06, Suburban/Tahoe/Yukon/Yukon XL/ Avalanche '00 thru '06
24067 Chevrolet Silverado & GMC Sierra '07 thru '10
24070 S-10 & S-15 Pick-ups '82 thru '93, Blazer & Jimmy '83 thru '94,
24071 S-10 & Sonoma Pick-ups '94 thru '04, including Blazer, Jimmy & Hombre
24072 Chevrolet TrailBlazer, GMC Envoy & Oldsmobile Bravada '02 thru '09
24075 Sprint '85 thru '88 & Geo Metro '89 thru '01
24080 Vans - Chevrolet & GMC '68 thru '96
24081 Chevrolet Express & GMC Savana Full-size Vans '96 thru '10

CHRYSLER
10310 Chrysler Engine Overhaul Manual
25015 Chrysler Cirrus, Dodge Stratus, Plymouth Breeze '95 thru '00
25020 Full-size Front-Wheel Drive '88 thru '93
K-Cars - *see DODGE Aries (30008)*
Laser - *see DODGE Daytona (30030)*
25025 Chrysler LHS, Concorde, New Yorker, Dodge Intrepid, Eagle Vision, '93 thru '97
25026 Chrysler LHS, Concorde, 300M, Dodge Intrepid, '98 thru '04
25027 Chrysler 300, Dodge Charger & Magnum '05 thru '09
25030 Chrysler & Plymouth Mid-size front wheel drive '82 thru '95
Rear-wheel Drive - *see Dodge (30050)*
25035 PT Cruiser all models '01 thru '09
25040 Chrysler Sebring, Dodge Avenger '95 thru '05, Dodge Stratus '01 thru 05

DATSUN
28005 200SX all models '80 thru '83

28007 B-210 all models '73 thru '78
28009 210 all models '79 thru '82
28012 240Z, 260Z & 280Z Coupe '70 thru '78
28014 280ZX Coupe & 2+2 '79 thru '83
300ZX - *see NISSAN (72010)*
28018 510 & PL521 Pick-up '68 thru '73
28020 510 all models '78 thru '81
28022 620 Series Pick-up all models '73 thru '79
720 Series Pick-up - *see NISSAN (72030)*
28025 810/Maxima all gasoline models, '77 thru '84

DODGE
400 & 600 - *see CHRYSLER (25030)*
30008 Aries & Plymouth Reliant '81 thru '89
30010 Caravan & Plymouth Voyager '84 thru '95
30011 Caravan & Plymouth Voyager '96 thru '02
30012 Challenger/Plymouth Saporro '78 thru '83
30013 Caravan, Chrysler Voyager, Town & Country '03 thru '07
30016 Colt & Plymouth Champ '78 thru '87
30020 Dakota Pick-ups all models '87 thru '96
30021 Durango '98 & '99, Dakota '97 thru '99
30022 Durango '00 thru '03 Dakota '00 thru '04
30023 Durango '04 thru '09, Dakota '05 thru '11
30025 Dart, Demon, Plymouth Barracuda, Duster & Valiant 6 cyl models '67 thru '76
30030 Daytona & Chrysler Laser '84 thru '89
Intrepid - *see CHRYSLER (25025, 25026)*
30034 Neon all models '95 thru '99
30035 Omni & Plymouth Horizon '78 thru '90
30036 Dodge and Plymouth Neon '00 thru'05
30040 Pick-ups all full-size models '74 thru '93
30041 Pick-ups all full-size models '94 thru '01
30042 Pick-ups full-size models '02 thru '08
30045 Ram 50/D50 Pick-ups & Raider and Plymouth Arrow Pick-ups '79 thru '93
30050 Dodge/Plymouth/Chrysler RWD '71 thru '89
30055 Shadow & Plymouth Sundance '87 thru '94
30060 Spirit & Plymouth Acclaim '89 thru '95
30065 Vans - Dodge & Plymouth '71 thru '03

EAGLE
Talon - *see MITSUBISHI (68030, 68031)*
Vision - *see CHRYSLER (25025)*

FIAT
34010 124 Sport Coupe & Spider '68 thru '78
34025 X1/9 all models '74 thru '80

FORD
10320 Ford Engine Overhaul Manual
10355 Ford Automatic Transmission Overhaul
36004 Aerostar Mini-vans all models '86 thru '97
36006 Contour & Mercury Mystique '95 thru '00
36008 Courier Pick-up all models '72 thru '82
36012 Crown Victoria & Mercury Grand Marquis '88 thru '10
36016 Escort/Mercury Lynx all models '81 thru '90
36020 Escort/Mercury Tracer '91 thru '02
36022 Escape & Mazda Tribute '01 thru '07
36024 Explorer & Mazda Navajo '91 thru '01
36025 Explorer/Mercury Mountaineer '02 thru '10
36028 Fairmont & Mercury Zephyr '78 thru '83
36030 Festiva & Aspire '88 thru '97
36032 Fiesta all models '77 thru '80
36034 Focus all models '00 thru '07
36036 Ford & Mercury Full-size '75 thru '87
36044 Ford & Mercury Mid-size '75 thru '86

36045 **Ford Fusion & Mercury Milan** '06 thru '10
36048 **Mustang V8** all models '64-1/2 thru '73
36049 **Mustang II** 4 cyl, V6 & V8 models
'74 thru '78
36050 **Mustang & Mercury Capri** '79 thru '86
36051 **Mustang** all models '94 thru '04
36052 **Mustang** '05 thru '10
36054 **Pick-ups & Bronco** '73 thru '79
36058 **Pick-ups & Bronco** '80 thru '96
36059 **F-150 & Expedition** '97 thru '09,
F-250 '97 thru '99 **& Lincoln
Navigator** '98 thru '09
36060 **Super Duty Pick-ups, Excursion**
'99 thru '10
36061 **F-150** full-size '04 thru '10
36062 **Pinto & Mercury Bobcat** '75 thru '80
36066 **Probe** all models '89 thru '92
36070 **Ranger/Bronco II** gasoline models
'83 thru '92
36071 **Ranger** '93 thru '10 &
Mazda Pick-ups '94 thru '09
36074 **Taurus & Mercury Sable** '86 thru '95
36075 **Taurus & Mercury Sable** '96 thru '05
36078 **Tempo & Mercury Topaz** '84 thru '94
36082 **Thunderbird/Mercury Cougar**
'83 thru '88
36086 **Thunderbird/Mercury Cougar**
'89 and '97
36090 **Vans** all V8 Econoline models '69 thru '91
36094 **Vans** full size '92 thru '10
36097 **Windstar Mini-van** '95 thru '07

GENERAL MOTORS

10360 **GM Automatic Transmission Overhaul**
38005 **Buick Century, Chevrolet Celebrity,
Oldsmobile Cutlass Ciera & Pontiac
6000** all models '82 thru '96
38010 **Buick Regal, Chevrolet Lumina,
Oldsmobile Cutlass Supreme &
Pontiac Grand Prix** (FWD) '88 thru '07
38015 **Buick Skyhawk, Cadillac Cimarron,
Chevrolet Cavalier, Oldsmobile Firenza
& Pontiac J-2000 & Sunbird** '82 thru '94
38016 **Chevrolet Cavalier & Pontiac Sunfire**
'95 thru '05
38017 **Chevrolet Cobalt & Pontiac G5**
'05 thru '09
38020 **Buick Skylark, Chevrolet Citation,
Olds Omega, Pontiac Phoenix**
'80 thru '85
38025 **Buick Skylark & Somerset,
Oldsmobile Achieva & Calais and
Pontiac Grand Am** all models '85 thru '98
38026 **Chevrolet Malibu, Olds Alero & Cutlass,
Pontiac Grand Am** '97 thru '03
38027 **Chevrolet Malibu** '04 thru '10
38030 **Cadillac Eldorado, Seville, Oldsmobile
Toronado, Buick Riviera** '71 thru '85
38031 **Cadillac Eldorado & Seville, DeVille,
Fleetwood & Olds Toronado, Buick
Riviera** '86 thru '93
38032 **Cadillac DeVille** '94 thru '05 **& Seville** '92
thru '04 **Cadillac DTS** '06 thru '10
38035 **Chevrolet Lumina APV, Olds Silhouette
& Pontiac Trans Sport** all models
'90 thru '96
38036 **Chevrolet Venture, Olds Silhouette,
Pontiac Trans Sport & Montana**
'97 thru '05
**General Motors Full-size
Rear-wheel Drive** - see BUICK (19025)
38040 **Chevrolet Equinox** '05 thru '09 **Pontiac
Torrent** '06 thru '09

GEO

Metro - see CHEVROLET Sprint (24075)
Prizm - '85 thru '92 see CHEVY (24060),
'93 thru '02 see TOYOTA Corolla (92036)
40030 **Storm** all models '90 thru '93
Tracker - see SUZUKI Samurai (90010)

GMC

Vans & Pick-ups - see CHEVROLET

HONDA

42010 **Accord CVCC** all models '76 thru '83
42011 **Accord** all models '84 thru '89
42012 **Accord** all models '90 thru '93
42013 **Accord** all models '94 thru '97
42014 **Accord** all models '98 thru '02
42015 **Accord** models '03 thru '07
42020 **Civic 1200** all models '73 thru '79
42021 **Civic 1300 & 1500 CVCC** '80 thru '83
42022 **Civic 1500 CVCC** all models '75 thru '79
42023 **Civic** all models '84 thru '91
42024 **Civic & del Sol** '92 thru '95
42025 **Civic** '96 thru '00, **CR-V** '97 thru '01,
Acura Integra '94 thru '00
42026 **Civic** '01 thru '10, **CR-V** '02 thru '09
42035 **Odyssey** all models '99 thru '04
42037 **Honda Pilot** '03 thru '07, **Acura MDX**
'01 thru '07
42040 **Prelude CVCC** all models '79 thru '89

HYUNDAI

43010 **Elantra** all models '96 thru '10
43015 **Excel & Accent** all models '86 thru '09
43050 **Santa Fe** all models '01 thru '06
43055 **Sonata** all models '99 thru '08

ISUZU

Hombre - see CHEVROLET S-10 (24071)
47017 **Rodeo, Amigo & Honda Passport**
'89 thru '02
47020 **Trooper & Pick-up** '81 thru '93

JAGUAR

49010 **XJ6** all 6 cyl models '68 thru '86
49011 **XJ6** all models '88 thru '94
49015 **XJ12 & XJS** all 12 cyl models '72 thru '85

JEEP

50010 **Cherokee, Comanche & Wagoneer
Limited** all models '84 thru '01
50020 **CJ** all models '49 thru '86
50025 **Grand Cherokee** all models '93 thru '04
50026 **Grand Cherokee** '05 thru '09
50029 **Grand Wagoneer & Pick-up** '72 thru '91
Grand Wagoneer '84 thru '91, Cherokee &
Wagoneer '72 thru '83, Pick-up
'72 thru '88
50030 **Wrangler** all models '87 thru '08
50035 **Liberty** '02 thru '07

KIA

54050 **Kia Optima** '01 thru '10
54070 **Sephia, Spectra & Sportage** all models
'94 thru '10

LEXUS

ES 300 - see TOYOTA Camry (92007)

LINCOLN

Navigator - see FORD Pick-up (36059)
59010 **Rear-Wheel Drive** all models '70 thru '10

MAZDA

61010 **GLC Hatchback** (rear-wheel drive)
'77 thru '83
61011 **GLC** (front-wheel drive) '81 thru '85
61012 **Mazda3** '04 thru '11
61015 **323 & Protogé** '90 thru '00
61016 **MX-5 Miata** '90 thru '09
61020 **MPV** all models '89 thru '98
Navajo - see Ford Explorer (36024)
61030 **Pick-ups** '72 thru '93
Pick-ups '94 thru '00 - see Ford Ranger (36071)
61035 **RX-7** all models '79 thru '85
61036 **RX-7** all models '86 thru '91
61040 **626** (rear-wheel drive) all models
'79 thru '82
61041 **626/MX-6** (front-wheel drive) '83 thru '92
61042 **626, MX-6/Ford Probe** '93 thru '01
61043 **Mazda 6** '03 thru '10

MERCEDES-BENZ

63012 **123 Series Diesel** '76 thru '85
63015 **190 Series** four-cyl gas models,
'84 thru '88
63020 **230/250/280** 6 cyl sohc models
'68 thru '72
63025 **280 123 Series** gasoline models
'77 thru '81
63030 **350 & 450** all models '71 thru '80
63040 **C-Class:** C230/C240/C280/C320/C350
'01 thru '07

MERCURY

64200 **Villager & Nissan Quest** '93 thru '01
All other titles, see FORD Listing.

MG

66010 **MGB** Roadster & GT Coupe '62 thru '80
66015 **MG Midget, Austin Healey Sprite**
'58 thru '80

MITSUBISHI

68020 **Cordia, Tredia, Galant, Precis &
Mirage** '83 thru '93
68030 **Eclipse, Eagle Talon & Plymouth Laser**
'90 thru '94
68031 **Eclipse** '95 thru '05, **Eagle Talon** '95 thru '98
68035 **Galant** all models '94 thru '10
68040 **Pick-up** '83 thru '96 **& Montero**
'83 thru '93

NISSAN

72010 **300ZX** all models including Turbo
'84 thru '89
72011 **350Z & Infiniti G35** all models '03 thru '08
72015 **Altima** all models '93 thru '06
72016 **Altima** '07 thru '10
72020 **Maxima** all models '85 thru '92
72021 **Maxima** all models '93 thru '04
72025 **Murano** all models '03 thru '10
72030 **Pick-ups** '80 thru '97 **Pathfinder**
'87 thru '95
72031 **Frontier Pick-up, Xterra, Pathfinder**
'96 thru '04
72032 **Frontier & Xterra** '05 thru '08
72040 **Pulsar** all models '83 thru '86
Quest - see MERCURY Villager (64200)
72050 **Sentra** all models '82 thru '94
72051 **Sentra & 200SX** all models '95 thru '06
72060 **Stanza** all models '82 thru '90
72070 **Titan pick-ups** '04 thru '09
Armada '05 thru '10

OLDSMOBILE

73015 **Cutlass** V6 & V8 gas models '74 thru '88

For other OLDSMOBILE titles, see BUICK, CHEVROLET or GENERAL MOTORS listing.

PLYMOUTH

For PLYMOUTH titles, see DODGE listing.

PONTIAC

79008 **Fiero** all models '84 thru '88
79018 **Firebird** V8 models except Turbo '70 thru '81
79019 **Firebird** all models '82 thru '92
79025 **G6** all models '05 thru '09
79040 **Mid-size Rear-wheel Drive** '70 thru '87

For other PONTIAC titles, see BUICK, CHEVROLET or GENERAL MOTORS listing.

PORSCHE

80020 **911** except Turbo & Carrera 4 '65 thru '89
80025 **914** all 4 cyl models '69 thru '76
80030 **924** all models including Turbo '76 thru '82
80035 **944** all models including Turbo '83 thru '89

RENAULT

Alliance & Encore - *see AMC (14020)*

SAAB

84010 **900** all models including Turbo '79 thru '88

SATURN

87010 **Saturn** all S-series models '91 thru '02
87011 **Saturn Ion** '03 thru '07
87020 **Saturn** all L-series models '00 thru '04
87040 **Saturn VUE** '02 thru '07

SUBARU

89002 **1100, 1300, 1400 & 1600** '71 thru '79
89003 **1600 & 1800** 2WD & 4WD '80 thru '94
89100 **Legacy** all models '90 thru '99
89101 **Legacy & Forester** '00 thru '06

SUZUKI

90010 **Samurai/Sidekick & Geo Tracker** '86 thru '01

TOYOTA

92005 **Camry** all models '83 thru '91
92006 **Camry** all models '92 thru '96
92007 **Camry, Avalon, Solara, Lexus ES 300** '97 thru '01
92008 **Toyota Camry, Avalon and Solara and Lexus ES 300/330** all models '02 thru '06
92009 **Toyota Camry**, includes Avalon and Lexus ES 350 '07 thru '11
92015 **Celica Rear Wheel Drive** '71 thru '85
92020 **Celica Front Wheel Drive** '86 thru '99
92025 **Celica Supra** all models '79 thru '92
92030 **Corolla** all models '75 thru '79
92032 **Corolla** all rear wheel drive models '80 thru '87

92035 **Corolla** all front wheel drive models '84 thru '92
92036 **Corolla & Geo Prizm** '93 thru '02
92037 **Corolla** models '03 thru '08
92040 **Corolla Tercel** all models '80 thru '82
92045 **Corona** all models '74 thru '82
92050 **Cressida** all models '78 thru '82
92055 **Land Cruiser** FJ40, 43, 45, 55 '68 thru '82
92056 **Land Cruiser** FJ60, 62, 80, FZJ80 '80 thru '96
92060 **Matrix & Pontiac Vibe** '03 thru '08
92065 **MR2** all models '85 thru '87
92070 **Pick-up** all models '69 thru '78
92075 **Pick-up** all models '79 thru '95
92076 **Tacoma, 4Runner, & T100** '93 thru '04
92077 **Tacoma** all models '05 thru '09
92078 **Tundra** '00 thru '06 & **Sequoia** '01 thru '07
92079 **4Runner** all models '03 thru '09
92080 **Previa** all models '91 thru '95
92081 **Prius** all models '01 thru '08
92082 **RAV4** '96 thru '10
92085 **Tercel** all models '87 thru '94
92090 **Sienna** all models '98 thru '09
92095 **Highlander & Lexus RX-330** '99 thru '06

TRIUMPH

94007 **Spitfire** all models '62 thru '81
94010 **TR7** all models '75 thru '81

VW

96008 **Beetle & Karmann Ghia** '54 thru '79
96009 **New Beetle** '98 thru '05
96016 **Rabbit, Jetta, Scirocco & Pick-up** gas models '75 thru '92 & Convertible '80 thru '92
96017 **Golf, GTI & Jetta** '93 thru '98 & **Cabrio** '95 thru '02
96018 **Golf, GTI, Jetta** '99 thru '05
96019 **New Jetta, Rabbit, GTI** '05 thru '10
96020 **Rabbit, Jetta & Pick-up** diesel '77 thru '84
96023 **Passat** '98 thru '05, **Audi A4** '96 thru '01
96030 **Transporter 1600** all models '68 thru '79
96035 **Transporter 1700, 1800 & 2000** '72 thru '79
96040 **Type 3 1500 & 1600** all models '63 thru '73
96045 **Vanagon** all air-cooled models '80 thru '83

VOLVO

97010 **120, 130 Series & 1800 Sports** '61 thru '73
97015 **140 Series** all models '66 thru '74
97020 **240 Series** all models '76 thru '93
97040 **740 & 760 Series** all models '82 thru '88
97050 **850 Series** all models '93 thru '97

TECHBOOK MANUALS

10205 **Automotive Computer Codes**
10206 **OBD-II & Electronic Engine Management**
10210 **Automotive Emissions Control Manual**
10215 **Fuel Injection Manual, 1978 thru 1985**
10220 **Fuel Injection Manual, 1986 thru 1999**

10225 **Holley Carburetor Manual**
10230 **Rochester Carburetor Manual**
10240 **Weber/Zenith/Stromberg/SU Carburetors**
10305 **Chevrolet Engine Overhaul Manual**
10310 **Chrysler Engine Overhaul Manual**
10320 **Ford Engine Overhaul Manual**
10330 **GM and Ford Diesel Engine Repair Manual**
10333 **Engine Performance Manual**
10340 **Small Engine Repair Manual, 5 HP & Less**
10341 **Small Engine Repair Manual, 5.5 - 20 HP**
10345 **Suspension, Steering & Driveline Manual**
10355 **Ford Automatic Transmission Overhaul**
10360 **GM Automatic Transmission Overhaul**
10405 **Automotive Body Repair & Painting**
10410 **Automotive Brake Manual**
10411 **Automotive Anti-lock Brake (ABS) Systems**
10415 **Automotive Detailing Manual**
10420 **Automotive Electrical Manual**
10425 **Automotive Heating & Air Conditioning**
10430 **Automotive Reference Manual & Dictionary**
10435 **Automotive Tools Manual**
10440 **Used Car Buying Guide**
10445 **Welding Manual**
10450 **ATV Basics**
10452 **Scooters 50cc to 250cc**

SPANISH MANUALS

98903 **Reparación de Carrocería & Pintura**
98904 **Carburadores para los modelos Holley & Rochester**
98905 **Códigos Automotrices de la Computadora**
98906 **OBD-II & Sistemas de Control Electrónico del Motor**
98910 **Frenos Automotriz**
98913 **Electricidad Automotriz**
98915 **Inyección de Combustible 1986 al 1999**
99040 **Chevrolet & GMC Camionetas** '67 al '87
99041 **Chevrolet & GMC Camionetas** '88 al '98
99042 **Chevrolet & GMC Camionetas Cerradas** '68 al '95
99043 **Chevrolet/GMC Camionetas** '94 thru '04
99048 **Chevrolet/GMC Camionetas** '99 thru '07
99055 **Dodge Caravan & Plymouth Voyager** '84 al '95
99075 **Ford Camionetas y Bronco** '80 al '94
99076 **Ford Camionetas, Expedition y Lincoln Navigator** '97 al '09
99077 **Ford Camionetas Cerradas** '69 al '91
99088 **Ford Modelos de Tamaño Mediano** '75 al '86
99089 **Ford Camionetas Ranger** '93 al '10
99091 **Ford Taurus & Mercury Sable** '86 al '95
99095 **GM Modelos de Tamaño Grande** '70 al '90
99100 **GM Modelos de Tamaño Mediano** '70 al '88
99106 **Jeep Cherokee, Wagoneer & Comanche** '84 al '00
99110 **Nissan Camioneta** '80 al '96, **Pathfinder** '87 al '95
99118 **Nissan Sentra** '82 al '94
99125 **Toyota Camionetas y 4Runner** '79 al '95

Over 100 Haynes motorcycle manuals also available